When Sex Counts

When Sex Counts

Making Babies and Making Law

Sherry F. Colb

ROWMAN & LITTLEFIELD PUBLISHERS, INC.
Lanham • Boulder • New York • Toronto • Plymouth, UK

ROWMAN & LITTLEFIELD PUBLISHERS, INC.

Published in the United States of America
by Rowman & Littlefield Publishers, Inc.
A wholly owned subsidiary of The Rowman & Littlefield Publishing Group, Inc.
4501 Forbes Boulevard, Suite 200, Lanham, Maryland 20706
www.rowmanlittlefield.com

Estover Road
Plymouth PL6 7PY
United Kingdom

Distributed by National Book Network

Copyright © 2007 by Sherry F. Colb

All rights reserved. No part of this publication may be reproduced, stored in a retrieval system, or transmitted in any form or by any means, electronic, mechanical, photocopying, recording, or otherwise, without the prior permission of the publisher.

British Library Cataloguing in Publication Information Available

Library of Congress Cataloging-in-Publication Data

Colb, Sherry F., 1966–
When sex counts : making babies and making law / Sherry F. Colb.
p. cm.
Includes bibliographical references and index.
ISBN-13: 978-0-7425-5150-3 (cloth : alk. paper)
ISBN-10: 0-7425-5150-4 (cloth : alk. paper)
1. Human reproduction—Law and legislation—United States. 2. Fetus—Legal status, laws, etc.—United States. 3. Sex and law—United States. 4. Rape—United States. 5. Abortion—Law and legislation—United States. I. Title.
KF3760.C65 2007
342.7308′4—dc22 2006029613

Printed in the United States of America

∞ ™ The paper used in this publication meets the minimum requirements of American National Standard for Information Sciences—Permanence of Paper for Printed Library Materials, ANSI/NISO Z39.48-1992.

I dedicate this book to Michael, Meena, Amelia, and Sheyna, and to the memory of Scooter and Mandy, the people and animals who have shaped my definition of who I am in the world.

Contents

Preface

Every woman is either pregnant or not pregnant. Though this statement may sound beyond obvious, it is in fact a deep truth about the lives of women and how they are viewed. A significant element of what it means for a person to be female in today's world is that she will, in a fundamental sense, view herself and be viewed by others as someone who could one day or may currently be (or might once have been) in the process of nurturing a developing human being inside her body. This is an essential distinction between women and men.

As a logical truism, of course, all men too are either "pregnant or not pregnant." But no one thinks of men that way. No one wonders, when a man vomits, whether he is experiencing "morning sickness." No one speculates, when a man puts on some weight, whether he is "with child." A man is fundamentally separate from the process of pregnancy, except as a supporting actor, and that reality inevitably affects the shape that his life will take.

In a case from three decades ago called *Geduldig v. Aiello*,[1] the United States Supreme Court managed to overlook the essential link between womanhood and pregnancy. The women who brought the case—Carolyn Aiello, Augustina Armendariz, Jacqueline Jaramillo, and Elizabeth Johnson—claimed that California law violated the constitutional rights of women to be free from sex discrimination. The law violated their rights, they alleged, by specifically excluding pregnancy-related disability from the class of disabilities covered by state unemployment insurance.

The Supreme Court had previously recognized that state-sponsored sex discrimination is unconstitutional. But it nonetheless rejected the women's claims in *Geduldig*. It held that because nonpregnant people included both males and females, it followed that discrimination against pregnant people was not sex discrimination. Specifically, the 6 to 3 majority concluded that "[t]here is no risk from which men are protected and women are not. Likewise, there is no risk from which women are protected and men are not."[2]

The decision received its share of well-deserved criticism.[3] The Court was correct, of course, to note that not all women are pregnant. Indeed, most of us would rightly criticize as sexist an employer who assumed that every female job applicant was, or was about to become, pregnant. Nonetheless, the all-male (at the time) Supreme Court failed in its analysis to recognize the potential pregnancy of every woman in her childbearing years. It made the mistake of characterizing men and women alike as "either pregnant or not pregnant," when in reality, men simply never occupy this pair of alternatives.

So what? Why should it matter that a woman is either pregnant or not pregnant? Is there not more to being female than that? There is. But a woman's identity is still intimately and inevitably bound up in her *potential* state of containing another life within her. And that reality seems unlikely to change unless human reproduction itself undergoes serious evolution. This truth goes a long way in explaining why the centrality of abortion in debates about women's rights never seems to go away.

This book is about how the law, public policy, and a general sense of fair play should respond to the fact that every woman is—in an essential way—a fundamentally different entity from every man, by virtue of her potential capacity to conceive and develop a human being inside her body. This distinction affects almost every feature of the disputes surrounding the status of women, including when it is unacceptable, acceptable, or even mandatory to treat women differently from men.

To a great degree, debates about abortion—as well as related debates about frozen embryos, birth control, and "unborn victims of violence"—ask when it is proper to think of a woman as a separate person from the developing child who either does now or might some day inhabit her body.

A feminist might be heard to say in one conversation, for example, that women of childbearing age should be allowed to work around chemicals that could harm a fetus, because many women are not pregnant and should not have to be lumped together with those who are. But in another conversation, that same feminist might assert—with equal force—that a workplace that refuses to provide maternity leave is insensitive to the needs of all women.

These positions might sound contradictory: the frustrated employer could ask, "do you want me to work on the assumption that women could become pregnant at any time or on the assumption that they are just like men and should be treated as such?" It is only when we understand that every woman is either pregnant or not pregnant that we see there is no contradiction here: an employer sensitive to women holds in his or her mind the full picture of a woman in her dual and paradoxical reality of being one person and potentially more than one person at the same time. Such an employer provides a workplace that accommodates potential mothers even as it permits women to opt out of that status and make their own judgments about where they can work accordingly.

Part I confronts this dual reality in a variety of contexts and grapples with the questions that inevitably arise when we seek fair treatment for a group of people who are, in an essential sense, *not* "similarly situated"[4] to the men with whom they seek equality. It can be as devastating to sex equality, I suggest, to disregard the special status of pregnancy for women, as it is to force women to enter or remain in that state against their will.

Sometimes, the answers I offer to questions about sex equality can be surprising. Though I defend the right to abortion in chapter 8, for example, I argue in chapter 3 that it is entirely proper for California to prosecute as a murderer the man who attacks a pregnant woman and deliberately causes the death of a first-trimester fetus. Furthermore, in chapter 31, I suggest that women who trick men into fathering children should perhaps forfeit their entitlement to collect child support. Just as the capacity for pregnancy can hamper the lives of women, it can also empower them, relative to men, in ways that call for legal recognition as well.

Part II addresses a reality of women's lives that is partly biological and partly social: the reality of rape. Though men and women alike can become victims of rape, it remains true—outside of environments like prison—that women are overwhelmingly more likely to fall prey to this crime and that, as a result, the fear of rape shapes the way women live their lives—from where they choose to reside to whether and when they feel they can safely go out alone in public—in a way that it does not do for men. Indeed, people regularly characterize prison rape by defining the male victims in feminine terms, thus emphasizing the male/female dynamic of rape, even when no woman is present.[5]

The chapters in this Part discuss the forced intimacy that rape represents for women, an intimacy that resembles—even as it differs in many ways from—the forced intimacy that an unwanted pregnancy can represent. One chapter confronts the Supreme Court's having gone out of its way to announce that capital punishment is a "grossly disproportionate" punishment for rape, while several others take up the view that many people hold that "date rape" is not a very serious offense and that women who claim to have been raped by acquaintances should perhaps be presumed to be lying. Together, these sorts of value judgments, I argue, evidence a view of the woman as appropriately available for sexual intimacy, at least to some subset of men, a presumed availability that both mitigates violations against her and reduces her credibility when she complains after having acted in a manner that "invited" a particular man to join the favored group. Other chapters in this Part consider a variety of other issues regarding rape and the role of women's status in driving the law regarding this unique crime.

Part III is about how the law does or ought to handle false attempts to "essentialize" women or artificially limit their options based on their biological sex. One chapter discusses why an employer that forces women to wear makeup while men need only have a well-groomed appearance is engaged in invidious sex discrimination.[6]

Another chapter explains how discriminating against gay men and lesbians is a straightforward example of discrimination on the basis of sex. And a third addresses the thorny question of how to define "reasonable doubt" in criminal prosecutions for date rape.

In a sense, these chapters represent the flipside of what it means for all women to be pregnant or not pregnant: when reproduction does not require accommodation and acknowledgement, or when it is not at issue at all, and women are nonetheless treated as a different walk of life from men, we have sex discrimination, pure and simple. Saying that men and women are simply "different" and then accordingly demanding distinct modes of behavior from them, rests on the fallacy that because there are essential differences between the sexes, there is no essential equality between them. This, in turn, is the power of stereotyping, a mode of thinking that properly triggers stringent legal prohibitions.

I teach law, and many of the ideas within this book come from conversations I have had with students and colleagues about sex equality. Sadly, some of the ideas have come from instances of gender bullying that I have witnessed among this same cast of characters. None of us is immune from the power of stereotypes, as Malcolm Gladwell so ably demonstrated in *Blink*.[7] But by becoming aware of both the truth of gender differences and the fraud that gender stereotypes perpetrate on women and on men, I hope that this book can bring us closer to a time when every woman and every man occupies a just and nurturing world that welcomes every one of us, regardless of our sex.

A version of each of the chapters in this book originally appeared as a column for Writ.Findlaw.com. I have added references to the chapters to clarify when the events described took place in real time, and I have inserted endnotes for those interested in locating the original column. I decided to combine edited and annotated versions of these columns as chapters in one book because they together reflect my own perspective on women's struggle for an equal place in our world. At the core of that struggle is the need to identify what makes women "different" from men and the consequences—if any—that ought fairly to flow from that "difference." As countless others before me have said, it is largely differences in power and not innate distinctions that determine who subordinates whom in this world.[8]

Innate differences have, however, long operated as a vehicle and platform for exercising power, and it therefore continues to be important to acknowledge the differences that cannot be ignored and to engage in reasoned (if heated) debate about what—if anything—should turn on them. One such difference revolves around the capacity—uniquely female—to gestate young members of the species inside one's body.

In every chapter of this book, I join in the struggle to say when human beings with control over others' lives have abused that power and perpetuated a long and ugly history of sexual subordination in the process. To achieve equality between the sexes, we must be able to define our terms: What is a man? What is a woman? And what exactly is equality? This book represents my own attempt to ask and begin to answer these questions.

Acknowledgments

I want to express my heartfelt gratitude for the tireless and expert research assistance provided by the following students and former students at the Rutgers School of Law in Newark: Michael Isaac, Brad Jarman, Robert Lipschitz, Stacy Posner, Monica Seth, and Diana Weeden. I also wish to express thanks to Michael C. Dorf, Larry Haveson, and Julie Hilden for reading and providing invaluable comments and suggestions on the chapters of this book in their original incarnation as columns. In addition, I want to thank Dean Stuart Deutsch of Rutgers Law School-Newark for providing the time and financial support that made it possible to complete this book on schedule. And last, but not least, I would like to express appreciation to Christopher Anzalone and Elaine McGarraugh at Rowman & Littlefield for their hard work, patience, and perfectionism in facilitating the conception, gestation, and delivery of this book. Responsibility for all errors, of course, rests squarely at my own feet.

I

PREGNANCY AND ITS DISCONTENTS: IGNORING THE INTIMATE LINK BETWEEN MOTHER AND FETUS

In this first section of the book, I explore some of the strange things that happen when the law or private actors disregard the way in which pregnancy differs from all other human conditions. Ignoring the special realities of pregnancy can take many forms. One can disregard, for example, the fact that to avoid "harming" her baby, a pregnant woman must engage in constant self-regulation and surveillance. A woman can harm her unborn child by inhaling pollutants, eating uncooked food, sleeping in the wrong position, or undergoing medical treatment essential to her own health. To understand the total nature of the mother-child link is to recognize that laws which regulate a pregnant woman's "treatment" of her fetus—however well-meaning—have the necessary effect of imprisoning a woman inside her own body, a prison that remains an utter impossibility for males of the species. And this sex-specific prison merits our attention, however old or young or bright or dull the prisoner happens to be.

In examining this risk of female imprisonment, we learn the singular importance of pregnant women's freedom. At the same time, though, we see that recognizing the consequences of the mother-fetus link allows and even invites the law to protect pregnant women from potential predators. That is because the pregnancy connection makes both the woman and her unborn child extremely vulnerable to those who would harm either one of them. In the service of protecting pregnant women, it is therefore crucial not to confuse the freedom of women to exercise agency over their own bodies with the failure to value her developing child. The view that one must choose between pregnant women and the babies that they carry presents a false choice, one that is detrimental to the well-being of all involved.

One feature of pregnancy that emerges as we focus our attention on its demands and vulnerabilities is the fact that it is a critical part of human reproduction. This may seem obvious, but we shall see that people have sometimes used language in a way that hides the plain truth that without pregnancy, there is no reproduction. I argue in this Part that referring to one-celled organisms as "human beings" or "persons" and encouraging the "adoption" of embryos obscures the role of pregnancy in giving rise to life. Because our images of reality affect our ultimate decisions about divisive issues, moreover, I suggest that the misuse of language can yield destructive and even catastrophic results by subtly shifting perception and creating a reality that is not and never was there.

Using language accurately, of course, does not dictate our substantive position on every issue. There are still difficult questions that challenge us to investigate our intuitions. Questions like "What makes a woman a mother?" can sometimes be difficult to answer. But the journey will be more satisfying and productive if we come prepared and ready to look at the unvarnished facts.

The first and second chapters in this Part discuss two women confronting creative—and, I contend, disturbing—applications of the criminal law. Both women make arguably wrong decisions about how to care for their own bodies during pregnancy and ultimately find themselves prosecuted under criminal statutes designed for people who reach out and harm other, separate people.

In the third and fourth chapters, the reader will encounter scenarios in which the interests of the pregnant woman and of her growing baby are in alignment. Into this peaceful coexistence enters a third-party who proceeds to cause harm to both the maternal and the fetal partner in the pregnancy team.

Chapter 3 describes a case in which a murderer takes the life of a pregnant woman in order to steal the new baby to raise as her own. Chapter 4 discusses a prosecution for homicide in which the murder victim is a first-trimester fetus and the attacker does not know about the pregnancy. In both cases, I explain, the pregnant woman and her baby suffer at the hands of a third party who fails to honor the integrity of the pregnancy bond, whether deliberately or inadvertently.

Chapter 5 addresses an innovative way in which public officials have chosen to ignore pregnancy—by calling the implantation of a donated embryo into a woman's uterus "adoption." Rather than ignoring the burdens of pregnancy or the loving bond that a willingly pregnant woman enjoys with her growing companion, the "embryo adoption" concept ignores the difference that pregnancy makes in the life of a few cells—turning a microscopic and undifferentiated mass into a highly complex human being. The language of adoption treats the embryo as the equivalent of a child who needs a home in which to thrive. In this context, such blinking at reality might, perversely, reduce the number of families willing and able to adopt children, all in the name of encouraging "adoption."

The next five chapters deal with the issue of abortion and women's rights. Chapter 6 takes on the question of whether a person can describe herself as a feminist and, at the same time, support the criminalization of abortion. Chapter 7 analyzes the tendency of pro-life advocates to focus on late-term abortions and suggests that this focus ultimately undermines the claim that killing an embryo is the equivalent of killing a child. Chapter 8 discusses Florida governor Jeb Bush's attempts to appoint a guardian for the fetus of a severely mentally retarded woman. In this discussion, I observe that Governor Bush, ironically, acknowledges the vulnerability of the unborn only by exploiting the vulnerability of the developmentally disabled.

Chapter 9 confronts the legitimacy of proposed legislation that would require abortion providers to tell patients that their fetuses might suffer during an abortion. On the one hand, it might seem that more information is better than less. On the other, however, most of us can successfully avoid unpleasant realities about the pain caused by our decisions (including the decision not to donate blood or cadavers after we die). To treat abortion as distinct from other refusals to help others is to miss the active sacrifice entailed in pregnancy.

Chapter 10 takes up an issue on which many pro-life and pro-choice Americans appear to agree: the right of parents to weigh in on the abortion decisions of their minor daughters. I criticize this view and expose the flawed reasoning that underlies the notion that in the absence of parental guidance, the right thing to do is to compel a minor to remain pregnant. This notion once again treats the state of being pregnant as a nonevent and its termination as an event, when the reality—as I explain—is otherwise.

Chapters 11 and 12 address the thorny question of what makes a woman a mother. In chapter 11, I present the story of a woman who carries a pregnancy to term, only to learn that the fertility clinic gave her the wrong embryo. After she gives birth, the genetic parents of the child claim that the woman has no maternal rights. I suggest that this position ignores the importance of pregnancy and implies that genetic contribution—that which defines biological fatherhood—is the defining essence of biological motherhood as well.

In chapter 12, I talk about a case in which the opposite problem emerges—the failure to place any weight on a woman's donating her egg to help create the embryo that becomes a child. Just as pregnancy makes biological motherhood more complicated than biological fatherhood, the role of genetic contribution is not the sole province of the biological father. Both chapters thus bring out the difficulty our law has in taking full account of maternity in all of its rich complexity: pregnancy is neither everything nor nothing.

The final two chapters in this Part discuss aspects of life after pregnancy that dominate the experiences of a subcategory of women. In chapter 13, I talk about breastfeeding in public, a challenge in spite of the laws that give women an absolute right to nurse their children in public places. Though this book is largely about the law, the challenge of public breastfeeding reminds us that the law cannot do everything and that social attitudes often lag behind legal imperatives.

Chapter 14 takes up the tragedy of post-partum psychosis, a rare disorder that afflicted Andrea Yates and that evidently led her to drown her five young children to death. In this case, I argue, a jury convicted a woman rather than acknowledge the dark side of pregnancy: its mental health consequences for a small but consistent proportion of those who give birth.

To a surprising degree, public dialogue about issues involving pregnancy fails to take account of simple truths about the world. In this Part, I take what I believe is a necessary step in achieving equality for women, recognizing the realities—both beautiful and ugly—that accompany the unique status of walking around while another living creature lives and grows inside one's body.

• 1 •

To Murder a Child by Refusing a C-section

In March 2004, Utah prosecutors charged a woman with murder for failing to undergo a Caesarean section ("C-section") delivery, a failure that allegedly resulted in the death of one of her unborn twins. Prosecutors have suggested that the reason the woman, Melissa Ann Rowland, refused the procedure was her desire to avoid an abdominal scar.

Ultimately, this prosecution raises a very simple question: Are we, as a society, prepared to demand more of pregnant women than of anyone else?

The answer to this question must be no, if we are sincerely committed to equality.

THE STATUS OF A FETUS IN THE WOMB

To avoid creating the impression that I take the responsibilities of pregnancy lightly, let me be clear in stating that I believe a woman who intends to carry her pregnancy to term has a moral obligation to attempt to avoid situations and activities that will harm her unborn child. Pregnant women who engage in drinking sprees or other high-risk behavior, without considering the impact on their children, are doing something that I consider selfish, reprehensible, and cruel.

The fact that the pregnant woman's child will suffer in the future rather than in the present because of her actions, moreover, does not—to my mind—mitigate the harm of those actions.

Further, if an uninvited third party were to inflict upon a pregnant woman the very same sorts of hazards to which she is exposing herself, I would have no hesitation about subjecting the third party to criminal responsibility for the harm caused to the unborn child. Indeed, I shall say as much in a later chapter.[1]

To make a principled case for opposing Rowland's prosecution for murder, someone who values fetal life must accordingly distinguish what the defendant allegedly did—failing to obtain a C-section against doctors' orders—from the actions that a third party might carry out to cause death or serious bodily harm to an unborn baby. And one cannot rely on the fact that the twin whose death Rowland allegedly caused was not yet born.

PREGNANT WOMEN VERSUS EVERYONE ELSE

Advocates for abortion rights sometimes fall into what I describe as the pro-life trap of arguing about whether a fetus is a person.[2] The only coherent defense of abortion, however, once a pregnancy has progressed beyond the early stages, is that in a free country such as ours, we do not demand that people give their bodies over to others—even their own children—in the way that forced pregnancy entails.

We do not make parents of physically separate children, for example, donate a kidney or bone marrow or even blood to save their children (though we might hope that parents would love their children enough to make these sacrifices voluntarily).

Though for many a welcome and beautiful event, it is nonetheless true that the experience of pregnancy physically taxes a woman's organ systems and health in ways that simply do not admit of analogy in the existing law of ordinarily required sacrifice.

Yes, individuals can be made to pay money to support their children, even when those children are unwanted. But as a matter of common sense, the mandating of financial payments, however burdensome, does not rise to the level of imposition upon bodily integrity implicated by pregnancy.

And once an imposition rises to that level, we no longer see the law making such demands, even of parents.

So what?, the reader might be thinking. That's all about abortion. Rowland chose not to have an abortion. Doesn't that obligate her to care for her children, as any mother who chooses to keep her baby must do? Indeed, far from demanding that she remain pregnant, her doctors asked her to stop being pregnant to save the lives of her children, and she was unwilling to do that. Does Rowland really have the right to remain pregnant and thereby to kill her children?

The question is a good one, but the distinction between punishing a woman for abortion, and punishing her for refusing surgery to terminate a pregnancy, is illusory. Just as a pregnancy represents a major physical intrusion, so then does surgery. In fact, one can readily understand the seriousness of major surgery without even knowing much about how difficult pregnancy can be.

Imagine a law that said that some sector of the population—defined by race, gender, or national origin—must undergo a particular surgical procedure, involving all of the risks and painful after-effects of surgery and anesthesia. Such a law would be objectionable and obviously unconstitutional no matter how helpful to others, including the children of the targeted group.

An example? It is difficult to invent one, but let us use our imaginations. Say a hypothetical (but devastating) disease—fabricitis—is quite common. Say also that one can cure the disease completely by injecting liver cells from men of Finnish descent. A surgeon must extract the liver cells from the men before they reach the age of forty-five, though, and the only way to accomplish the extraction is through abdominal surgery.

The criminal law could not demand of Finnish-American young men that they undergo the surgery to save victims of the disease, even those victims who are close relatives of the patients. Altruistic individuals could choose to make the sacrifice, of their own free will, and some would surely do so. But to incarcerate those who did not as murderers would here represent unconstitutional discrimination on the basis of national origin and would place a grossly unfair demand on the relevant minority.

TARGETING A LIMITED POPULATION

Why do I focus on a minority rather than saying that the law could not force everyone to undergo abdominal surgery? The reason is that a nation of enforced altruism would not necessarily be inferior to or less desirable than our own. It would, no doubt, be highly burdensome and intrusive to live in a country in which everyone is legally obligated to donate bone marrow and blood routinely and to undergo surgery to help others in need. In addition, such a regime would almost certainly violate existing constitutional liberty and privacy rights in the United States.

Nonetheless, if the demand were evenhanded, then we would have some assurance that a majority of the public sincerely felt that the benefits—in the saving of lives and the prevention of extreme suffering—outweighed the costs in liberty and autonomy. In other words, there is no reason why the costs of demanding universal altruism would be systematically undervalued or the benefits systematically overvalued if every member of society were subject to both.

MINIMIZING COSTS TO OTHERS

Consider how different it would be, on the other hand, if a particular portion of the population were legally bound to carry burdens that the rest of us could avoid. The targeted group could be Finnish-American young men or pregnant women (or perhaps pregnant women like Rowland, who apparently had little money and lacked strong ties to her treating doctors). In such a situation, it is quite plausible to expect that advocates for imposing this burden would minimize the costs and trivialize the objections while focusing primarily on the real or imagined benefits of the compulsory sacrifice.

We see this phenomenon in anti-abortion rhetoric that portrays women as casually terminating their pregnancies to avoid "inconvenience." And we see it as well in the prosecutor's attempts to suggest that Rowland allowed her child to die in utero in order to avoid an unsightly scar—a claim that conflicts with her own statement that she had already had C-sections (and scars) in the past and was thus not simply trying to preserve a scar-free aesthetic.

Most of us—that is, men, women who are not pregnant, and many women who are pregnant but who do not have adversarial relationships with their doctors—will never be in Rowland's position and are well aware of that. A majority of the population might therefore find it quite easy to tolerate such criminal prosecutions, when the prosecutions would cost most of us nothing.

EXAGGERATING BENEFITS THAT WILL COME FROM OTHERS' SACRIFICES

In addition to minimizing burdens borne by somebody else, there is also a human tendency to overvalue the benefits to be derived from reducing others' liberties. This tendency has been a great source of concern, for example, for those who have suffered the effects of racial profiling and heightened surveillance in the years since the attacks of September 11, 2001.

In addition to noting the unfair distribution of liberty, many have claimed that using racial profiling to investigate terrorism gives us the illusion, but not the reality, of greater safety. The same could be true of forced C-sections.

THE TRUTH ABOUT C-SECTIONS

Up until now, this chapter has proceeded on the assumption that a doctor who tells a pregnant patient that she needs to have a C-section is generally providing sound advice that ought to be followed if the woman cares about her unborn children. Even if that assumption were accurate, I have argued that it is unacceptable to require pregnant women to undergo major surgery for the sake of their children (and on pain of criminal prosecution) when no one else is forced do so.

As it turns out, though, the premise that an obstetrician's surgical recommendation ought necessarily to be followed is itself questionable. In the United States, approximately one-quarter of all babies are delivered by C-section.[3] According to the World Health Organization's Safety Standards, however, there is no justification for a C-section rate of higher than ten to fifteen percent.[4]

That is, roughly one-half of the C-sections in the United States are performed unnecessarily. Furthermore, as it turns out, the risk of maternal death is between twice and four times greater when a woman has a C-section than when she undergoes a vaginal delivery.

But doesn't the United States offer the best obstetrical care in the world? No. If we look at comparative C-section numbers across industrialized nations, the U.S. rates—as of 1995—were higher than those of at least ten other countries, including England, France, and Spain, *where infant mortality rates were also lower.*

C-sections are thus risky not only for pregnant women but for their babies as well—a fact that certainly has some bearing on whether doctors who recommend surgery are necessarily practicing good medicine.

But what do these surgical rates have to do with the Rowland prosecution? Didn't one of her twins die, just as the doctors had feared? And doesn't that death show that at least in her situation, it was—from her babies' perspective—an obvious mistake for her to refuse a C-section?

In light of C-section rates across the United States, the death of Rowland's baby does not necessarily support the conclusion that refusing the surgery was wrong. The alarmingly high numbers of C-sections in this country evidence a tendency for doctors to intervene surgically in many instances in which such intervention is inappropriate and thereby to create unjustified risks for mothers and their babies.

When it comes to recommended C-sections, it is therefore difficult to know in advance that a particular doctor's recommendation represents sound advice.

Specific court cases bear out this concern about C-section recommendations as well. In three of the first five cases in which providers sought court ordered C-sections in the United States, the women delivered vaginally without incident. In two of the three, significantly, the doctors predicted that both the woman and her offspring would *die*, though the women went on to deliver healthy babies without surgery.

Even in the Rowland case itself, doctors said that her twins would likely die without a C-section, but in fact, one of the two survived. This is not to say, of course, that a fifty percent infant mortality rate is acceptable. It is not. However, the surviving twin does—even in hindsight—point to a serious problem in allowing courts to place unquestioning reliance upon medical judgment about the need for C-sections.

Unlike court orders, moreover, criminal prosecutions can take advantage of 20/20 hindsight. They allow prosecutors to ignore the many cases in which doctors said the very same things that they said to Ms. Rowland, and outcomes proved the doctors wrong.

THE CASE IN FAVOR OF ROWLAND

In short, the arguments against the homicide prosecution of Melissa Ann Rowland for failure to have a C-section are substantial and ultimately decisive.

To undergo surgery to help another person—even one's own child—is a decision currently left up to the individual in our society. The criminal law does not enforce moral obligations to risk life and limb for one's children.

To select a subgroup—pregnant women—to face mandatory surgery is thus patently unfair. And in addition to embracing a double-standard, the advocate of forced C-sections must confront the wealth of data suggesting that the professionals deciding a C-section is necessary for a child's well-being are consistently making errors that risk the lives and well-being of women and their babies alike.

If we wish to become a nation of good Samaritans, a step that this country does not appear poised to take at this time, we must make sure that the obligations of such a choice rest equally upon all of us. We otherwise risk subjugating a minority, and, in the process, systematically failing to assess the real-life costs and benefits of what we do.

POSTSCRIPT

Melissa Ann Rowland pleaded guilty to two counts of third-degree felony child endangerment. Besides refusing a C-section, Ms. Rowland also admitted that she had used cocaine during her pregnancy. She received a sentence of eighteen months probation.

Had her prosecution gone forward, Rowland might have had the opportunity to challenge the constitutionality of the charges against her. She would also, however, have risked a murder conviction with no guarantee of reversal on appeal. Her decision to plead guilty almost certainly reflected a fear of the alternative, in the way that a mugging victim might surrender his wallet in the hopes that his life will be spared in return. In addition to losing one of the children to whom she had hoped to give birth, a pregnant woman thus came to occupy the status of criminal—a parent who abuses or neglects her children—simply by refusing a surgeon's advice to place herself under the knife, something that every competent adult male has an absolute right to do.

We turn next to the status of a woman charged with using illicit drugs—unquestionably a criminal act—while pregnant. In examining these charges, we shall see yet another creative equation between the solitary behavior of pregnant women—individuals who contain other individuals inside their bodies—and the parental conduct of mothers and fathers toward their physically separate children.

•2•

Drug-Dealing to Unborn Children

In August 2004, Tracy Ward of Amarillo, Texas, went on trial for delivering drugs to her unborn child. She allegedly "delivered" the drugs by using cocaine.

As Ward was pregnant at the time, her own ingestion of the controlled substance would necessarily have passed it along to her developing baby. The authorities discovered Ward's act after her child was born and tested positive for cocaine

As of 2003, Texas law has defined an "individual" to include "an unborn child at every stage of gestation from fertilization until birth." The legislature's apparent purpose in expanding the definition of an "individual" was to allow for prosecutions and lawsuits against third parties who harm unborn children.

For some purposes, the law exempts the mother from criminal liability. But prosecutors and defense attorneys disagree on whether the exemption should apply in Tracy Ward's case.

Let us put aside the question of whether an appellate court would ultimately read the statute to apply to the use of cocaine by a pregnant woman. For purposes of this chapter, we will assume that the statute applies and we consider an independent question: Is such a prosecution appropriate, from a constitutional and policy perspective?

Resolution of this issue turns out to be far less simple than might appear at first glance.

AN EASIER CASE THAN ABORTION?

One argument for opposing a "delivery of drugs to a child" prosecution concerns the right to abortion. If there is a right to kill an embryo or fetus prior to birth, then surely it must follow, on this argument, that there is a right to harm that same embryo or fetus in a manner that falls short of causing death. The greater power to kill, in other words, must include the lesser power to injure.

Though seemingly logical, this argument is unpersuasive for three reasons. First, abortion is not a per se right to kill. Second, the authority to kill does not necessarily include the authority to injure. And third, abortion and prenatal cocaine use cause harm to distinct entities, a fact that has legal and constitutional significance.

ABORTION IS NOT A RIGHT TO KILL

The right to abortion, as I will argue in chapter 3, is not truly a right to kill an embryo or a fetus. It is instead a right to choose not to remain pregnant. That is why, I explain, the right to kill the fetus in utero ends at viability—the point at which choosing not to remain pregnant no longer entails the necessary death of the fetus, for it can then survive outside the womb.

Once understood in this way, it is clear that a woman does not have the legal right simply to injure an embryo or fetus. Being able to choose not to be an altruist, in other words, does not entail being able to choose to cause injury to another person.

Abortion, so understood, is an on/off proposition—not a license to hurt one's embryo or fetus. Prosecuting a woman for injuring her child during pregnancy could therefore be consistent with preserving her right to abortion.

AUTHORITY TO KILL DOES NOT INCLUDE AUTHORITY TO INJURE

Furthermore, even if there were a right to kill one's fetus, there would not necessarily be a right to injure it. Injuring, in other words, is not simply a lesser form of harm than killing. It is qualitatively different. For that reason, for example, our Constitution is understood to permit a person to be executed for a capital offense but not to have a limb severed or to be tortured or to be used involuntarily in a medical experiment.[1]

Similarly, though the law permits some homicides (called "justifiable homicides"), such as self-defense, it does not thereby permit a person to say "I won't kill the guy now, but I will steal his wallet or give him a blanket containing smallpox instead."

The right to abortion, even if conceptualized as a right to kill, is thus consistent with the prosecution of a defendant for delivering drugs to her unborn child.

ABORTION AND DRUG USE HARM DIFFERENT ENTITIES

Finally, the harms that are committed in abortion and in the use of a toxic substance during pregnancy, respectively, victimize a baby at two very distinct points in his development.

Abortion commits a harm against a fetus or embryo at whatever stage of maturation it has reached. For that reason, many consider it worse, as a moral matter, to abort a six-month fetus than to terminate during the first month of pregnancy. The further along the gestation, the greater the presumed entitlement of the developing human being to our respect and empathy.

Using a toxic drug during pregnancy, however, is harmful to the baby later on, once he or she is born with an impairment that results from the toxin. To protect that future baby, in fact, the most crucial period of time during which a pregnant woman should refrain from exposing herself to harmful substances is the first trimester, the period during which abortion is widely considered less objectionable than it is later on.

The relevant moment of *impact* for prenatal exposure to toxins is therefore the time after birth, when the fully developed baby will experience the harm. In this sense, the use of cocaine during pregnancy is a potential harm to a child who is later born, rather than to an existing fetus or embryo. If there is an abortion, then the harm of the cocaine delivery accordingly never comes to pass.

Consider an analogy. High school prankster Jim Roe places a highly potent laxative in his rival John Doe's lunch thermos, knowing that John will drink from the thermos in three hours. Sure enough, John drinks his grape juice from the thermos at lunch and soon afterward suffers severe diarrhea. John is scheduled to take an important exam at exactly that time, but he misses the test, because he is in the bathroom for several hours. Though Jim drugged John's thermos in the morning, the foreseeable impact of Jim's actions was to make John sick at lunchtime and thus to interfere with John's subsequent examination.

Similarly, a pregnant woman's use of cocaine will foreseeably have any destructive impact after she gives birth to her child (rather than in utero) so that the relevant moment of harm is when the child is outside the womb and, hence, uncontroversially a full human being. It is because of the harm that occurs at that time (rather than during pregnancy) that the criminal law might step in and hold the woman responsible.

Logically, then, the right to abortion does not include the right to use drugs during pregnancy that will harm the child once he is born.

DOES COCAINE'S ILLICIT STATUS JUSTIFY THE WARD PROSECUTION?

In addition to identifying these distinctions between abortion and prenatal exposure to toxic substances, there is another reason that one might favor prosecuting women who use cocaine during their pregnancy: No one has the right to use cocaine, a controlled substance the possession of which is criminally banned. By demanding that pregnant women refrain from using cocaine, the law accordingly places no greater burden upon them than it places upon everyone else.

Furthermore, when a nonpregnant person uses an illicit drug, it generally harms only the user him- or herself. When a pregnant woman, by contrast, uses a drug, it has a potentially harmful direct effect on another person, the woman's child. Her use of the substance is therefore more destructive than its use by her nonpregnant counterpart and perhaps ought, for that reason, to be subject to greater punishment, as Tracy Ward's cocaine use could have been.

Though apparently reasonable, again, like the arguments regarding abortion, the drug use argument is flawed. The regulation of a pregnant woman's use of cocaine is legally questionable *not* because she has a right to use cocaine. She does not have such a right, and if she were prosecuted for possession in the same way as a nonpregnant man or woman might be prosecuted, she would have no cognizable cause for complaint.

The problem, however, is that Ward was prosecuted for harming another person when all she had literally done was to ingest a substance herself. In other words, it was her uniquely female status as a pregnant woman rather than anything distinctive about what she was doing with cocaine that turned *her* use of drugs into a delivery to a child. When the law punishes the pregnant woman more harshly for drug use than it would another person, it consequently burdens her uniquely by virtue of her sex-based status.

Such regulation, moreover, does not admit of a logical stopping point at cocaine. The medical evidence shows, for example, that alcohol use by pregnant women is more destructive to babies than the use of cocaine. The same is true for smoking cigarettes or working at factories in which substances such as lead circulate in the air. It would accordingly make little sense to single out cocaine if the concern were truly the welfare of children.

If we start down the road of prosecuting pregnant women for doing things to their developing children, then there is almost no activity—however private and protected for the rest of the population—that would not present itself as a potential target for regulation.

In the end, pregnant women would effectively become wards of the state whose every action could subject them to criminal penalties.

PRAGMATIC ARGUMENTS

As I have argued, then, neither the right to abortion nor generalized prohibitions against cocaine use resolve the question of whether the law ought to punish mothers specifically for taking a controlled substance during pregnancy. One could logically prosecute them without endangering the right to abort, and one could oppose their prosecution without questioning the state's authority to prohibit everyone, including pregnant women, from using illicit drugs.

How, then, do we decide whether to support such prosecutions, if not ideologically? One useful way to approach the issue is pragmatically.

What can we expect pregnant women to do if faced with the possibility of prosecution for delivering drugs to children when they use cocaine? One possibility is that they will not use cocaine. If we believed that would happen, then prosecution might be worthwhile.

Another scenario, however, seems far more plausible, given the general failure of the war on drugs to curb use or demand (and the likelihood is that a woman using drugs during pregnancy is either addicted or less than fully compliant with the criminal law, in any event). The probable consequence of prosecuting pregnant women who use cocaine is therefore that such women will try to avoid getting caught.

The fear of detection will accordingly motivate women to do one of two things. First, they might refrain from seeing a doctor, particularly when they are about to deliver their babies (who might test positive for cocaine and provide evidence against their mothers). Second, and perhaps more likely, the women might simply terminate their pregnancies.

If our concern is the well-being of children once they are born, we will want to avoid the first scenario. The babies of women who receive no prenatal care or who deliver their babies without some support (whether from a midwife or a doctor) are unlikely to thrive in the face of post-partum complications. Scaring women away from the healthcare system is therefore a dangerous proposition, if one wants the best outcome for their newborn babies.

If our concern is to protect born and unborn children alike, then the correct decision is obvious: Do not prosecute pregnant cocaine users. Offer them opportunities for rehabilitation instead, because there is a good chance that at least some of them are addicted and would like to stop using drugs, if only for their children's sake.

If, however, our concern is to avoid the birth of injured babies, then we face a painful dilemma: if women will have already used drugs before their babies are due to be born, do we wish for these women to abort?

I would suggest that the answer is no. Regardless of one's position on the right to choose, few would propose that the government pressure women to abort "imperfect" children. And it would be ironic indeed, as well as unfortunate, if—as I suspect—the successful prosecution of pregnant drug abusers resulted not in healthier pregnancies but in more abortions, performed under pressure from the government.

POSTSCRIPT

Tracy Ward pleaded guilty to the charges in this case but retained her right to appeal. She received a sentence of five years probation and was ordered to attend a drug treatment program. The 7th Circuit Court of Appeals in Texas overturned Ms. Ward's conviction on March 29, 2006. It reasoned that there had been no actual transfer of drug possession from mother to unborn child because the mere presence of drugs in the child's body does not alone constitute physical possession of drugs.

Like Melissa Ann Rowland, profiled in chapter 1, Tracy Ward faced a prosecution that could never confront a man: actions or omissions related to her own body classified as criminal aggression against the child within her.

Even if the law did nothing distinctive to prosecute pregnant women, however, a woman expecting a child would nonetheless feel her own similar sense of self-criticism. Any risk undertaken is a risk for her child, any food or medicine ingested a potential toxin to her baby. And whatever harm a third party inflicts on her may seriously injure or kill the developing child who lives within her.

The next chapter takes up the question of whether the law can explicitly protect the pregnant woman's special vulnerability to the actions of third parties without betraying her right to equality and fairness.

•3•

The Inadvertent Murder of an Ex-Girlfriend's Fetus

In January 2004, the California Supreme Court heard argument in a case raising important issues about how the crime of fetal murder should be defined in the State of California. The Justices' questions and comments to counsel during oral argument suggested an inclination to rule that a defendant may be guilty of murder for killing the fetus of a woman who, unbeknownst to the defendant and the woman herself, was pregnant.

Though seemingly draconian, upon close analysis, this result is both sensible and fair.

FAILING TO COUNT THE FETUS AS A HUMAN BEING: THE OLD CALIFORNIA RULE

In 1970, the California courts faced the question whether a viable fetus could count as a "human being" for purposes of the state's murder law.

The defendant in the case, *Keeler v. Superior Court*,[1] had assaulted his ex-wife after learning that she was carrying another man's child. Upon seeing her swollen belly, the defendant pushed her, shoved his knee into her abdomen, and struck her until she fainted, announcing to her his intention to "stomp it out of you." He succeeded in his objective and the fetus—whom doctors attempted to deliver by Caesarean section, at five pounds—died in utero of the trauma sustained during the assault.

The man who brutally attacked his pregnant ex-wife was subsequently charged with both the attack on her and the murder of her baby. On a special application to arrest the proceedings, Keeler argued that the word "human being" in the homicide statute does not include a fetus who dies prior to birth.

The Supreme Court of California agreed with the defendant. It concluded that in light of the statute's legislative history, prosecuting the defendant for murder for killing an unborn fetus would violate the Due Process Clause of the Fourteenth Amendment.

When I teach the *Keeler* case in my criminal law course, most students who voice an opinion oppose the result. Pro-life members of the class are understandably upset with the ruling. And pro-choice students point out that the choice of abortion belongs to the mother. Taking away that choice by killing her fetus without her consent accordingly does as much—or more—violence to reproductive freedom as a prohibition against abortion would.

Many students agree, moreover, that an unborn baby has moral worth that requires that as long as the mother is prepared to sustain the physical and emotional burdens of pregnancy, others must refrain from harming her fetus. In response to the ruling in *Keeler*, the California legislature amended its murder statute to add "fetus" to the class of victims whose malicious killing would qualify as murder, coupled with an exception for consensual abortions obtained by the mother.

THE RECENT CALIFORNIA CASE: UNKNOWING FETAL MURDER

The recent case with which I opened this chapter presents a different set of facts. That prosecution, reviewed by the California Supreme Court, was distinct from the 1970 *Keeler* case in at least two different respects, either of which could prove significant.

First, in the current case, when defendant Harold Taylor shot his ex-girlfriend Patty Fansler to death in 1999, neither the victim nor Taylor knew that Fansler was pregnant. In killing her, the defendant accordingly did not intentionally or knowingly cause the death of anyone *other than* his ex-girlfriend.

Second, unlike in *Keeler*, where the fetus was viable and could probably have been born alive and healthy on the very day that the defendant attacked the mother, Patty Fansler's fetus was nowhere near viability, at somewhere between eleven and thirteen weeks gestation—that is, within, or just at the end of, the first trimester of pregnancy.

WHY INTENT MIGHT NOT MATTER

Upon first considering the Taylor prosecution, it might seem that the killer's ignorance of his ex-girlfriend's pregnancy should be an absolute bar to a murder conviction. Having had no idea that the fetus even existed, how could Taylor possibly be guilty of "murdering" it?

The answer is that he could not, *if he had lacked any sort of murderous intention, knowledge, or recklessness*. Had Taylor, for example, accidentally caused a miscarriage by slipping on a crowded subway platform and, in the process, knocking a pregnant woman to the ground, he could not be prosecuted for murder. Our case, however, is notably distinct from this hypothetical scenario.

The actual Harold Taylor intentionally killed his ex-girlfriend by shooting her to death. His behavior was in no way accidental, and he was in fact subsequently convicted of second-degree murder for killing Fansler. In the process of deliberately killing his intended victim, moreover, he also, unwittingly, killed her fetus.

A truer analogy, then, is not to the man who slips on a subway platform but rather to the man who shoots at a woman who is lying in her bed but whose bullet kills not only the woman but also a child concealed underneath the woman's blanket or underneath her bed. Though the shooter did not know about the child when he aimed his gun, his actions were nonetheless intentional, and he specifically meant for those actions to result in a person's death.

When confronted with a hypothetical scenario like this one at oral argument, Harold Taylor's attorney conceded that the shooter in the example would probably be guilty of murder for both deaths. This concession logically amounts to an acknowledgment that intent with respect to one murder victim can be understood to extend to all victims killed by the same deliberately homicidal action directed against one of the victims, even if the presence or existence of other victims was unknown to the killer.

FETUS VS. HUMAN BEING: DOES THE DISTINCTION MAKE A DIFFERENCE HERE?

There remains, of course, the distinction between a "fetus" and a "human being," as the two classes of potential homicide victims are designated in the California Code. This distinction might seem especially significant in Taylor's case, where the fetus he killed was not even close to viability yet. One might ask: How could the death of such a creature—however regrettable—be equated with the death of a person who has already been born?

There are two answers to this question, one statutory and the other moral. The statutory answer is that California law does not draw a distinction either between a "human being" and a "fetus," or between an early fetus and a late fetus, as long as the killer's actions fall outside of the limited exception for consensual abortion.

Clearly, in murdering his ex-girlfriend, Harold Taylor did not perform a consensual abortion when he unwittingly killed her fetus as well. Therefore, under the criminal law of California, the death of the three-month-old fetus in this case has the same legal import as the death of any living human being.

The moral answer is a bit different, because it must respond to disparities that the law does not take fully into account. "Viability" represents an important milestone in fetal development for purposes of abortion law, because the viable fetus can be said to have an existence "independent" of that of its mother. Simply removing the viable fetus from its mother's womb no longer automatically entails the death of the fetus, in the way that it would have done earlier in pregnancy. Therefore, the right to terminate an unwanted pregnancy no longer physically necessitates a death.

Because the right to choose abortion is a right on the part of the woman to physical integrity and not a per se right to kill an unwanted fetus, the moment that her physical integrity becomes compatible with fetal life, the right to maintain one no longer includes the right to terminate the other. (For similar reasons, a genetic mother has no right to terminate a surrogate mother's pregnancy, no matter how much the former wants to avoid becoming a genetic parent.) The constitutional right to abortion is simply a right to stop being pregnant, nothing more and nothing less.

UNDERSTANDING FETAL "VIABILITY" AS AGAINST THE MOTHER'S ASSAILANT

Viability, then, is the time at which a person who does not want to be pregnant with a child can walk away from the fetus in question without the fetus having to die. If instead of the mother, therefore, it is an unlawful assailant or murderer who kills a woman's fetus, then the fetus is effectively "viable" for that assailant's purposes, as long as the mother has not obtained an abortion. In other words, a fetus whose mother is not planning to obtain an abortion is as "viable" relative to the mother's assailant as the truly viable fetus is vis-à-vis the woman who seeks a late term abortion. In either case, killing the fetus terminates the life of a creature who could—consistent with the bodily integrity of the killer—continue to live.

With the willing participation of the pregnant woman in sustaining the life of her fetus, it is no longer morally relevant to ask whether the fetus's lungs could breathe air if its mother were to deliver it immediately. The fetus is "viable," as against an assailant, because if left in its mother's consensual care, it will probably continue to survive. If a woman is willing to be pregnant, the fetus is thus "viable" as long as it is alive.

Harold Taylor killed a pregnant woman before she even learned of her pregnancy. He is thus in no position to invoke the possibility that she might have had an abortion if she had only lived. He eliminated that option with his gun.

HAROLD TAYLOR WAS PROPERLY CHARGED WITH THE MURDER OF AN UNDISCOVERED FETUS

So it was with good reason that the Justices on the California Supreme Court found themselves unconvinced that Harold Taylor's conviction for the murder of a fetus should be overturned if the prosecutor failed to prove that Taylor knew of the fetus's existence.

The discussion at oral argument focused largely on the failure of the law in question to specify that a defendant must intend or know of the death of the fetus. But the underlying moral principles are sound as well. The death of Patty Fansler's fetus was no "accident"; it was instead the direct product of intentionally (and successfully) homicidal behavior by the defendant.

The fact that a fetus is not yet born, or even viable, speaks not to the value of that fetus but only to the consequences of terminating an *unwanted* pregnancy through consensual abortion. Lack of viability—given the fact that a growing fetus lives inside a woman who is prepared to carry that fetus—thus does nothing to mitigate the homicide of a living creature. California law in its current incarnation properly affirms that premise.

POSTSCRIPT

On April 5, 2004, the California Supreme Court reversed the Court of Appeals decision and returned the case to the lower court for resolution consistent with the opinion.[2] The Supreme Court held irrelevant the question of whether Taylor knew of his victim's pregnancy in reviewing a finding of malice murder. The court reasoned that the law of murder contains no requirement that a defendant know of the existence of each victim. In addition, the court concluded that an unborn child need not be viable for his or her killing to be characterized as fetal homicide in California. In a fetal homicide prosecution, the State need only prove that the fetus was beyond seven weeks along at the time of its death. Taylor received a sentence of 65 years to life in prison.

Like Harold Taylor, most people who attack a pregnant woman mean to harm the woman herself. Their attitude to the unborn baby is either one of indifference or, as in the *Keeler* case discussed in this chapter, one of overt hostility. In the next chapter, we turn to a very different sort of attack against a pregnant woman, one in which the assailant means to kill the woman and leave her child unharmed. Though the attacker spares the baby, we shall see that such an attack is in some ways even more depraved than the more common assault against a pregnant woman.

·4·

Kidnapping Unborn Children from their Murdered Mothers

In late 2004, Kansas resident Lisa Montgomery reportedly cut open a pregnant woman's womb and stole her baby. The baby's mother died of her injuries, and Montgomery was arrested a few days later.

Charged with kidnapping resulting in death, the alleged perpetrator could face execution.[1] The crime is shocking and cruel and leaves many feeling that capital punishment is as appropriate as it could ever be. But other than the brutality of the crime, what accounts for the widely shared intuition that what Montgomery did constitutes an especially heinous act, worthy of the most severe penalty available?

THE BACKGROUND FACTS: A BRUTAL ASSAULT AND KIDNAPPING

The name of the victim in this case was Bobbie Jo Stinnett. Stinnett lived in Kansas and was eight months pregnant when she met Montgomery. Though the two women were strangers, Montgomery had allegedly procured an invitation to her victim's home by feigning interest in a dog whom Stinnett had advertised on an Internet message board.

Once Montgomery arrived at the pregnant woman's home, she savagely attacked Stinnett, a month shy of her due date, cut her open, and kidnapped the baby girl from inside her. Stinnett's mother found Stinnett lying in a pool of her own blood, barely breathing, her baby gone.

Bobbie Jo Stinnett's baby survived. In fact, the woman charged with murdering Stinnett intended for the baby to survive and become her own child. Shortly after the kidnapping, Montgomery was showing off the newborn as hers at a Kansas restaurant. Yet this fact does not seem to mitigate our perception of the severity of her crime. Indeed, it appears only to make it worse. But why?

WHY IS MONTGOMERY'S CRIME WORSE?

One answer lies in Montgomery's motive for killing her victim.

A killer's reason for deciding to take another's life is extremely important in determining her level of culpability. Consider, for example, self-defense, a form of justifiable homicide. Such a killing is not a crime at all. The law has long recognized that each of us has the basic right to defend ourselves from being killed or seriously injured by another person.

Other killers are considered blameworthy, but not quite as blameworthy as a murderer. For example, a person who kills in a state of legitimate rage induced by provocative behavior on the part of the victim of the killing, is—in many jurisdictions—guilty only of manslaughter, rather than of murder.

Though there are flaws in the manslaughter defense, it does reflect the sense in which we understand a person's lashing out at someone who has provoked him. Though we still consider it wrongful and reprehensible, we view a killing in the course of reasonable extreme anger as a lesser species of evil than murder. That is because the victim has—in some way—acted to harm the killer first, and the self-protective impulse that animates self-defense law provides some mitigation for an otherwise inexcusable reactive crime as well.

And finally, there are even moral gradations of murder.

WHAT MAKES SOME MURDERS WORSE THAN OTHERS?

Murder itself is wrong because the murderer decides to end the life of another person without that other person's having posed a threat to the murderer's life or even acted in a manner that might mitigate some of the blame. For no good reason, or for reasons having to do only with the murderer's own desires, she ends the life of another person. Such an act denies the inherent worth of each and every life and uses another's life as a means to her own objectives.

Now consider Montgomery's crime against Stinnett. The victim posed no threat to the perpetrator's life. Furthermore, Stinnett did nothing to Montgomery that would have justified rage. Indeed, Montgomery did not choose to kill Stinnett because of a personal grievance against her victim, or even because of a petty or foolish disagreement with her.

Instead, Montgomery chose Stinnett because she was pregnant with a child that Montgomery wanted to take as her own. The killer killed, in other words, purely to gain access to the child who was living inside the victim's body.

Montgomery's actions thus represent the extreme of regarding another person as a mere means of serving one's own interests. Montgomery treated her victim as a vessel carrying loot that she could plunder. Not simply a means to the killer's own objectives, the victim here became a container. The killing was accordingly an absolute assault on Stinnett's personhood.

A CASE THAT PROVOKES COMPARABLE OUTRAGE: KILLING THE FETUS, BUT NOT THE MOTHER

In criminal law, as I discussed in the last chapter, I teach *Keeler v. Superior Court*, a California Supreme Court case involving a man who beat his pregnant ex-wife's abdomen with the intention of killing the fetus inside her.[2] That case, too, attracts a great deal of outrage when students read it each year. Though the woman in that case survived, and the child died, the assault on the pregnant victim's intrinsic dignity was quite similar to that committed against Bobbie Jo Stinnett in the case before us.

In both attacks, the perpetrator's actions derived from a view of the woman as a living incubator. In *Keeler*, the ex-husband attacked the incubator to kill the baby inside, as though the mother's physical being were incidental and irrelevant.

In the Montgomery case, by contrast, the killer cut open the living incubator, killing her in the process, because she wanted to have the baby who rested inside. When the victim's mother came home to find her own daughter dying, the anguish of losing her beloved child could only have been compounded by the killer's apparent and blatant indifference to the independent existence and value of the woman whom she had attacked.

A WOMAN'S LIFE IS AN END UNTO ITSELF

As is reflected in debates about abortion, a pregnant woman is in a condition that distinguishes her from all other people—men and women alike—who are not pregnant. She holds a second life within her body.

That distinction places special burdens upon the pregnant woman and renders her vulnerable to outside harms in a unique way. She cannot expose herself to danger without risking her baby's life and health at the same time. Indeed, her right to abortion rests, I have argued, on the importance of allowing her to bear such burdens and risks voluntarily, because we do not live in a world of compulsory altruism and therefore cannot ask more from women than we do of anyone else. In our world, then, to see the pregnant woman as a resource to be mined—instead of as a precious being who voluntarily holds within her a second precious being—is to rob her of her dignity as a person.

Lisa Montgomery's alleged crime is thus an outrage in several respects. In addition to killing a human being, and thereby also depriving a baby of her mother before the two had finished the journey of pregnancy together, the killer here treated her victim as a thing instead of a living creature. For that, she might well have forfeited her own entitlement to the mercy that a jury could otherwise have accorded her.

POSTSCRIPT

Lisa Montgomery was charged under the federal kidnapping statute, and the prosecution plans to seek the death penalty. Her trial had been set for October, 2006, but the judge granted a motion to continue the trial to April 30, 2007.[3] Fetal kidnapping—a rare occurrence—has apparently been increasing in frequency over the last few years. Most recently, in October of 2005, a Pennsylvania woman, Peggy Jo Conner, appears to have carried out a fetal kidnapping, the tenth since 1987 and the fourth since 2003.

Up until now, we have examined the law's response to pregnant women—women who contain other, unborn lives within their own bodies. But there are a growing number of unborn human entities that exist outside of any womb. Some such entities are implanted and grow into fetuses and ultimately children. Others become material for stem cell research. And still others are preserved for a time and then ultimately discarded. How the law should characterize and treat such entities is the subject of the next chapter.

•5•

Adopting Embryos from the Frozen Orphanage

In mid-August 2002, the Associated Press reported that the Bush administration would soon distribute almost a million dollars for public awareness campaigns promoting "embryo adoption." Embryo adoption occurs when couples undergoing in vitro fertilization (IVF) produce too many embryos and decide to donate the extras to other infertile couples.

If a couple does not donate or hold onto its excess embryos, the embryos are either destroyed or used in stem cell research. Under guidelines announced by President George W. Bush in an August 9, 2001 speech, however, federal funding will not go to support organizations doing research with embryonic stem cells (unless the cells were developed prior to the date of the president's speech).

Senator Arlen Specter (R-Penn.) was reportedly responsible for inserting the little-noticed grant provision (concerning embryo adoption) in a Health & Human Services (HHS) spending bill. Though Senator Specter publicly supports stem cell research, he asserts that it should occur only if the biological parents prefer not to give up their embryos for adoption by other couples. The better alternative, according to Specter, is to "try to find people who will adopt embryos and take the necessary steps on implanting them in a woman to produce life."

PRESIDENT BUSH'S UNPRINCIPLED POSITION ON STEM CELL RESEARCH

President Bush's opposition to most stem cell research, he has explained, comes from the belief that a person exists from the moment of conception. Bush's position lacks moral coherence.

First, if an embryo is a person, then its parents should not be able to choose between keeping it, discarding it, donating it to research, and giving it to another family. Biological mothers and fathers of real children must either keep them or give them up for adoption. Experimentation and destruction are simply not options.

Second, the entire practice of IVF in the United States—a practice on which both stem cell research and embryo adoption are parasitic—is hostile to the personhood of embryonic life. IVF involves the knowing creation of thousands of embryos that will never be implanted and that will ultimately be destroyed.

FROM WHENCE STEMS SENATOR SPECTER'S POSITION?

Like President Bush, Senator Specter expresses no opposition to fertility medicine. Unlike Bush, however, Specter also has no problem with stem cell research, though he apparently thinks that it should remain a last resort. In the context of advocating embryo adoption, he reportedly says that "[i]f any of those embryos could produce life, I think they ought to produce life."

Given Specter's view that an embryo is not a person entitled to life, it is hard to know what to make of his statement. Perhaps he believes that raw materials ought to be used to support life whenever possible. That could explain a preference for embryo donation over embryo disposal, for example. But it does not explain why he would favor embryo adoption over stem cell research.

After all, the use of stem cells for research also sustains life. People who might otherwise have suffered and died of diseases such as Alzheimer's could potentially live longer and more comfortable lives through the use of embryonic stem cells. Why should this prospect strike the Senator as less worthy than implantation?

One possibility is that Senator Specter and others who support the HHS grant provision believe that when it comes to human beings, more is better. If raw materials can be used to create additional people, in other words, then that's how they ought to be used.

EVERY SPERM IS SACRED

If this population expansion principle is the basis for Specter's view, it is fair to ask: why stop at embryos? Though fertility clinics sometimes implant a donated embryo, for instance, they regularly inseminate patients with donated sperm. Perhaps the federal government should therefore encourage people to give up more of their sperm for "adoption" as well.

The Red Cross could receive a special grant for adding sperm drives to its regular blood drives. Instead of wastefully masturbating at home, men could contribute to the important project of producing as many human beings as possible.

It is hard to imagine a groundswell of support for such a grant program. We are not likely, for example, to hear Specter saying any time soon that "if any of the sperm expelled every day could produce life, I think they ought to produce life," as he said of embryos.

When viewed from this perspective, the adopt-an-embryo program might even seem amusing, although I know it will not amuse my pro-life readers, and for that, I apologize. If one were truly pro-life, of course, Specter's position would be offensive as well, because it accepts the use of IVF as well as a couple's prerogative to discard any excess embryos.

But for anyone who rejects the notion that an embryo is a person with human rights, the promotion of embryo adoption reflects something very ugly and not especially amusing about our nation's priorities. It shows a willingness to waste money, even a relatively small quantity like a million dollars, at a time when Americans are being asked to tighten their belts and forego such luxuries as prescription drug coverage and housing for the poor.

There is independently good reason, moreover, to question a program intended to increase the population, when we have thus far done such an inadequate job of providing for those people who are already here.

THE COSTS TO REAL CHILDREN

A federal program promoting embryo adoption has one final disturbing implication. It encourages people who might otherwise adopt a real child—an already-existing person who waits hopefully for a loving home—to implant a donated embryo instead.

Though every person has the right to decide how to build her own family, the government has no business putting a thumb on the scale against adoption. Supporters of a grant that encourages families to adopt an embryo instead of a child must therefore answer to the thousands of babies and children awaiting permanent families in orphanages and foster homes in the United States and around the world, while our government embraces the six-cell embryo.

POSTSCRIPT

Embryo adoption has proven to be an emerging industry. As of August 2005, the Snowflakes Frozen Embryo Adoption Program has assisted in the successful implantation and subsequent birth of eighty-six babies. In May of 2005, President Bush invited Snowflake babies wearing "former embryo" t-shirts to visit the White House.

Viewing embryos as the moral equivalent of fully formed children might seem absurd to many people. If one sincerely takes the pro-life position that personhood begins at conception, however, then this view follows inexorably and embryonic stem cell research comes to resemble human experimentation. Though the issue of frozen embryos is not a trivial one, pro-life activists are best known for their views regarding abortion, when the embryo or fetus finds itself inside the body of a woman who would prefer that it not be there. Accordingly, people who support abortion rights may perceive stem cell arguments as an attempt to resolve the abortion issue behind the scenes. In fact, though, some people who support stem cell research nonetheless oppose abortion, perhaps because in the absence of an unwanted pregnancy, the interests of the embryo seem less compelling. Such activists place themselves squarely on the side of the fetus in the ultimate maternal/fetal conflict—abortion.

It might therefore come as a surprise to many to learn that there are women who consider themselves feminists—people who are committed to a strong vision of equality for women—and who nonetheless join in the pro-life cause. There is indeed an organization dedicated to the explicit synthesis between the two positions.

·6·

Are "Feminists for Life" Feminists for Real?

In July 2005, after Justice Sandra Day O'Connor announced her intent to retire, President George W. Bush announced his nomination of Judge John Roberts to a seat on the United States Supreme Court. In some respects, Judge Roberts represented an ideal candidate, from the president's standpoint. Extremely smart and able, he did not have much of a paper record to betray a bias on hot-button issues such as abortion. Though he argued repeatedly for overturning *Roe v. Wade*[1] before the very Court he was poised to join, he did so for the Solicitor General's office and not on his own behalf. As a good lawyer—which he unquestionably is—Roberts would be quite capable of making arguments for positions that were not in fact his own.

All of this was true. Yet it was hard to escape the sinking feeling (or the sense of elation, depending on one's perspective) that accompanies the instinctive knowledge that this man would vote to overturn *Roe* as soon as he had a real opportunity to do so. Perhaps we should call such instinctive knowledge "women's intuition," though the woman in question was the nominee's wife, Jane Sullivan Roberts.

The commitments of a candidate's spouse can be quite revealing, and Ms. Roberts served for four years on the board of "Feminists for Life," a group that opposes abortion rights in the name of feminism.

IS FEMINISM CONSISTENT WITH OPPOSITION TO ABORTION?

Upon hearing about an organization opposing reproductive freedom called "Feminists for Life," one might immediately think of other Orwellian titles. "Jews for Jesus," "Swift Boat Veterans for Truth," and the Bush administration's "Clear Skies Initiative" come to mind. But is it fair to assume that Feminists for Life must be an enemy of feminism? Is opposition to abortion necessarily inconsistent with feminism, defined as the pursuit of equally safe, happy, and productive lives for men and women?

The answer is complicated. As the organization's web site will tell you, many early feminists, including Susan B. Anthony and Elizabeth Cady Stanton, opposed abortion as an act of violence against a helpless unborn child. (As the web site does not tell you, though, the early suffragettes opposed contraception as well).[2] And a portion of the group's mission statement, "Women Deserve Better Than Abortion," also on the web site, suggests the beginning of an argument that an anti-abortion position could also be pro-woman.[3]

What positive implications might the statement that "women deserve better than abortion" have?

To assert that women deserve better than abortion is to say that women who want to experience the good life should not have to consider abortion a mandatory path to that goal. A woman who becomes pregnant ought to feel free to bear her child without risking her career or endangering the financial prospects of her existing family.

Feminists for Life (FFL) correctly observes—as many pro-choice feminists have in the past—that our workplaces penalize pregnancy and maternity. In *Geduldig v. Aiello*, for example, the U.S. Supreme Court drew the preposterous conclusion that discrimination against pregnant women is not sex discrimination, because not all women are pregnant.[4]

Fortunately, Congress has since passed the Pregnancy Discrimination Act,[5] officially prohibiting employers from singling out pregnant women for inferior treatment. Still, for many women who seek an education or a demanding career, abortion can feel like the only alternative. Borrowing from FFL's mission statement, "abortion" in those instances "is a reflection that we have not met the needs of women."

If the workplace and our social safety networks were more supportive of women with children, fewer—maybe many fewer—women would even want to have an abortion. And for those who fall into this category, abortion "choice" may truly sound like a cruel joke: a decision that they feel forced to make because the other options are even worse. FFL rightly criticizes the status quo in this regard.

ABORTION "GUILT" AND WHAT IT SAYS ABOUT FFL

To spread its feminist anti-abortion message, the FFL website carries an ad campaign targeting college students. The ads include two posters of young (though not fetal) babies, one white and one African-American, captioned "Is This the Face of the Enemy?" A third poster pictures a young woman, whom we are told was conceived during the rape of her mother, captioned, "Did I Deserve the Death Penalty?" And a third poster shows an unhappy-looking student who has had an abortion, captioned "Been There. Done That. Hated It."

Interestingly, few of the FFL posters address feasible alternatives for women at risk for an undesired abortion. And crucially, not one poster criticizes the dearth of safe, effective, and affordable contraception, a glaring omission if women are to be allowed to have sex even when they do not want to bear a child.

In one of the essays on abortion supplied by FFL, the writer says the following of birth control: "Contraceptives fail, and half of all aborting women admit they weren't using them anyway. Thus, preventing unplanned pregnancies will involve a return to sexual responsibility. This means either avoiding sex in situations where a child cannot be welcomed, or being willing to be responsible for lives unintentionally conceived, perhaps by making an adoption plan, entering a marriage, or faithful child support payments."[6]

Rather than encouraging the use of contraceptives (perhaps by the "half" of aborting women who admit they were not using them, and by their sexual partners), the FFL solution appears to be abstinence, marriage, or giving up children for adoption.

Child-support payments—one solution offered by a poster captioned "If She's In Trouble He's In Trouble, Too"—are only effective when the father is financially capable of supporting a child; the failure to pay child-support, however, can often be a product of poverty rather than male selfishness. Yet that reality—and the consequent fact that the man is "in trouble" along with the woman—do nothing to ease the burden of unwanted motherhood.

And what about women who do follow the abstinence regime but fall victim to rape? Must they remain pregnant too? FFL's response is unmistakable. The poster of the woman conceived in rape asks, "Did I Deserve the Death Penalty?" Presumably, the correct answer to this rhetorical question is "no."

The content of this and several other posters (including "Is This the Face of the Enemy?") appears designed to induce feelings of guilt in women considering abortion, rather than to help them avoid unplanned pregnancies in the future or fight the forces that make childbearing potentially catastrophic to their lives as equal members of society.

IS GUILT NOT APPROPRIATE?: TWO IMPORTANT GAPS IN GUILT-INDUCTION

An FFL member could, of course, respond that guilt is an appropriate emotion when one is considering killing a fellow human being, regardless of what has brought one to that place. Perhaps that is true, but there are two important gaps in this response.

First, the posters mislead the viewer by suggesting visually that babies and young women are the victims (or potential victims) of abortion. As I will discuss in chapter 7, though, a majority of abortions occur early in pregnancy, when a fetus or embryo is not what many people would consider a baby at all.

A lot of discomfort with the prospect of terminating a pregnancy results from the characteristics that a fetus is presumed to share with a baby, including the capacity to feel pain or pleasure and the general ability to have a sensory experience of one's environment. These are capacities that a late-term fetus has but that an early embryo or fetus lacks. Yet the pro-life movement—including FFL—does not appear to draw any such distinction. In another essay provided by FFL's web site, for example, the writer encourages readers to think of the unique, developing child within her and says, "there are no generic zygotes." The implication is that even a fertilized egg is a child, entitled to human rights.

It is, of course, true that the babies and the young adult pictured in the posters would not exist if their mothers had had abortions. However, it is also true that they would not exist if their mothers had used contraception or, in the case of the young adult, if her biological father had not raped her mother. Does that mean that we should consider contraception murder or that when an ovulating woman is being raped, people should not intervene?

Many of us in the world would not be here if our parents had made even slightly different plans—often having nothing to do with either sex or abortion. But this plain truth does not render the alternative scenarios reprehensible. An adult must say more, in other words, than that "I would not have been born if my mother had had an abortion" to make a persuasive argument that abortion is tantamount to a "death penalty" for that living adult, rather than a simple fortuity that would have prevented a baby from coming into being in the first place.

There is a second flaw in the "guilt is appropriate" contention, as well, one that is perhaps more fundamental to the project of criticizing an organization that calls itself "*Feminists* for Life." It is that there is nothing particularly revolutionary or equality-oriented about making women feel guilty for seeking to terminate a pregnancy.

This is an old story of condemnation, perhaps dressed up in feminist garb and trendy photographs and expressions. It says that "women deserve better than abortion." But what about when "better" is not available yet? Should abortion nonetheless become a crime?

DOES FFL WANT ABORTION TO BE A CRIME?

An explicit answer to this question is surprisingly difficult to locate on the FFL website. The mission statement does not mention the issue, and it also cannot be found among the answers to "Frequently Asked Questions."

In reading the arguments presented on the website, however, the conclusion that the group supports criminal bans on abortion is virtually inescapable. And indeed, the president of FFL, Serrin Foster, acknowledged in an interview with the *New York Times* that "[r]eversing *Roe v. Wade*, the 1973 decision that recognized a constitutional right to abortion, is a goal."[7]

If so, then why would the group be coy or evasive about saying explicitly in its college outreach materials or mission statement that it supports criminal laws banning all abortion?

Given the close attention to detail evident on the website, it is hard to imagine that such a statement was left out by accident. The omission instead seems calculated to mislead—to give the impression that FFL is a moderate and mainstream group on the issue of abortion, though the organization in fact supports laws that would force rape victims to undergo nine months of pregnancy and the pain of labor, no matter what their wishes might be and no matter how responsibly they had behaved.

FEMINISTS FOR REAL?

In calling itself a "feminist" group, FFL is therefore misleading as well, suggesting as the name does that the group's priority is improving the lives of women, rather than curtailing an option, whatever the circumstances happen to be.

Viewed in this light, the group's literature and its name come across as a velvet glove covering the iron fist of pro-life extremism.

WHAT DOES ANY OF THIS HAVE TO DO WITH JOHN ROBERTS?

John Roberts did not serve on the Board of FFL for four years; his wife did. Can't his wife do whatever she wants without implicating her husband? Shouldn't her work be, as Senator Edward M. Kennedy (D-Mass) said, "out of bounds"?

Of course, in general, one spouse may do what she pleases, without necessarily reflecting on the views of the other spouse. There are even rare cases of couples (such as Mary Matalin and James Carville) holding high-profile jobs at political cross-purposes.

Jane Sullivan Roberts's leadership role in an anti-abortion group, however, sheds light on John Roberts's participation in writing briefs and arguing orally for the Supreme Court that *Roe v. Wade* should be overturned.

A picture emerges of a family that does not consider abortion—either the procedure itself (however early in pregnancy or even when conception results from rape or incest) or the political issue—a private, personal matter. It is instead a political matter on which advocacy at the highest levels is appropriate.

This picture should have been an unsettling one for those who strongly support a woman's right to decide whether or not she will bear the burden of what Justices Kennedy, O'Connor, and Souter described in *Planned Parenthood v. Casey* as "suffering . . . too intimate and personal for the State to insist, without more, upon its own vision of the woman's role, however dominant that vision has been in the course of our history and our culture."[8]

Judge Roberts may be an unknown quantity on some other issues, but on this one, it is clear that President Bush deliberately selected a pro-life candidate and that a future Justice Roberts would very likely work to turn back the clock on *Roe v. Wade*. Like the glossy appearance of "Feminists for Life" and its own cageyness about expressly stating its ultimate view on criminalizing abortion, there is every indication that Judge Roberts's seeming openness on women's issues represented a glossy and misleading fiction as well.

POSTSCRIPT

After President Bush renominated Roberts on September 5, 2005, to fill the vacancy left by the death of Chief Justice William H. Rehnquist, Roberts was confirmed as Chief Justice of the United States on September 29, 2005. Meanwhile, his wife, Jane Roberts, continued to serve as "Feminists for Life" legal counsel on a pro bono basis.

During the confirmation hearings, many senators grilled Roberts about his views on abortion in general and *Roe v. Wade* in particular. The nominee declined to give his personal views but stressed instead the importance of stare decisis, saying that Roe is "settled as precedent of the court, entitled to respect under the principles of stare decisis." In addition, Roberts said, "I do think that it is a jolt to the legal system when you overrule a precedent . . . there are situations when that's a price that has to be paid."

On November 30, 2005, the Court heard oral arguments in its first abortion case in five years and the very first before the new Chief Justice Roberts.

The case involved the constitutionality of New Hampshire's parental notification statute. The Supreme Court decided *Ayotte v. Planned Parenthood* on January 18, 2006, and in its unanimous decision, authored by Justice O'Connor, chose not to revisit its prior abortion precedents. The Court found unconstitutional the lack of an exception for medical emergencies.[9] Even the Texas statute struck down in *Roe v. Wade*[10] contained an exception for the life of the pregnant woman. The pro-life camp therefore did not suffer a significant defeat in *Ayotte*, though it might nonetheless perceive the case as a setback.

However sincerely one might hold the pro-life vision of morality, of course, one necessarily confronts a difficulty in selling this vision to the general public: Most Americans feel that there is a difference between abortions that occur early in pregnancy, on the one hand, and those that occur closer to birth, on the other. The legal framework of the right to abortion has incorporated this sentiment into existing law, with the point of fetal viability defining the moment at which abortions may be prohibited outright (provided exceptions for the mother's life and health). The pro-life movement has accordingly focused its energy on graphically exposing and attempting to criminalize late-term abortions. This focus, however, betrays an inconsistency between the pro-life philosophy and the pro-life legislative agenda, an inconsistency that may lead to unexpected consequences for pregnant women in the real world.

·7·

Sending out Partial Birth Announcements: Pro-Life Symbolism and Deception

During the first week of June 2003, the House of Representatives approved a ban on a procedure that opponents call "partial birth abortion." President George W. Bush expressed support for the ban, reportedly saying that "[p]assage of this important legislation is a shared priority that will help build a culture of life in America."[1]

The abortion bill in question, however, would be unlikely to survive in the face of an already developing judicial challenge. The Supreme Court struck down similar legislation in *Stenberg v. Carhart*[2] and would likely do the same to the newest ban.

To take care of these contingencies, the president might continue to carry out an evident plan to replace retiring personnel on the Supreme Court with abortion opponents. If the balance on the Court shifted, *Carhart* and other pro-choice decisions (notably *Roe v. Wade*[3]) might make their way to what one abortion opponent called "the big abortuary in the sky."

But retirements take time, and unless and until they occur, "partial birth abortion" bans are likely to remain unenforceable. So why does Congress (and the lobbyists who provide its financial incentives) bother to conceive a statute that is headed for an almost certain stillbirth?

AESTHETICS: THE PUBLIC RELATIONS ADVANTAGE OF ENACTING THE BILL

Whether or not the law "lives," it makes wonderful copy. The lead sponsor of the bill, Representative Steve Chabot (D-Ohio), described the procedure at issue as follows: "Partial birth abortion is the termination of the life of a living baby just seconds before it takes its first breath outside the womb."

Even more dramatic were the words of then House Majority Leader

Tom DeLay (R-Tex), who urged lawmakers to "think of the frantic wriggling of that little body in that gloved hand, think of that moment of pure terror when those sanitized scissors puncture the baby's neck."[4] Such descriptions provide legislators and their constituencies with a vivid and profoundly disturbing image of abortion-as-infanticide, an image that fosters a very misleading impression of what is at stake in abortion debates.

The pro-life lobby has recently focused on a relatively rare type of abortion that resembles infanticide (and that therefore generates revulsion in the public). In doing so, it distracts our attention from two facts: First, 88 percent of abortions occur during the first trimester of pregnancy, long before the fetus is capable of experiencing "pure terror" or pain.[5]

Second, those who describe themselves as pro-life oppose abortion at *every* stage of pregnancy, no matter how early and therefore no matter how *unlike* infanticide the procedure might actually be. Even a zygote—a fertilized egg—is a person entitled to life, in the view of self-described pro-lifers.

THE PRO-LIFE POSITION: UNDIFFERENTIATED CLUMPS OF CELLS ARE PEOPLE TOO

Consider the controversy over stem cell research. It arose because fertility clinics deliberately produce many more embryos than will ever be implanted in a woman's uterus. The large number maximizes the odds of a pregnancy for each specific patient but necessarily creates a surplus of embryos as well.

This surplus could, in theory, provide a wealth of material for research and promising breakthroughs for people suffering from such conditions as Alzheimer's and Parkinson's diseases. But alas, such potential has gone and will continue to go almost completely untapped.

In the second week of August 2001, a month before the terrorist attacks on the World Trade Center and the Pentagon, the president aborted the promise of surplus embryos. He determined that only research involving preexisting stem cell lines could continue in institutions receiving federal funding. With respect to these lines, he explained, the embryos had already perished and thus the "life-and-death decision has already been made."[6]

The president accordingly prohibited research institutions that receive federal dollars from working with discarded, frozen embryos created after the date of his speech. At least in part as a result, according to recent reports, the number of embryos currently in frozen storage in this country approaches 400,000.[7] They are kept in suspended animation while neurological disorders destroy human lives, because President Bush and, more importantly, his core supporters, believe that personhood begins at conception.

Do the true commitments of the pro-life movement really matter? After all, if most Americans are horrified by so-called partial-birth abortion, then isn't it appropriate for lawmakers to seek to ban it, rare as it is, if only to send a message?

Not necessarily. To press such legislation is to imply a deceptive level of urgency. The reality is that late-term abortions are rarely undertaken, and almost never in the absence of medical necessity. Yet the singling out of these procedures for censure suggests otherwise.

Further, feeling, caring people react as they do to images of late-term abortion not because of some abstract philosophical or theological position on when "life" begins. They react with revulsion because the procedure looks violent and cruel, particularly when observed outside of the context in which it actually occurs.

Pro-lifers thus adhere to a pretense when they say "we oppose this specific procedure." The pretense is that, like nonpartisan members of the public, they recoil from what is *distinctive* about late-term abortions. But in truth, they do not make such distinctions; they likewise oppose the destruction of a six-cell, undifferentiated mass, or a woman's taking of a morning-after pill that prevents such a mass from attaching to her uterus in the first place.

To press a ban on "partial birth abortion," then, is the equivalent of holding up a color poster of a late-term abortion in front of a clinic at which the vast majority or all of the procedures occur during the first trimester. To put forward late-term abortions as representative of what pro-lifers oppose, in other words, misrepresents both abortion itself and the position for which the pro-life speaker stands.

HYPOCRISY ON THE PART OF PRO-CHOICE FORCES

Hypocrisy is, of course, hardly unique to those who oppose abortion. Proponents of reproductive choice often publicly accept the faulty premise of the pro-life movement that abortion is only acceptable as long as a fetus has not yet become a "person." They therefore oppose statutes that would classify the fetus as a "person" for any purpose, including the punishment of assault against a pregnant woman.

Refusing to experience empathy for a late-term fetus whose mother is assaulted by a third party, however, only exhibits an apparently callous prejudice against fetuses—not a principled position in favor of choice. If a late-term fetus suffers when its life is terminated, then that suffering ought to be acknowledged, regardless of one's position on abortion.

Especially when there are no valid interests in opposition to those of the fetus—such as when an assailant beats a pregnant woman to death—consideration of fetal interests is entirely proper. Accordingly, it is troubling to hear that supporters of women's rights are reflexively up in arms in opposition. It is no more appropriate for pro-choice people to pretend that a late-term fetus is a nonentity for all purposes than it is for pro-life people to pretend that stem cell research or first-trimester abortion resembles the work of Nazi Doctor Josef Mengele.

SYMBOLISM AS OVERSIMPLIFICATION, AND ULTIMATELY AS DECEPTION

I have suggested here that engaging in symbolic gestures, through posters, slogans, or legislation, is a species of lying. On the pro-life side, people lie by implying (or by projecting images that subliminally convey the view) that abortion looks (to spectators) and feels (to the fetus) like the killing of an infant during delivery. That equation of abortion and infanticide is simply inaccurate on the facts.

On the pro-choice side, people lie by pretending that up until the moment of birth, the fetus lacks any characteristics that would justifiably trigger a decision to extend cognizable interests to it under any set of circumstances.

Each side deliberately erases the merits of the other side's arguments and suggests that any nuanced consideration of reality at the margin is tantamount to a betrayal of the cause.

As a teacher, I find the lies and symbolic oversimplification troubling. As a supporter of reproductive choice, moreover, my sense is that the lies of pro-choice advocates have been largely unsuccessful. When a prominent leader of a pro-choice organization says that a law protecting the fetus from violence by third-party assailants would be outrageous, she sounds shrill and unconvincing.

Much more effective have been the deceptive tactics of the pro-life movement in pulling at our heartstrings with pictures of violence against a full-term fetus inside an invisible woman.

In the face of the propaganda war I have described, people on the fence will begin (or continue) to focus on the violence of late-term abortion. They will ask themselves whether such violence is troubling enough to force women to sustain the burdens and pains of pregnancy. And their views on abortion might change.

IMPORTANT FACTS THAT SHOULD INFORM THE ABORTION DEBATE

My hope is that as people agonize over these issues, they remember three things.

First, the easier it is to obtain an early abortion (in which a nonsentient creature is destroyed), the fewer late-term (and far more troubling) abortions there will be.

Second, right now, an overwhelming majority of abortions occur before the fetus is capable of experiencing pain.

And third, as food for thought, consider another kind of cruelty that occurs regularly without event. The animals that many people eat without a second thought, including pigs, cattle, lambs, and chickens, unquestionably experience horrible pain as they are subjected to excruciating "living" conditions and procedures on factory farms in preparation for a merciless slaughter. The only interest on the other side of the ledger in the case of meat production, moreover, is the tastiness of these intelligent, warm-blooded animals' flesh.[8]

Though I leave further discussion of animal rights for another day, it is worth pondering the reality of animal pain when considering whether, as a matter of compassion for those who are helpless, a non-sentient embryo that happens to share our DNA ought to have the right to occupy a grown woman's body against her will, while baby and adult mammals and birds, whose capacity to feel pain and terror closely resembles our own, suffer torture and cruel deaths to satisfy our cravings.

POSTSCRIPT

Tom Delay is now the former House Majority Leader and no longer occupies a seat in the Congress. The Partial Birth Abortion Ban was signed into law in November of 2003 but has never taken effect because of three separate challenges to the constitutionality of the ban, in New York, in California, and in Nebraska. The three district court judges all found the ban unconstitutional, because it lacked a health exception. In July of 2005, the U.S. Court of Appeals for the Eighth Circuit affirmed the Nebraska ruling.[9] The United States filed a petition for certiorari (review) with the U.S. Supreme Court on September 23, 2005. The U.S. Supreme Court granted certiorari on February 21, 2006 and heard argument on November 8, 2006.[10]

We have seen that test-case abortion statutes tend to address a variety of pregnancy termination techniques that are dramatic, gruesome, and very likely to upset the public. The implicit contest is clear: a vulnerable infant's right to live, balanced against a selfish and powerful woman's desire to destroy that infant. But sometimes it is the pregnant contestant's powerlessness that makes her an appealing target of pro-life intervention.

·8·

Pro-Life Bullies and Mentally Retarded Women

In mid-2003, Florida Republican Governor Jeb Bush tried to stop a mentally retarded woman from having an abortion. He did it by intervening in her case (in which her own guardian sought an abortion for her) and moving to appoint a guardian for the fetus.[1] The court denied Bush's motion, so he sent lawyers to assist in the appeal.

The fetus in question was believed to have been the product of the rape of a severely retarded twenty-two-year-old woman, who police described as having the mental capacity of a one-year-old. At the time of the governor's appeal, it was unknown whether the woman—referred to as J.D.S.—was still pregnant.

Both pro-choice and pro-life groups viewed Governor Bush's efforts as an assault on abortion rights. But it may in fact have amounted to a far broader assault on the ideals of this nation.

THE CONFLICT BETWEEN FETAL GUARDIANSHIP AND THE RIGHT TO CHOOSE ABORTION

Appointing a guardian for a fetus conflicts with the right to abortion in two separate ways. The first has to do with the status of the fetus; the second, with the status of the pregnant woman.

If a court can appoint a guardian for a fetus's protection, it may follow that the fetus is a "person" with entitlements independent of, and perhaps in tension with, those of its mother. In a maternal/fetal conflict, in other words, the guardian signals a rise in the status of the fetus. In addition, if a fetus's interests can, potentially, circumscribe a pregnant woman's legally available actions, as the appointment of a guardian necessarily implies, then it is difficult to imagine much protection for the deliberate decision to end the fetus's life.

In short, as a matter of logic, it would seem, guardianship for a fetus enhances the legal status of the unborn and simultaneously diminishes that of pregnant women. Neither move bodes well for abortion rights.

GOVERNOR BUSH'S TARGETING A RETARDED WOMAN SHOULD BE TROUBLING TO ALL

Yet the case of J.D.S. also raises a different issue—one that should perhaps cloud its initially evident appeal for abortion opponents. Utilizing an advocate for a fetus to clash in court with an advocate for a retarded pregnant woman has an undesirable implication. It looks as though, for Jeb Bush, people with developmental disabilities occupy a lower rung of the moral ladder than healthy people, for whose fetuses the governor does not seek guardians.

The message—that a retarded woman has a lesser status than her "normal" counterparts—discredits the pro-life agenda in two ways. First, it might imply that some kinds of abortion—those of babies with Down Syndrome, for example—are less objectionable than others. And it does so, not on the neutral ground that no woman should be forced by the state to bear the substantial physical and emotion burdens of pregnancy. Instead, it rests on the eugenics ground that not all lives are equal.

Second, the unequal treatment of a pregnant retarded woman suggests that if a disabled person does remain pregnant, her own medical best interests—as voiced by her legal guardian—ought to be subordinated to, or at least balanced against, those of her fetus. No such balancing occurs when the pregnant woman is "normal."

The fact that the pro-life governor Jeb Bush selected a retarded woman as a target for adversarial fetal protection law thus has disturbing implications for the value a pro-life society might place on its most vulnerable members.

THE FACT THAT J.D.S. HERSELF HAS A GUARDIAN DOES NOT JUSTIFY TARGETING HER

Pro-life readers might object that Governor Bush selected the J.D.S. case for intervention only because there was already a guardian involved (the retarded woman's), and it thus seemed appropriate to bring in a second guardian.

This explanation, however, ignores the fact that J.D.S. only had a guardian because of her mental retardation. Her guardian thus held the power to protect J.D.S. in much the same way as a competent woman would ordinarily protect herself.

Introducing a *fetal* guardian, by contrast, would change the picture substantially. Before the motion to appoint a fetal guardian, there was one decision-maker for J.D.S.'s body—a guardian who stood in the place of J.D.S. If a fetal guardian were added, however, there would exist competing decision-makers, one of whom would be specifically installed to view J.D.S.'s body as little more than a live incubator. Recall that Lisa Montgomery, the woman accused of kidnapping a fetus after butchering the mother, viewed a pregnant woman's body that way as well.

Consider an analogy to the fetal guardian scenario. Say a four-year-old child named Jane has a rare blood type, and an unrelated adult named John desperately needs a transfusion of such blood. Assume further that Jane is injured, and her parents are advised to obtain a transfusion for their daughter. Before they can obtain the needed blood for their daughter, however, a lawyer for John intervenes and attempts to enjoin the transfusion. Jane will not die without the blood, the lawyer argues, but if she gets a transfusion, her blood will become unsuitable for transfusion to John, who does need a small quantity of it in order to survive.

Jane's parents would ordinarily make transfusion decisions on their daughter's behalf, because she is too young to do so on her own. But that fact does not make it any more appropriate for John's attorney to weigh in on the matter in court, than it would be if Jane were thirty years old and making the decision for herself. John has nothing to say, in other words, about whether or not Jane obtains a transfusion. If he wants her to donate blood to him, then he can take it up with her (or with her parents).

WHY PROHIBITING ABORTION MANDATES ALTRUISM

This analogy will bother opponents of abortion, because it suggests that abortion prohibitions mandate altruism, an anomaly in U.S. law. Pro-life advocates prefer to view an abortion ban as a prohibition against violence, no more or less controversial than a homicide statute.

The flaw in this perspective is that refraining from murder does not, in any other context, demand that a person share the contents of her body with another human being for a lengthy period of time. Because the fetus takes oxygen, nutrients, and internal space from a woman, compulsory pregnancy is far more like an extreme version of forced blood and tissue donation than it is like a homicide prohibition.

Prior to fetal viability, moreover, simply removing a fetus from inside a woman will end the fetus's life. Though abortions generally involve killing the fetus prior to removal, the fetus could not survive a normal delivery. Even if it were carefully removed intact, in other words, with the best of intentions, the fetus would die, and no one could do anything to save it. Pregnant women who go into labor prior to term know this reality only too well.

This fact is significant, because it means that to obey a prohibition against terminating a pregnancy, it is not enough for a woman to refrain from killing another being or otherwise doing violence against another. She must also hold a fetus inside her body and allow it to absorb everything it needs for nine months. Asking that of her is far more intrusive than asking a person simply to eschew violence.

WHY J.D.S.'S IS AN EXCEPTIONALLY WEAK CASE IN WHICH TO REQUIRE ALTRUISM

The common response to the forced altruism argument is that someone like the four-year-old Jane in our earlier example is not responsible for creating the person who needs her blood (or for creating the need itself). A woman who has sex with a man, by contrast, does create both the fetus and its need for sustenance. Having invited the fetus into her body, where it consequently depends on her for life, the argument goes, she should not be able to order it to leave and face a certain death.

Even under normal circumstances, this response is weak. Given the slim odds of pregnancy any one time people have sex, the act can hardly be described empirically as a fetal invitation. One could, as plausibly, describe the failure to lock one's door as a burglary invitation. In both cases, people take a risk, but that is all. And when people use contraceptives, the "risk equals invitation" argument becomes that much weaker.

In any event, this response—poor as it is generally—is entirely unavailable in the case of J.D.S. She is believed to have conceived during a rape that took place in a group foster home where she lived. She therefore did not consent to—indeed, was not mentally capable of consenting to—anything that might be construed (however implausibly) as an invitation to use her body to sustain another life.

WHY TARGETING J.D.S. IS NOT ONLY WRONG, BUT TRAGIC

Tragically, J.D.S.'s disability—which should have entitled her to special governmental accommodation—instead led Governor Bush and his pro-life constituents to single her out for discriminatory treatment.

It is because of J.D.S.'s severe disability that she was incapable of consenting to sex. It is because of her severe disability that she was incompetent to make medical decisions on her own behalf and thus required a guardian. And it is thus inescapable that it is also her severe disability that made her such an appealing candidate for pro-life activist intervention.

The governor's defenders may counter that the selection of J.D.S. was purely opportunistic. Were it possible to appoint guardians for every fetus, Jeb Bush would happily do so. But regrettably, the law seems to provide an opening only in the case of the severely retarded pregnant woman.

This response is morally repugnant. Whenever people choose to pick on the retarded (or the vulnerable generally), they do it at least in part because they expect to get away with it. Indeed, if not for her disability, J.D.S. might not have become the target of a rapist who probably anticipated that his crime would go undetected if committed against a woman who could not speak or complain of the outrage committed against her. Unlike a normal, functioning adult woman, J.D.S. was apparently impaired enough to tempt the governor of her state as well, to try to elevate her fetus's interests over her own.

POSTSCRIPT

In August of 2003, J.D.S. gave birth to a healthy baby girl. The 5th District Court of Appeals in Florida subsequently affirmed the trial court's denial of Governor Bush's request to appoint a legal guardian for the fetus.[2] It turned out that the baby girl's father was the husband of J.D.S.'s caregiver, Hester Strong. Both Hester and her husband were arrested, but Mr. Strong was found not competent to stand trial, and Ms. Strong's felony neglect charges were dismissed.

When a woman's right to abortion is at issue, courts are, for the moment, unwilling to appoint fetal representatives to resist a woman's right to terminate a pregnancy, regardless of how impaired the mother might be. But can anti-abortion advocates take their appeals directly to the pregnant women themselves? The next chapter considers the wisdom and constitutionality of a proposed federal law that would require providers to tell their patients about fetal suffering before performing an abortion.

·9·

Forcing Pregnant Women to "Know" about Fetal Pain

Recently, the *Journal of the American Medical Association* (*JAMA*) published an article concluding that a developing fetus does not experience pain prior to twenty-eight weeks of gestation.[1] The study might prove significant not only for pregnant women considering whether and when to terminate a pregnancy, but also for the law.

Before publication of this study, Senator Sam Brownback (R-Kansas) sponsored a bill, known as the "Unborn Child Pain Awareness Act," which would require abortion providers to discuss fetal pain with their patients after twenty weeks of pregnancy and offer to administer fetal anesthesia during the procedure.[2] Based on the new scientific findings, such counseling would seem completely inappropriate. But what about after the twenty-eighth week? Is it then acceptable to mandate such counseling?

Quite apart from the empirical conclusions outlined in *JAMA*, the article's appearance provides a useful occasion for public discussion of the question whether the law should *ever* mandate the exposure of women seeking an abortion to information about fetal pain.

IMPLICATIONS OF THE *JAMA* FINDINGS FOR UNBORN CHILD PAIN AWARENESS ACT

If one finds persuasive the findings negating fetal pain in the first two trimesters of pregnancy, *JAMA*'s announcement has obvious implications for the Unborn Child Pain Awareness Act. If the fetus does not experience pain prior to twenty-eight weeks of gestation, it would plainly be improper for the law to require health care providers to tell their abortion patients otherwise.

Providing material misinformation to patients considering a procedure is medical malpractice, and the law has no business demanding malpractice of the nation's physicians. (Sadly, even without a federal mandate, there is plenty of medical malpractice to go around.) Offering fetal anesthesia to such women would be equally inappropriate, for similar reasons, as it could expose patients to unnecessary risks with no benefit to anyone, including the fetus.

An interesting question that the *JAMA* article does not answer, however, is whether it is *ever* appropriate to require that health providers tell abortion patients about fetal pain. That is, if an abortion *does* take place after a fetus has become capable of suffering, should doctors have to tell women of that fact?

Those who favor the bill in question say yes.

Someone who opposes the right to terminate a pregnancy would, almost by definition, wish to do whatever he or she legally could do to make abortion more difficult for women to obtain. Like a mandatory waiting period, an information session about an unborn child's suffering during abortion is likely to discourage at least some women considering the procedure from going through with it. Furthermore, if a woman does decide to terminate her pregnancy notwithstanding what she has learned, the discussion could contribute to the emotional distress she might feel after having done so, a desirable effect if one views abortion as properly criminal.

It is, not surprisingly, precisely these anticipated consequences of the Unborn Child Pain Awareness Act that opponents cite as reasons to oppose it. If women have the right to abortion, then the law should not burden them with compelled information sessions that serve to discourage them from carrying out their plans or contribute to the anxiety accompanying the choice.

Is this a sound argument? The answer may depend in part on *why* one thinks the law does, or ought to, recognize the right to abortion.

WHY THE LAW PROTECTS ABORTION

Some would protect abortion on the theory that until an individual human being is born, he, she, or it does not count as someone entitled to rights. If one accepts this premise, then it would seem to follow that a pregnant woman should be allowed to terminate the life of the nonperson in her body at any time during gestation. Indeed, answering the question would be no more difficult than saying whether the law should permit a couple to refuse to donate its extra frozen embryos to another couple (which, of course, a couple may indeed refuse to do). Until birth, then, the embryo or fetus is a kind of property that the pregnant woman can decide to keep, donate, or destroy, as she wishes.

From this perspective, the notion of compelling doctors to tell women about fetal pain would seem preposterous. The only "person" present with the doctor is the woman, and only if she *wants* information about the property she holds within her body should the doctor be giving her that information.

A second account of the abortion right, however, stems from the very different idea that no person should be forced to sustain another living creature with her body, an idea that I have defended in earlier chapters. The experience of pregnancy, on this view, is far too intimate and demanding for the law to require it of women, particularly when the law generally requires no similar physical altruism of men, who can choose not to donate blood or organs to relatives (or others) in need.

Far from demanding blood and organs from its citizenry, in fact, the law in this country protects even a dead person from compulsory organ donation. And this is true notwithstanding the fact that such organs—which will otherwise decompose in a graveyard or go up in flames—could be used to save and preserve many lives.

When bodily integrity is so prized, it must not give way just because it is the bodies of pregnant women at issue. Otherwise, the law engages in arbitrary sex discrimination.

Unlike the first nonpersonhood account of reproductive freedom, this second account of the right to abortion does not take a position on the question of when life begins, or whether or not the fetus is (or at some point becomes) a person holding rights and entitlements. Even a full person, it maintains, does not have the right to inhabit another person or demand blood or organs from her.

Because this second account of abortion protection does not denigrate the status of embryos or fetuses, it might accordingly allow for women's exposure to facts about abortion that could bear on the moral significance of the procedure. It allows—though it does not require—the belief that the fetus is a person, and the corresponding view that women should be informed of the consequences of their abortion to what may be fairly characterized as a third-party.

If continuing a pregnancy is in fact an act of kindness, and abortion an act of cruelty (albeit a legally permissible act of cruelty) against another valuable living creature, then a woman making a decision about how to proceed should perhaps know what she is (or is not) doing in taking the next step.

ARE INFORMATION SESSIONS INSULTING TO WOMEN?

There is a common response to the argument that women should know what they are choosing to do, even if no one has the right to stop them. It is that this argument assumes that women do not consider the moral implications of abortion before proceeding. Such an assumption might seem presumptuous and insulting to women. But it need not be.

Most of us—male and female alike—are probably ignorant about the degree to which a fetus at a particular stage of gestation may or may not experience sensations. It is no insult to recognize this fact and to provide information that might bear on the decision that a woman will make.

By the same token, many women considering abortion might find comforting the newly published data about fetal suffering; these data help to dispel some of the misinformation propagated by various actors within the pro-life movement. And learning of the data might cause women to schedule—and doctors to provide—abortions timed to avoid fetal pain, thus lessening some of the guilt or other trauma that could follow an abortion.

AN EQUAL RIGHT TO REMAIN IGNORANT

But there is a second, more compelling, response to the argument that women should know the moral consequences of what they do. It has more to do with equality than with (potentially inaccurate) claims about what women already know and therefore need not be told.

That second response is this: Even with respect to facts that we might consider morally relevant to our decisions, most of us can avoid information that we prefer not to hear.

Suppose you go to the doctor and ask about donating blood. The doctor will probably tell you that if you give blood regularly, then with virtually no risk to your own health, you can save several lives every couple of months. In spite of chronic blood shortages, however, the law does not *require* doctors to tell us this information. Thus, those of us who simply dislike needles can move through our lives blissfully ignorant about the numbers of people who need us for their very survival and whose deaths can accordingly be attributed to our petty squeamishness.

The same is true when it comes to donating organs after we die. We no longer need them at that point, and people who are suffering from organ failure do. Yet we can choose to turn away from that information, and consequently leave others to suffer painful, horrible, and unnecessary deaths, just as surely as if we were to leave them drowning in a swimming pool, when we could easily have rescued them.

To give one more example, people choose to remain happily unaware of the suffering inflicted on animals killed for consumption. Most people know in their gut that if they were to read about or pay a visit to a slaughterhouse, what they learned would likely induce feelings of guilt about the decision to continue eating meat and thus finance the shocking cruelty. So they don't pay such a visit (or its Internet equivalent); they shield themselves from unwelcome revelations—again, remaining blissfully ignorant. Society, moreover, permits the ignorance to flourish and does not, for instance, require that every package of meat feature graphic photographs of animal suffering that would more fully inform the choice to consume flesh.

We tell ourselves that animal's lives are relatively good prior to slaughter and that their deaths are quick and painless, though, as a general matter, nothing could be further from the truth. Animals are kept in inhumane conditions of crowding and disease, and their deaths are generally terrifying and painful. But waiters need not tell us any of this when they read us the specials of the day. A person can feast on suckling pigs and baby calves without giving their suffering or terror a second thought.

For purposes of terminating a pregnancy, then, we might ask whether women contemplating an abortion should be forced to confront the moral implications of their course of conduct, when others who cause pain and death—of other people, by declining to donate blood and organs, or of other sentient creatures, by consuming meat—are not required to do so.

In answering this question, we might conclude that no one should have the right to choose ignorance, and that the government ought to be telling people about the consequences of refusing to donate blood, of refusing to sign the "donate organs" line on their driver's licenses, of making the choice to consume the flesh of animals, *and* of choosing to terminate a pregnancy.

Though such an approach would be internally consistent, it is far from the position that society currently takes. The fact that only the last of these—the one that affects women alone—might be subject to mandatory disclosure says a great deal about gender equality.

We might, on the other hand, decide that the government is ill-suited to select which information is most relevant to the moral choices that people in a free society—men *and* women—must make. If we take that view, then the government should not be forcing anyone to confront unpleasant information about their actions.

It is also clear that given the meat lobby's power over government, it is unlikely that the law would ever compel disclosure of the facts about animal cruelty to consumers of dead animals as food or clothing.

The government is, thus, far from a neutral arbiter of which facts its citizenry needs in order to act wisely and justly in the world. When the government gives us morals information, it usually does so for a reason: because it wants to influence our ultimate decision. Similarly, the government's failure to offer pertinent facts indicates that it likes or is at least complacent about the kinds of decisions that we are already making, given the information readily available and known to most, if not all.

In light of that reality, it may be best to embrace a general freedom to avoid government-mandated information sessions. Such freedom may ultimately amount to a right to reject the majority's selection of which facts a person ought to consider material to the significant moral choices that every one of us must make during our lives. In a country where public libraries feature Internet terminals for all, it has never been easier to inform ourselves. We delegate this responsibility to the government at our peril.

POSTSCRIPT

Senator Brownback introduced the Unborn Child Pain Awareness Act in 2004 and again in 2005.[3] The bill would require abortion providers to tell mothers that fetuses after twenty weeks are capable of feeling pain, to offer anesthesia for the fetus, and to have the mother sign a consent form. The bill is currently in committee.[4]

Pro-life activists have approached their abortion-reduction mission in a variety of creative ways. Telling women that a fetus suffers during abortion is one example. Another, which also involves the compelled provision of information, has taken the form of parental notification statutes. By and large, the public favors laws that require providers to notify parents when their children wish to obtain an abortion. But is this favor misplaced?

• 10 •

The "Minor" Issue of Abortion

In mid-July 2002, the United States Senate held hearings on whether to confirm Priscilla Owen, a Texas Supreme Court Justice, for a position on the U.S. Court of Appeals for the Fifth Circuit. Owen has held an extremely narrow view of a minor's right to abortion—one that a majority of her colleagues on the Texas high court has rejected as inconsistent with state law. In part for this reason, her nomination provoked considerable controversy.

President George W. Bush may have chosen to nominate Owen precisely because of her politics. Accordingly, her politics—and especially her views on abortion—are relevant to the confirmation process.

Regardless of its outcome, the fight over Priscilla Owen will have been worthwhile if it motivates the nation to confront a question it has often seen fit to ignore: how important is a minor's right to terminate a pregnancy?

THE PRO-LIFE ANSWER: MINORS SHOULD NOT HAVE ABORTIONS AT ALL

We know the pro-life answer to that question, but how far outside the mainstream is it? Many Americans share the intuition that minors ought to consult with their parents before obtaining an abortion. But there is a crucial and often-overlooked distinction between believing that girls *ought* to talk to their parents, and supporting a law that *requires* them to do so.

For a person who holds the view that all abortions should be illegal, the parental consent issue is easy. If a minor should ideally be forced to carry her pregnancy to term, then it follows necessarily that she should not be allowed to abort without her parents' input. Short of an outright ban, in other words, a substantial obstacle (or any obstacle) is better than nothing. But why might someone who generally supports abortion rights come to this conclusion?

THE ARGUMENT THAT MINORS HAVE LESS AUTONOMY ACROSS THE BOARD

The main defense of pro-choice Americans who support parental consent and notification requirements is that parents can decide for a sick child which medical procedures she will undergo or whether to consent to treatment at all. A child who prefers to keep his swollen tonsils may have them forcibly removed, if a parent agrees, on the advice of a physician. And an overweight child who wants liposuction may be barred from the surgery by a parent's refusal to consent. We generally presume that parents will act in the best interests of their children in such matters.

Abortion, moreover, in addition to being a medical procedure might seem similar to other sorts of important decisions that minors are not empowered to make for themselves. A fourteen-year-old boy or girl, for example, can be criminally punished for having sex—through statutory rape laws—because we believe that only adults are entitled to sexual autonomy. The decision to have an abortion, once pregnant, may strike many as a logical extension of the decision to have sex. Though adults have a right to it, children do not.

Although superficially appealing, this reasoning is flawed, for both philosophical and practical reasons.

THE ABORTION DECISION DIFFERS FUNDAMENTALLY

Consider the circumstances of a pregnant minor who wishes to abort. The burden of carrying a child in her body against her will is just as great as, if not greater than, the analogous burden on an adult woman. (Indeed, the possibility of an unplanned pregnancy is one of many reasons to prohibit minors from engaging in sexual relations in the first place.)

Pregnancy draws nutrients such as calcium out of the still-maturing young mother's body, and the emotional costs of being forced to remain pregnant against her will may be inestimable. To that extent, the youth of the petitioner—rather than undermining her interest in self-determination, as it normally might—enhances the strength of her claim.

To compare an abortion to an appendectomy or liposuction, moreover, is to miss perhaps the most important feature of the burden faced by a minor who wishes to terminate a pregnancy but cannot: her body is subjected to a severe and major intrusion in order to give life to someone else.

Remaining pregnant against her will is therefore more like a nonconsensual organ donation or nonconsensual surrogate motherhood than it is like an unwanted throat culture that parents elect for their child's own good.

THE ORGAN DONOR ANALOGY

Imagine a fourteen-year-old boy whose father needs a kidney transplant. Assume that the adolescent, after learning the pros and cons of the procedure, refuses to give consent. Without the transplant, his father will die.

Is this decision one that we would want the father to force upon his son? Would we not consider such an imposition tantamount to child abuse?

Keep in mind, moreover, that this analogy assumes an existing man (the father) whose status as a person is incontrovertible. At least in the early stages of pregnancy, the same can by no means be said of the developing embryo or fetus.

THE SURROGATE MOTHERHOOD ANALOGY

Now assume that a married couple creates four frozen embryos with the intention of implanting them in the uterus of the wife. Unforeseen circumstances, however, make it physically impossible for her to become pregnant. Her fourteen-year-old daughter, on the other hand, could carry a pregnancy to term and is fertile enough to make implantation extremely likely.

What if the parents in these circumstances were to force surrogate motherhood on their unwilling daughter? That would unquestionably constitute child abuse, despite the fact that the alternative for the embryos is a certain death. In fact, it may be that even if the girl did consent, the physical and emotional burdens of pregnancy at the age of fourteen would be too great to justify.

These analogies illustrate why parents should not be in a position to make a choice on an unwilling child's behalf when two conditions are present: first, the choice categorically runs counter to the child's medical interests; and second, others—whether her parents, a fetus, or someone else—stand to benefit from that choice. The risks to the child are too immense—and the temptation too great—under these circumstances to allow parents to discount her interests in favor of another's.[1]

Of course, both conditions are present when a minor chooses whether to abort. Most minors' lives will not be improved by being pregnant and giving birth while they are still children themselves. Yet in considering the abortion decision, the minor may be pressured to ignore her own interests to honor her parents' religious beliefs or vindicate the embryo's interest in a potential life. She might reasonably be expected to listen to the parents' views on religion, and think about the embryo. But in the end, the decision should be hers.

PRACTICAL REALITY

Though the abstract arguments for a minor's right to abortion are strong, the practical case is even stronger.

The Supreme Court has held that states may require minors seeking an abortion to notify a parent, as Texas law requires, or to obtain a parent's consent, as Pennsylvania law does.[2] There is one caveat, however. To pass constitutional scrutiny, the law must provide for a "judicial bypass."

A judicial bypass is an opportunity for the minor who prefers not to consult with her parents about a planned abortion to convince a judge that she is mature enough to make the decision on her own (or that an abortion would be in her best interests). At such hearings, judges often ask girls irrelevant questions about their grades at school or embarrassing and unnecessary questions about how the girls became pregnant.

In an abortion case that came to the Texas Supreme Court while Priscilla Owen served, she wrote a dissenting opinion that interpreted the Texas judicial bypass provision so narrowly as to provoke the following words from then-Justice (now Attorney General) Alberto Gonzalez: "To construe the Parental Notification Act so narrowly as to eliminate bypasses, or to create hurdles that simply are not to be found in the words of the statute, would be an unconscionable act of judicial activism."

As Columbia Law Professor Carol Sanger has said, a girl's appearance at the hearing is a ritual of humiliation, one that is experienced (and may indeed be intended) as punitive and intrusive.[3]

Given this reality, Justice Owen's desire to block the girls who appear in court from obtaining an abortion is truly alarming. It necessarily entails a decision that a girl who has managed to find her way to a judge to petition for her rights is too immature to decide that she should *not* have a child.

And under Supreme Court precedent, it must also reflect a finding that being forced to carry a pregnancy to term and give birth against her will is in the best interests of the immature teenager. In the real world, such a girl can be expected to turn next to a substantially less reputable source of assistance than Justice Owen.

OUR IDEALS AND REALITY CLASH WHEN IT COMES TO MINORS' RIGHT TO CHOOSE

The notion of pregnant minors consulting with their parents is unquestionably appealing. No one—whether pro-choice or pro-life—likes the idea of a child going alone to an abortion clinic. Ideally, a girl can depend on a parent at a time like that. Unfortunately, however, the law only comes into play in situations far from ideal.

To a girl who would automatically go to Mom about an unwanted pregnancy, the law of parental notification is irrelevant. And to a girl who would not, the law cannot forcibly create the warmth and trust that are absent. Many minors will seek guidance from their parents, regardless of the law. Nonetheless, and as the Court has held with respect to an analogous spousal notification provision struck down in *Planned Parenthood v. Casey*, "[t]he proper focus of constitutional inquiry is the group for whom the law is a restriction, not the group for whom the law is irrelevant."[4]

The truth is that few minors in this situation have the wherewithal to find their way to court to petition for an abortion. For a judge to look those who do in the eye and say "No; you must carry your pregnancy to term" is to speak volumes about that judge's ability to exercise empathy and compassion, a capacity that is rightfully considered a hallmark of an enlightened and fair judiciary. If Priscilla Owen lacks that quality, then she does not belong on the federal bench, and the Senate should have said so.

POSTSCRIPT

Priscilla Owen indicated her belief that a judge's stance on parental-notification should not play any role in the assessment of that judge's views on *Roe v. Wade*. The Senate confirmed Judge Owen on May 24, 2005, as part of the Senate deal to prevent the "nuclear option," i.e., the elimination of the filibuster from Senate practice. Her confirmation signaled a further weakening of women's and girls' freedom from discriminatory intimate coercion in this country.

As we discuss the many issues surrounding reproductive rights, it is important to observe that abortion disputes often come down to a fight over how to characterize the events that occur between conception and birth. Pro-choice advocates say that such events represent "reproduction," in which raw cellular material metamorphoses into a full, rights-holding human being inside a woman's body. Pro-life activists assert instead that pregnancy is more of a custodial time when a rights-holding person lives and thrives in the environment best suited to his or her present needs, the uterus.

Though crucial to abortion debates, moreover, the importance of these characterizations goes well beyond the issue of whether a woman should have the right to terminate her pregnancy. How we characterize the process of zygote-to-birth development affects the definition of what it takes for a woman to become a biological "mother" when there are several contenders for that title. It is to this question that the next two chapters turn.

• 11 •

Who Gets Custody When the Fertility Clinic Makes a Mistake?

In August 2004, Susan Buchweitz recovered a million dollars in a settlement with a fertility clinic. Doctors at the fertility clinic had erroneously given her an embryo intended for another family.

That same year, when the boy who had come from that embryo was three, Buchweitz's right to remain his mother came under attack. The possibility that she could lose her son—by virtue of the DNA that he shares with a different family—reveals a kind of sex discrimination that often goes unnoticed.

THE DOCTORS' ERROR

For many years, Susan Buchweitz dreamed of becoming a mother. Like other women, she had initially hoped to find a partner in her quest for parenthood. But when things did not work out that way, she decided to pursue the difficult alternative path of having a baby and raising him by herself. At the age of 47, Buchweitz visited a fertility clinic and had an embryo implanted in her womb. She carried the developing child for nine months and then delighted when her plan came to fruition and she gave birth to a baby boy.

Ten months later, however, Buchweitz learned that she might lose her son. This was not because she had done anything wrong or had failed to lavish sufficient love and attention on him. It turned out that her doctor had made a mistake and implanted an embryo that was intended for someone else.

The doctor in question reportedly told Buchweitz that he knew of his error almost immediately after making it. He testified that he failed to tell her, however, for fear of what the revelation might unleash for all involved.[1] He reportedly said he had decided instead to leave it "in God's hands."[2]

THE ENSUING TORT LITIGATION

As noted above, Buchweitz subsequently sued and received a million dollar settlement. The case was straightforward. The doctors should have taken greater care to ensure that they did not implant an embryo in a woman whose status as the child's parent would, foreseeably, come under attack.

The fertility specialists' job was to help Susan Buchweitz and the other couple (whose identity has not been disclosed) conceive babies whom each, respectively, would be entitled to keep and raise as their own. The doctors failed spectacularly at that job.

Because of the clinic's negligence, Buchweitz faced much more daunting litigation: defending a lawsuit in which another couple sought custody of her son. Before the ultimate resolution of the case, a family court in California awarded the biological father twice-weekly access to the child and gave Buchweitz temporary custody.

THE ESSENCE OF MOTHERHOOD

The man and woman for whom the embryo was originally intended, according to Buchweitz, "don't accept me as my son's mother." In their view, the woman who took care of the boy had no legitimate claim to him at all. Buchweitz remarked that this was the worst part of the mix-up.

The couple competing with Buchweitz for custody were not to blame, of course, for the error. Indeed, they too may have a legitimate interest in a parental relationship with the little boy who had, for a long time, known only one parent. But compared to what Buchweitz invested in the existence of the boy, the superiority of the couple's claims is anything but obvious.

As chapter 12 details, the attributes that define a biological and legal "mother" ordinarily assemble in one person, all at the same time. Therefore, it is typically unnecessary either to rank these attributes in order of importance or to determine which, if any, are superfluous and which are essential to the status in question. Salient among the attributes are pregnancy, a genetic link, and an expressed intention to raise and care for the child as one's own.

In this case, both Buchweitz and the couple did what would ordinarily have resulted in their respective acquisition of full parental rights. The couple went to a fertility specialist and asked for the retrieval and implantation of an embryo created from the husband's sperm and a donor egg. Buchweitz requested an embryo that had been donated precisely for someone like her, who would implant it and give birth to a child who would be her own. Buchweitz was not a volunteer surrogate mother, and the couple did not voluntarily donate an embryo to a stranger.

In the light of what each of the parties did, it is therefore troubling that the couple would consider it so obvious that the "real" parent is the one with a genetic connection. The willingness to leap to this conclusion reflects a very male-centered orientation to the essence of what it is to be a mother.

FATHERHOOD SHOULD NOT REPRESENT THE PARADIGM BY WHICH MOTHERHOOD IS JUDGED

Think about how a man becomes a father. Ordinarily, a man achieves biological paternity by providing a sperm cell that unites with an egg cell to divide and ultimately grow into a human being. Once a child is born, the man is a father simply by virtue of that initial contribution. Over time, he may prove to be a good or a bad father. To acquire the status in the first place, however, usually demands only a sperm contribution and a nine-month wait.

Consider, by contrast, the meaning of biological motherhood. Conception (and the DNA input entailed) only begins the process of maternity. Pregnancy makes significant demands of a woman. For women, the phrase "biological motherhood" is at least as likely to evoke an image of pregnancy as it is of egg donation. Unlike in the case of paternity, then, one can find oneself the biological child of two women, if one woman gestates and the other contributes an egg. Chapter 12 addresses this possibility.

In this particular controversy, there is not even a colorable argument that Buchweitz waived her parental rights or that she otherwise knowingly carried a child in her body who could subsequently be claimed by other people. Still, when it comes to women and maternity, many fixate on DNA when a controversy arises.

IGNORING GESTATION AS A CLAIM TO BIOLOGICAL MOTHERHOOD

To characterize pregnancy as a nonessential ingredient of biological motherhood is to dismiss as irrelevant the unique (and clearly essential) contribution that women make to the perpetuation of our species. To focus exclusively upon Buchweitz's failure to contribute DNA is to suggest that the *only* important aspect of biological parenthood is the part in which men participate—the contribution of DNA.

Some might respond here that by focusing on DNA, we treat men and women equally. It is not, after all, a man's fault that he cannot gestate a child, so why shouldn't he be treated as an equal partner in creating life?

This question assumes that pregnancy is simply an advantage that women have over men, for which they should get no credit, much as men should not be given points for their (on average) superior height and physical strength. Such an approach ignores the reality that carrying a pregnancy is not simply a capacity that women alone have; it is also a difficult and burdensome job that women alone perform.

If a woman does not carry a pregnancy to term, the fact that she theoretically could (i.e., her sex-based capacity) does not alone entitle her to call herself a child's mother. But if she does make this special contribution, then it is a form of sex discrimination to pretend that she did nothing of value, simply because what she did is uniquely female.

To be sure, there are other ways of becoming parents beside the biological. Adoptive parents are rightfully offended when people ask about their children's "real" parents, referring to the biological mother and father. In Buchweitz's case, however, she has not offered to give up the little boy she raised for three years. Two different families attempted to create a child, and each succeeded in that attempt. The dispute here thus concerns who the *true* biological parent is—who is entitled to hold that office.

To factor Buchweitz out of the equation would, accordingly, have not only done her an individual injustice, but would have treated paternity as the paradigmatic way of becoming a parent. This would represent a biased approach to reproduction. Susan Buchweitz should not have to rely on financial compensation to make her whole. She should be able to take her rightful place among the class of people who are legitimately the parents of the baby to whom she gave birth.

HAS BUCHWEITZ GIVEN UP HER MATERNAL RIGHTS BY SUING HER DOCTORS?

One issue remains. Buchweitz sued and recovered money from the insurer of her fertility providers. Should this recovery weaken her claims to the boy?

It might seem so, for two reasons. First, her suit against her providers might look like a statement from her that she is somehow dissatisfied with the child that resulted from her fertility treatment. Second, her financial recovery might appear to stand as a substitute for the relationship that she had hoped to have (but has now resigned herself to giving up) with her child.

On closer scrutiny, however, neither conclusion follows from the earlier litigation. First, Buchweitz evidently had been and continued to be happy with the child to whom she gave birth, even during her lawsuit against the fertility clinic. She had considered him her son and herself his mother all along. Her suit and recovery reflect the fact that because of the fertility doctors' errors, she faced the possibility of losing her child, and she had to fight for rights that should have been hers automatically. She was not dissatisfied with the child, in other words, but with her own precarious status vis-à-vis that child. (And for the very same reason, the couple suing for custody should perhaps also be able to recover from the fertility specialists' insurers.)

Second, the cost—in money and emotional anguish—of having to fight for custody is real, precisely because Buchweitz *does* love her son and does not want to give him up to another family. It is for that cost that she could legitimately claim recovery against the fertility clinic.

But these costs and Buchweitz's recovery do not tell us who is and who should be the parents of the boy over whom three people have fought. For that, we must rely on the Solomonic wisdom of the courts.

POSTSCRIPT

The biological father ultimately sued for full custody of the child, and after mediation, the two parties settled for joint custody. In April of 2005, the fertility doctor lost his medical license.

• 12 •

Is That Egg Donor My Mommy?

Within twenty-four hours of Mother's Day 2004, a California appeals court had held that E.G., a woman who gave birth to twins conceived with her lesbian lover's eggs, was the *sole* legal parent of the twins.[1]

The ruling came as a terrible disappointment to K.M., the woman whose eggs had been used to conceive the twins. K.M. had petitioned to establish her parental relationship with the children, but the trial court, affirmed by the appellate court, dismissed K.M.'s petition. The court based its conclusion largely on a consent form that K.M. had signed, waiving parental rights prior to the retrieval of her eggs.

The decision in this case exposes the complexity of defining the term "mother" as well as the discriminatory impact that traditional default rules can have on nontraditional families in which women seek to have children without a male partner.

THE FACTS OF THE CASE: HOW THE DISPUTE AROSE

To make it easier to follow the identities of the parties, I will refer to E.G. as "Birtha" (since she is the birth mother) and to K.M. as "Ova" (because her ova gave rise to the twins).

Birtha and Ova were together as a couple when they decided to use Ova's eggs to try to conceive a child in 1995. A doctor at the fertility clinic where both women had received treatment suggested that they use Ova's eggs and Birtha's womb to have children, because each woman suffered from medical problems that prevented one from becoming pregnant and the other from becoming a genetic parent.

The result of the chosen arrangement would be children that would have biological connections to both women. (Notably, this would create a variant on the classic family in which one person—the father—contributes genetic material and the other—the mother—contributes genetic material as well as gestates and gives birth to the child.)

Prior to retrieving her eggs, the hospital required Ova to sign a consent form that included, among other things, a waiver of parental rights to any resulting offspring. She signed the form—as so many of us routinely do on request when we go into the hospital. Doubtless, she believed that without her signature, the procedure could not go forward.

When Birtha gave birth to the twins, the two women were living together and proceeded to share the work of raising the children, work that is traditionally associated with mothers and fathers. As so many married couples do, though, the two women eventually split up and found themselves in litigation over their respective rights vis-à-vis the children.

OVA'S INTENTIONS

The standard egg donation consent form that Ova signed became a very significant document in this litigation, because it contained the boilerplate (standard) waiver of parental rights with respect to children resulting from any retrieved eggs.

Ironically, Ova appeared to have signed the form in order to facilitate the creation of children for whom she would in fact bear responsibilities and to whom she would maintain rights. Ova said that she planned to adopt the children later to formalize their relationship, though some construed this statement as further proof that she understood that she was not their legal mother in the absence of an adoption.

But Ova acted like the twins' mother in countless ways—actions that suggested that she wanted to be their mother but did not understand the law to protect that desire without an official adoption.

Ova likely thought, moreover, that she would stay with Birtha and live as one of two mothers of the twins and that the issue of "legal parent" would never prove to be as important as the reality of her connection to the two children.

Though perhaps naïve, this is all a far cry from Ova's intending to give up her parental rights.

A CONSENT FORM PREMISED ON TRADITIONAL ASSUMPTIONS DISCRIMINATES IN PRACTICE

The premise of the consent form that Ova signed is that if someone other than the genetic mother gestates a child, then either the genetic *or* the gestational mother (but not both) will be the "real" legal mother. The presumed situation is therefore that a woman is donating her eggs to another woman who will then become the mother. If, on the other hand, the gestational mother is a surrogate, then there is no need to sign a consent form, because the law tends to view genetic parenthood as the paradigm of biological parental connection, as we saw in chapter 11.

Even in theory, as the last chapter explained, this perspective on parenthood tends to elevate men over women. It does so by ignoring the uniquely female role of gestation in reproduction and accordingly requiring the "real" mother (whose contribution matches that of the biological father) to give up her rights before the "gestational" mother may occupy the status of biological parent.

In practice, moreover, these implicit assumptions foster discrimination against same-sex couples. Paradoxically, for example, to permit the in vitro fertilization (IVF) to proceed according to plan, Ova had to sign a form that included a declaration of her intention to do precisely the opposite of what she apparently intended to do.

The California appellate court, however, pointed to the terms of the consent form as evidencing Ova's intention that Birtha be the sole legal parent, possessing all parental rights that Ova might otherwise have had. "The ultimate determination of parenthood depends not upon the existence of a binding contract but rather, as *Johnson* instructs, upon the woman's *intention* to bring about the birth of the child to raise as her own."[2]

But can the court truly infer intention here primarily from a signed default consent form?

Imagine the analogous male/female situation. Husband and Wife are the members of a couple that wants Wife to become pregnant. Unable to conceive through sexual relations, the couple undergoes a course of IVF.

When the doctors prepare to collect Husband's sperm, they ask him to sign a default consent form, one under which he relinquishes paternity rights over any resulting children. He signs the form, which also contains provisions indicating his understanding of the process of preparing the sperm for fertilizing his wife's eggs and the potential risks involved. Husband and Wife raise the resulting child until the age of seven, when they divorce.

It would be strange to say that Husband had explicitly manifested his *intention* to relinquish paternity rights. Both his relationship with his spouse and his interactions with his children belie any such intention.

Of course, the idea that a father would, as a default matter, have to relinquish his paternity rights as part of fertility treatment is preposterous. Our default rule is that there can be *both* a mother and a father, not just one or the other, and therefore, such a default consent form would undermine rather than foster the intentions of most couples seeking fertility treatment.

THE ESSENCE OF MOTHERHOOD

When Husband and Wife in the real world conceive and bear a child in the conventional way, the various meanings of "mother" converge, and it is accordingly unnecessary for the law or society to articulate exactly what features define the essence of maternal status. The mother in such a case is the person who conceives, bears, and cares for the child.

Once a family departs from this picture, however, it is no longer possible to avoid the question. Is the woman whose egg was fertilized the mother? Is the woman who gave birth to a child the mother? Or alternatively, is the woman—or are the women—who care(s) for the baby the mother(s)?

There are circumstances in which we would answer "no" to each of these questions, although all three together conventionally define motherhood.

An egg donor, for example, like a sperm donor, can intentionally and prospectively relinquish contact and relations with her genetic progeny. The problem here is that Ova does not really fit the "egg donor" profile.

Similarly, a surrogate can decide to bear a child for someone else, although there is no evidence at all that Birtha meant to occupy the role of surrogate.

Finally, there are people who care for others' children, either as part of a support network or extended family, or as paid childcare. While these people may be valued caregivers, they do not ordinarily occupy the special status of "mother" either.

We can thus isolate each respective component of motherhood and determine that it is not *the* essential component. What this means is that defining the "essence" of motherhood through an across-the-board rule may not be desirable nor even possible.

WHERE LEGAL RULES FAIL

In some ways, it might seem that the most reliable, predictable, and thus legally sound result in the Birtha/Ova case would place a great deal of weight, as the appellate court did, on the consent form that Ova signed. The legal significance of such a form is clear and unambiguous, and no one forced Ova to sign it.

But common sense pulls many of us in a different direction. The behavior of the two women—who were in a committed relationship with each other at the time of conception—supports an intention by each to become a parent to the children to come.

To ignore this context and rule as the appellate court did is to exhibit insufficient respect for the connection between the parties in this case. It is also to focus far too much attention on the very common willingness among people to waive rights that they are asked to waive and that most people imagine will never be called into question because they trust their life partners, whether or not they are married.

It appears, based on the facts of this case, that Ova is a mother to the twins for whom she has cared with Birtha. Her desire to fill that role now must therefore come as no surprise to anyone following her story. And though a fact-sensitive inquiry is less neat and clean than the path taken by the appellate court here, it nonetheless appears to be the wiser course in this case.

It would be tragic to define "mother" exclusively by reference to oral or written waiver agreements. The injustice of proceeding in this fashion, moreover, would profoundly affect not only the person who has mothered the children in the past and wishes to do so in the future but also the children, who stand to lose as much in these legal battles as the named parties to the litigation.

POSTSCRIPT

The California Supreme Court reversed the Court of Appeals and held that both parties were mothers. K.M. (Ova) was a mother because under the Uniform Parentage Act, a genetic connection with a child is sufficient to establish parentage. The court reasoned that K.M. should not be viewed as comparable to a sperm donor because she did not merely donate her ova but believed that the resulting child would be raised in her and her partner's joint home. As a result, her waiver was irrelevant and neither diminished her obligations of support nor relinquished her parental rights.

When a woman takes her pregnancy to term and gives birth to a child whom she keeps in her custody, there ordinarily follows no dispute about whether she is the mother of that child. She does not, however, thereby escape entirely from society's efforts to define what mothers are or ought to be. Two extremely different contexts in which these questions of definition arise are, respectively, that of public breastfeeding and that of infanticide.

In the breastfeeding context, the question is how the public will react when women who choose to nurse their children (ordinarily the healthiest way to nourish a baby) also wish to leave their homes and join the community in its public spaces, a choice that has—at least formally—been accepted as uncontroversial for a very long time. In the second, tragic, context of infanticide, the question is whether society will acknowledge that, contrary to the myth that real mothers are inevitably nurturing and kind to their babies, a small percentage of new mothers suffer from a mental illness the symptoms of which threaten the lives of the small, vulnerable creatures in their care. The following two chapters take up these questions, in turn.

· 13 ·

Battles over Public Breastfeeding

Modern medicine has, relatively recently, acknowledged what has been obvious to mothers throughout the ages: breastfeeding confers unique and substantial benefits upon babies.

Nursing provides a baby with her mother's immunity to pathogens, along with exactly the right mix of nutrients needed for her to thrive. Breastfeeding also significantly reduces an infant's inevitable ingestion of air while she drinks and the consequent distress that bottle-feeding frequently entails. In addition, it does a lot to facilitate bonding between mother and child.

As a result of these benefits, obstetricians, pediatricians, and hospital nurses today encourage patients to breastfeed their new children. Expressions like "Breast is best," stores like the "Upper Breast Side" in Manhattan, and the proliferation of La Leche League groups throughout the world reflect the zeitgeist. Perhaps most tellingly, a majority of states have enacted legislation specifically protecting the right of a mother to breastfeed in public, and one finds similar legislation abroad.

Not all mothers breastfeed, of course. Some cannot do so for medical reasons, and others cannot afford to take the time away from work. Still others find the process uncomfortable and opt for the bottle. Breastfeeding is fortunately not a life-or-death necessity for babies, and most of those who drink formula do just fine.

Statistically speaking, however, the superiority of breast milk for a baby's first months is undeniable. Mothers with the opportunity and desire to breastfeed have accordingly welcomed legal developments that protect their ability to do so.

SOCIAL ATTITUDES LAG BEHIND THE LAW

Unfortunately, social attitudes and practices do not always keep pace with the law. In the United States and elsewhere, women who breastfeed outside the house must often be prepared to face hostility.

In Illinois, during the summer of 2004, a woman who tried to breastfeed an infant at her older daughter's Girl Scouts event was reportedly asked to vacate the public area and feed the baby in a toilet stall.

And in New York State, where a woman has an absolute legal right to breastfeed her baby any place she is otherwise authorized to be, hostility to public nursing persists as well.

Consider a personal (if minor) example. During the same summer, I went to the Guggenheim Museum and attempted to feed my baby in a corner of the reading room (where an official at the museum had recommended I go when my infant became hungry). The space at first seemed perfect, because it was quiet and calm, with few other people present.

The librarian in the reading room was friendly toward me initially. She swiftly became surly, though, the instant she realized what my baby and I were up to. She periodically looked over and glared at me while I nursed my newborn infant. (Ironically, one of the photographs of a featured artist at the Guggenheim Museum that day exhibited a nude woman breastfeeding a baby.) As a result, instead of enjoying the miracle of nourishing a child with my own body, I felt embarrassed and eager to finish up as quickly as possible.

This experience and those of mothers around the world led me to ask the following question: Why are some people so hostile to public breastfeeding?

The answer is about more than just breastfeeding. It is about women's bodies and the customary rules that demand shame, also known euphemistically as "modesty," from females.

BREASTFEEDING AND "PUBLIC INDECENCY"

Society today views women's breasts as presumptively sexual and accordingly dirty and taboo. Breasts cannot appear on television during the Super Bowl, for example, without resulting in a firestorm of protest, an investigation, and a debate about just how offensive one might have a right to be, as a matter of free expression.[1]

But isn't breastfeeding different from Janet Jackson's infamous performance? Even if it is "indecent" to bear one's breast in a sexual way, it is pure and beautiful to do so to feed a hungry baby. Inhibiting nursing, moreover, forces mothers to choose between staying home and thus abandoning the public sphere, on the one hand, and giving up breastfeeding, on the other. That choice has far greater implications—for women and for their children—than does the decision about whether to expose one's nipples for entertainment value.

Yet the difference between the two has a decidedly mixed pedigree—it is the distinction between the Madonna and the whore.

THE MADONNA/WHORE DIVIDE

The Madonna and the whore literally refer, respectively, to Mary, the mother of Jesus, a woman who is believed by Christians to have conceived her son without any sexual interaction, and Mary Magdalene, a reportedly fallen woman whom Jesus befriended despite her status as a sinner.[2] Because her maternity was unsullied by sexuality, Jesus's mother can be pictured breastfeeding throughout the world without a hint of impropriety. Mary is in that sense a pioneer of public breastfeeding.

In feminist discourse, the "Madonna/whore" split describes the choice women have traditionally been forced to make between being good girls—girls who are wholesome, remain virgins until marriage, and subsequently dedicate themselves to the private sphere—and bad girls—those who seek out sexual satisfaction and place their own fulfillment ahead of others'. The good girl was pure and innocent, while the bad girl was dirty, sinful, and sexy.

Other than Mary, mother of Jesus, however, few women—whether "good" or "bad"—can boast a virgin birth. Breasts are, therefore, a double-edged sword. If sexuality is suspect, then breastfeeding will be as well, no matter how maternal and self-negating the woman involved.

A TACTIC FOR BREASTFEEDING MOTHERS: "IN YOUR FACE"

Anyone who wants to create wide-scale acceptance of public breastfeeding will therefore have to do more than change the law—which in many places already reflects the split between "whore breasts" (topless indecency, which is impermissible in public) and "Madonna breasts" (the exposure of which is protected). To avoid the dirty looks, breastfeeding women may have to expose the people around them to breasts often enough for desensitization to set in.

The same was and continues to be true for people's exposure to gay and lesbian couples, interracial couples, and people with disabilities. The need to saturate public consciousness to eliminate a taboo is well captured in the chant, "We're here! We're queer! Get used to it!" If nursing outside the home continues to be a novelty, the taboos are likely to remain firmly in place.

For this reason, at least fifty nursing mothers appeared with their babies, ready to breastfeed, at the Esplanade in Singapore early in the summer of

2004. The women were engaged in a form of protest, reacting to an incident in which a security guard there reportedly asked a nursing mother to leave the premises.

As long as people see public breastfeeding as a taboo or a curiosity, there will be those who either explicitly or subtly drive nursing women into the dark recesses of their lives, regardless of the law. It may take an "in your face" approach, like that adopted by the women in Singapore, to counter that pressure.

Not that many years ago, otherwise tolerant people would say that gay couples could do what they wanted behind closed doors but that they didn't have to "flaunt" their relationships by holding hands or kissing in public. It turned out, however, that flaunting was exactly what the doctor ordered. It is hard to stay shocked by something that you see on a daily basis.

PRIVATE BREASTFEEDING IS A LUXURY

The other side of the argument over public nursing is that breastfeeding is private. If offered a choice, for example, I would have preferred to use a comfortable nursing room to feed my baby than to do it in full view of strangers—even nonobnoxious strangers—at a museum. Part of this preference is the reality that I can avoid perverts and misogynists best when I am alone with my child.

As one U.K. commentator put it, however, "there are a thousand places a mother may find herself when a baby demands—absolutely demands—food, and if she feels she has to be running for the nearest cubby hole, or toilet cubicle, she may decide it is simply not worth the hassle—whether it is better for baby or not."

Privacy is accordingly a luxury that mothers and their babies (and those who would rather not see them engaged in breastfeeding) can ill afford.

POSTSCRIPT

Thirty-two states[3] allow mothers to breastfeed in any private or public location (with most statutes allowing breastfeeding wherever the mother has the right to be, and others limiting the allowance to any place where the mother and the child both have a right to be). Fifteen states exempt public breastfeeding from indecency laws, ten states require workplaces to set aside locations for and develop policies regarding breastfeeding, and ten states explicitly exempt breastfeeding mothers from jury duty.[4]

Women have begun to organize in protest of those who would deny them their right to nurse their children.[5] Women staged a "nurse-in" at a Starbucks in Maryland on August 10, 2004, where they gathered with their infants and breastfed as a group. In May of 2005, Representative Carolyn Maloney (D-New York) led a nurse-in on Capitol Hill to reintroduce the Breastfeeding Promotion Act. And in June of 2005, there was an ABC nurse-in as well, after Barbara Walters made disparaging comments on her women's talk show, *The View*, about having been forced to observe public breastfeeding. Such protests are productive, not only because they help promote breastfeeding—a public good—but because they help make women who give birth to babies feel as welcome in the public sphere as they would have felt if they had made different life choices than they did.

· 14 ·

What Kind of Mother Would Drown Her Children?

After a jury trial that drew the nation's attention, a woman who had confessed to drowning all five of her young children found herself convicted of murder. The jury had unanimously rejected her insanity defense. This result was not entirely surprising, in light of public attitudes. Many people who read the story of her methodical slaughter found it hard to believe that Andrea Yates was insane when she killed her children. And indeed, one cannot really blame them, because in judging Yates, they were simply drawing on widespread—and misinformed—beliefs about insanity.

While understandable, this common perspective—shared by the Yates jury—did not accurately reflect the likely reality of Andrea Yates's mental state at the time of the killings. It underlines instead the dramatic chasm that divides public perceptions and myths about mental illness from what psychiatrists and other experts know to be its reality.

WHY YATES SEEMED SANE TO MANY

Why did people resist the conclusion that Andrea Yates was insane when she killed her children? The evidence seemed to negate insanity in a number of ways.

First, Yates planned her actions carefully. She waited for the one hour in the day when no other adults would occupy the house with her. (Her husband had already left for work, and her mother-in-law had not yet arrived to babysit.)

In addition to the careful planning, she seemed efficient and unrelenting in her actions. Rather than being overcome with emotion, she appeared strangely numb and under control when police arrived on the scene—more like a merciless soldier than a distraught mother. She killed her five children, one after another. And when her oldest son, Noah, resisted and fought for his life, Andrea overpowered him and did not let go. She forced him to die in the same tub water in which she had killed his four siblings, several of whom had vomited and defecated as they died.

Further, even after the terrible killings, Andrea was able to speak coherently, to sound rational, and to retain her composure. Immediately after drowning her defenseless children, Andrea called the police and confessed. She was calm as she explained what she had done. And when the police arrived at her home, she continued to act unperturbed about the grotesque slaughter that she had, only moments ago, carried out. The police found the children's bodies lined up neatly, still wet, on Andrea's bed.

Moreover, Andrea Yates apparently understood the nature of her actions. She did not mistakenly believe that she was washing the laundry or putting out a fire. She had in fact premeditated the deaths of her four young sons—Noah, John, Paul, and Luke—and her six-month-old daughter, Mary, prior to that fateful day. These facts left many skeptical, even among those generally sympathetic toward defendants standing trial in criminal court. How could Andrea have been insane, they wondered, if she knew exactly what she was doing the whole time?

And finally, Andrea understood that society—including her husband, her mother-in-law, and the police—would profoundly disapprove of her actions. She knew, in other words, that she was committing a criminal act that would be condemned by all, and she therefore acted when no one was around to stop her.

That might have been all she needed to qualify as sane. The test for insanity in Texas, quite similar to that in most states, is whether the defendant understood that what she was doing was wrong.

For all of these reasons, Andrea did not resemble the image many of us have of the truly insane. In the popular imagination, an "insane" person is disheveled, raving, and has no idea what she is doing. She is full of passion and rage and cannot respond to reason or manifest an awareness of her community's moral commitments.

An insane person accordingly, by the lights of many, could not coldly plan and premeditate killings of children and then calmly talk about what she had done. Such behavior is the mark of a rational, depraved, and evil heart. A person who would perpetrate these acts in this manner deserves to suffer punishment.

The defense accordingly faced substantial obstacles stemming from both the law and social expectations when it attempted to convince the jury that Yates was not guilty by reason of insanity.

THE REALITY OF MENTAL ILLNESS: A PORTRAIT FROM A POE STORY

The image of mental illness that dominates the popular imagination is, unfortunately, an inaccurate one. It ignores the reality of mental illness, even at its most serious and debilitating.

For a more accurate portrait of madness, consider the narrator in "The Telltale Heart," a short story by Edgar Allan Poe. The narrator stresses that he is not mad—indeed, could not possibly be mad—given how calmly and carefully he planned and carried out the unjustifiable homicide of a man with a deformed eye.

Poe's narrator challenges the reader, "How, then, am I mad? Hearken! and observe how healthily—how calmly I can tell you the whole story." He later comments, "Madmen know nothing. But you should have seen me. You should have seen how wisely I proceeded—with what caution—with what foresight—with what dissimulation I went to work!"

It is hard to read these descriptions now and not think of Andrea Yates—her calm, her caution, and her foresight, and yet her utter madness.

Like Yates, Poe's narrator suffers from a psychotically distorted perception of the world. He "hears" the beating of a dead man's heart and boasts that, "I heard all things in the heaven and in the earth. I heard many things in hell." Yates too claimed to have "heard" Satan's message that her children had to be killed if they were to be saved from eternal damnation.

Any reader of the Poe story can tell that the narrator, despite his protestations, is completely out of his mind. Under the Texas criminal law, of course, he might not have qualified for the defense—since he seemed to have understood both *what* he was doing and that it was wrong.

YATES'S DEPRESSION AND POST-PARTUM PSYCHOSIS: WHEN "GOOD PEOPLE" KILL INNOCENT CHILDREN

Andrea Yates was (and is) a very sick person. No one in the case has disputed that. The delusions from which she suffered distorted the reality around her almost beyond recognition. She had loved her five children—as every witness who knew her and her relationship with her family confirmed. She had not physically or mentally abused her offspring, prior to the homicide, nor had she neglected their needs. Until she came under the spell of the belief that they had to die, she had adored them and treated them with affection, kindness, and love.

When she killed her children, Yates apparently suffered from two kinds of mental illness: post-partum depression and post-partum psychosis. Both of these conditions are painful, frightening, and crippling. Though she had suffered from the same disorders after giving birth to her fourth child, she and her husband nonetheless proceeded with a fifth pregnancy, with tragic consequences.

According to Andrea's husband, Rusty Yates, he had brought her to a psychiatrist several days before she killed their children. The psychiatrist, Rusty claimed, refused to put Andrea on Haldol, an anti-psychotic medication that had worked for her in the past. As an alternative, the doctor adjusted the dosage of her anti-depressants and told Andrea to think positive thoughts. Had he instead prescribed Haldol, he might have averted the horrors that ensued.

Andrea and her husband, like the surrounding society, underestimated the power of mental illness. They believed that since Andrea was a good person, she would never harm her beloved children. Strangers have now embraced the logical flipside of that view, believing that since Andrea killed her children and did so in a cold and methodical fashion, she must never have been a good person or a loving mother in the first place.

The shared assumption underlying both these beliefs is the notion that mental illness cannot affect one's essential nature: A good person cannot be compelled by psychosis to do bad things. Unfortunately, this assumption is false.

Yates did not rant and rave like a Hollywood portrayal of a mentally ill woman, nor did she mistake her own actions for something other than homicide. She believed, however, that her children had to die or they would suffer the fires of hell. We do not know with certainty what put such an idea into her head. She had apparently been close with a traveling preacher, a spiritual mentor who told Andrea that she was evil, that her children were damned, and that only death could save her. Perhaps this "spiritual counsel" played some role in the particular shape that her pathology took, though we may never know.

However it got there, the idea possessed her consciousness. To understand how she felt, one might try to imagine the motives of Jewish mothers about to be discovered with their children in their hiding places during World War II. Knowing that their children would otherwise be taken to Auschwitz, some mothers might have given them cyanide and done so out of love.

In Andrea's case, of course, Nazis were not pursuing her family, and neither—so far as we know—was Satan. Her children could have been safe and happy if she had not brutally snuffed out their lives. Because of mental illness, however, Andrea experienced an urgency that misguidedly and insanely could have led her to feel as strongly as the mothers facing Nazis that what she was doing was in the best interests of her beloved children. Indeed, the prosecutors themselves acknowledged that this might have been the case.

Yates's was not a rational point of view. It was the product of an obsessive, psychotic delusion. It was, in a word, insane and—in particular—insane in a way that a very small category of mothers who have recently given birth are. The law, and our society, should have counseled the Texas jury so to find, and Yates should now be provided with treatment, not consigned to a prison term.

A DIFFERENT APPROACH TO INFANTICIDE

As we contemplate Andrea Yates's fate, we should consider for a moment how other Western nations have dealt with similar cases. Infanticide statutes in at least twenty-nine countries rule out murder charges and usually impose sentences of probation and counseling instead of prison.[1] These statutes reveal an understanding of the reality of post-partum mental illness, and a willingness to presume that maternal sickness, rather than malevolence, explains most such cases.

Andrea Yates, by contrast, could spend the next forty years in prison or even be sentenced to execution in the State of Texas. It is time for the United States to cultivate more of the compassion and enlightenment that other countries have exhibited in responding to the ravages of what we sometimes call "insanity."

POSTSCRIPT

In January of 2005, the 1st Court of Appeals overturned Yates's conviction because her trial had included false testimony from a psychiatrist. The psychiatrist had claimed that Yates was influenced by a Law & Order episode in which a mother drowns her children in a bathtub and then receives an acquittal by reason of insanity. As it turned out, though, that supposed episode never aired on television (and therefore could not have influenced Andrea Yates's prior contemplation of her course of action). The appeals court determined that the trial judge erred in failing to declare a mistrial due to this error. The Texas Court of Criminal Appeals subsequently affirmed the appeals court decision. After Yates was tried a second time, the jury brought back a verdict of not guilty by reason of insanity.[2]

II

NORMALIZING RAPE: THE PRESUMPTION OF INTIMACY BETWEEN WOMEN AND MEN

The first section of this book explored the role of pregnancy in shaping women's lives. This section explores a different kind of intimacy that women experience without their consent. That form of intimacy is rape. Rape is, of course, distinct from pregnancy in a variety of ways. First, a man can become a victim of rape, so the experience is not a uniquely female one.[1] Second, pregnancy can often represent a desired and miraculous experience for a woman, whereas rape is always, necessarily, a harmful and destructive one. And third, even when a pregnancy is unwanted, the unborn baby is not a predator or a perpetrator, as the rapist in a rape case is.

Despite the differences, however, there is a parallel that connects pregnancy and rape, and it is this: just as women are all either pregnant or not pregnant, women are all potential rape victims. Though men are vulnerable to rape if they serve time in prison, men on the outside typically do not feel the need to plan their days with the threat of rape in mind. Women, on the other hand, typically do, even when they do not consciously think about it. The threat of rape, for example, motivates many women to walk with a man or in groups when it is dark outside and they need to leave their offices or homes. And the possibility of rape keeps many women indoors when men feel free to go wherever they want. The "Take Back the Night" rallies—where large groups of college women gather at night and walk without fear—represent a protest against precisely this way of living—in the shadow of rape.

The chapters in this section ask how the law responds to rape. Though forcing a woman to have sex against her will is now and has long been a crime, the law remains ambiguous in some respects. And the ambiguity paints a picture of rape that is perhaps consistent with the reality that women inhabit—even though rape is wrong, it happens often enough that women expect (and are expected) to conduct their lives differently because of it. And when women refuse to do so, they are far more likely to be blamed for what happens.

Chapter 15, the first in this Part, is about the notorious "female serial killer," Aileen Carol Wuornos. The State of Florida executed Wuornos on October 9, 2002, for killing a series of johns whom she had picked up as a prostitute. She claimed that in every case, the man attempted to rape her, and she killed him in self-defense. Her jury, however, did not believe her claims, in part because she robbed some of the men whom she killed, and in part because she continued to turn tricks after each of the alleged attempted rapes. In describing the Wuornos case, I raise the following possibility: the jury may have concluded that as a prostitute, Wuornos did not possess the same legal and moral entitlement to protect herself from rape as that which other, more "virtuous" women possess. A woman's decision to invite men to have sex with her for money, in other words, may give rise—in many people's minds—to an irrebuttable presumption of consent. If this is the case, then a prostitute's right to be free from unwanted sexual intimacy does not find actual protection in the law, regardless of what it may say on the books.

Chapter 16 addresses a question somewhat related to that raised in Chapter 15: how harmful is it when a man rapes an adult woman? Because we are here no longer discussing a prostitute, everyone agrees that the rape in question is a criminal offense. Nonetheless, the Supreme Court tells us, rape is not bad enough—at least if the victim is an adult—to punish its perpetrator with the death penalty. After all, people recover from being raped, and they continue to live. I propose in this chapter that regardless of what one thinks of the death penalty, the categorical refusal to punish rapists with death, when other crimes (including, perhaps, the rape of children or adult men) might occasion execution, treats the violation of a woman's bodily integrity as less destructive and annihilating than it actually is. In doing so, it denies a fundamental predicate for true equality—safety from violation and attack.

Chapters 17 and 18 take on the issue of "date rape"—a crime that falls somewhere between the rape of a prostitute and the rape of a stranger in triggering people's sense of outrage. Specifically, these chapters address the failure of our legal system and our society to take the crime of rape by an acquaintance (or "date") sufficiently seriously. In chapter 17, we examine how the presumption of innocence applies in a date rape case. Many court-watchers and some defense attorneys believe, I explain, that presuming innocence, in the case of a date rape (a case in which the victim is unlikely to make a factual error in identifying the defendant as her assailant), means presuming that the victim is making a false accusation. In other words, the Constitution—on this view—requires the jury to presume that the rape victim witness is a liar, unless she or the prosecutor can persuade them that she is not. The chapter explains why such a mistaken view has taken hold in this one context and what it reflects about our view of a woman who consents to join a man on a date but then refuses to give the man sexual access (also known as a "tease"). Chapter 18 addresses more generally our collective failure to take the occurrence and prevalence of date rape seriously. This failure, I argue, betrays a view of virtually every woman as "fair game" to some man and under some circumstances, regardless of the woman's expressed wishes, a view that denies women's equal status in an essential way.

Chapter 19 advances the above argument about women as "fair game" in a case raising a novel question: whether women have the right to withdraw consent from a man once intercourse has commenced between them. The chapter contends that the fact that this question must arise at all in a court of law signals a presumption that at some point—whether it is when a woman agrees to exchange sex for money, when she decides to go out on a date with a man, or when she consensually begins an act of intercourse—she waives her right to say no and have her wishes honored. In a regime that truly values women's bodily integrity, no such concept of "waiver" of the right to refuse consent could survive.

Chapter 20 considers a proposal to abolish the statute of limitations (which limits the window of time during which a prosecutor may bring charges) in rape cases. The chapter explains the various justifications for statutes of limitations and suggests that because rape is extremely serious, it should—like murder—be subject to prosecution no matter how much time has passed. The existence of a rape statute of limitations, like the express prohibition on executing rapists, implicitly devalues women's absolute right to be free of rape.

Chapters 21 and 22 consider disturbing intimacies that do not rise to the level of rape. Chapter 21 takes up the subject of "statutory rape"—sexual intimacy involving a "victim" under the age of consent. I analyze the reasons that we choose as a society to define a crime in which we use the term "rape" to describe conduct in which a woman's expressed desires are legally irrelevant. In chapter 22, the unwanted intimacy in question is a governmental breast exam at the airport aimed at the prevention of terrorism. I suggest in this chapter that the harm of such unwanted intimacy is great enough to require the government to demonstrate some reason to suspect a particular woman of wrongdoing before embarking on it. Like all of the chapters in this Part, chapter 22 suggests that the government (as reflected in both laws and security policies) might be failing to view as truly deviant the violation of women's freedom from rape and other unwanted bodily intimacies. If the context is right, saying "no" and even resisting are somehow not enough.

•15•

A Female Serial Killer's Claims of Rape

On October 9, 2002, the State of Florida executed Aileen Carol Wuornos by lethal injection. Described in the media as a "serial killer," a phrase that brings to mind such sadistic characters as Ted Bundy and Jeffrey Dahmer, Wuornos might instead have been a serial victim.

Aileen Wuornos was a prostitute. Over a span of two years, the evidence showed, she killed at least six men whom she encountered as customers. Wuornos claimed initially that she had killed these johns after they assaulted or raped her. But she would necessarily have faced a significant obstacle to claiming self-defense before any jury: the fact of her profession.

WHY PEOPLE REJECT THE RAPE CLAIMS OF PROSTITUTES

Because she was a prostitute, Wuornos's rape accusations would strike a lot of people as implausible. Many view a prostitute as willing to have sex, indiscriminately, with any stranger or acquaintance, provided he is ready to pay. As such, people often conclude, a woman like that simply *cannot* be raped, as a matter of logic. Like a railroad obligated to serve all interested customers, the prostitute becomes a metaphorical common carrier, from whom anyone prepared to pay the price may demand service without facing serious criminal charges.

The law, of course, does not contain a literal exclusion for prostitutes from the class of people protected by the criminal law against rape. Indeed, such an explicit exclusion would almost certainly run afoul of the Equal Protection Clause of the Fourteenth Amendment. The law in theory, however, does not always translate well into practice. To become a prostitute may be—in the eyes of customers, jurors, and our society more generally—to hand over a blanket consent to sexual relations.

HOW PROSTITUTES' PLIGHT EXPOSES THE PRECARIOUS NATURE OF RAPE PROSECUTIONS GENERALLY

Though the prostitute may represent an extreme case, her status reveals the precarious nature of a woman's right to protection from rape. Until a few decades ago, for example, most states refused to extend their rape laws—even in theory—to cover sexual assaults by men against their wives.

When she chooses a man as her life-long partner, legislators reasoned, a wife gives herself over to her husband for sex at his pleasure. When we combine that absolute sexual accessibility with a man's legal obligation to support his wife financially, the analogy to prostitution becomes difficult to escape.

While marital rape has become a crime in theory, it is in fact almost never prosecuted. At the same time, the promiscuity of an unmarried rape victim persists—to this day—in substantially reducing the odds of a criminal conviction. The man who rapes a non-virgin, for example, still faces a far more forgiving jury than the attacker who deflowers a virgin.[1]

A STRANGE TWIST IN THE WUORNOS CASE: HER CONFESSION

Aileen Wuornos could therefore have expected little or nothing in the way of legal consequences for any man who raped her. And an intending rapist might himself have predicted in advance that he could assault her with impunity.

Perhaps because of this knowledge or because of the nature or sheer number of men who frequent prostitutes, rape is an occupational hazard for women in the oldest profession. And for the reasons outlined, its prosecution is as rare as its occurrence is common.

In the Wuornos case, however, there is a twist. After being convicted and sentenced to death, Wuornos admitted that she had deliberately robbed and killed her victims. This confession makes the claim that she was truly innocent of murder a difficult one to defend.

WHAT WOULD HAVE HAPPENED HAD THERE BEEN NO CONFESSION?

Let us, however, conduct a thought experiment. What if Wuornos—probably a guilty woman—was sentenced to die simply because of her profession?

Imagine, in other words, a different version of the case as it might have unfolded if Wuornos had not confessed. What would such a case tell us about how we, as a society, view prostitutes?

The convicting jurors in our hypothetical almost-Wuornos case could have believed one of two things. They might have concluded that the victims never tried to rape the defendant in the first place. Or alternatively, they might have believed that even if the men did try to rape her, she implicitly accepted this treatment by failing to quit her job, as a reasonable person would have done for self-preservation. Either way, responsibility for whatever occurred would have rested squarely on the shoulders of the defendant.

The underlying assumption, in other words, would be that even if the men did try to rape her, she—as a prostitute who, by hypothesis, had been raped before—had no right to kill them in self-defense. She had assumed the risk of rape by remaining a prostitute.

A COMPARISON BETWEEN AILEEN WUORNOS AND BERNHARD GOETZ

For a useful comparison, consider the case of Bernhard Goetz. Goetz was mugged on a number of occasions and decided to get even. Because prior assailants had been members of minority groups, he chose to carry out his own informal sting operation on minorities as well.

In 1984, Goetz took an unlicensed firearm, concealed it on his person, and boarded a subway car. He then deliberately sat near a group of young, African-American men who looked threatening to him. Saying nothing, Goetz waited for the men to pounce. They did, apparently attempting to rob him, and he responded with deadly force.

Goetz hated minorities and admitted to having hoped for exactly the scenario that transpired. His one expressed regret was having only paralyzed one of the men and critically injured two others, rather than killing all four of them.

Bernhard Goetz was acquitted of all charges save for illegal possession of a firearm, which carried a one-year minimum sentence.

In the cases of both Wuornos and Goetz, former alleged victims knowingly placed themselves in harm's way and ultimately tried (one successfully, one not) to kill the next potential assailant to come along.

But that is where the similarity ends. Despite his explicit racial hatred and the questions that many critics legitimately raised about the necessity for his repeatedly firing at a man who was no longer assaulting him, Goetz was acquitted. Jurors gave him the benefit of the doubt—a benefit that the criminal law demands. To sit near hostile people on the subway, they implicitly said, is not to assume the risk of being mugged, even if the victim has acted in a knowingly (or deliberately) provocative fashion.

Wuornos, in contrast, died at the hands of the State of Florida. She, a prostitute, would probably not have received the benefit of the doubt. She did not become a heroine in the media, even for a short time, as the subway gunman had. Rather, she was consistently depicted as a heartless villain.

WHY THE WUORNOS CASE REMAINS TROUBLING

There are unlikely to be many tears shed for Aileen Carol Wuornos. And assuming her actual guilt, that is perhaps as it should be. But the case remains a troubling one.

That is because of the possibility that Wuornos never stood a chance of receiving a fair trial. She might have been convicted and sentenced to death, even if she truly had acted in self-defense.

Wuornos was at best a prostitute who refused to retreat from danger. For too many people, that would not have been enough to entitle her to the law's (or her own) protection from rape.

POSTSCRIPT

When a person kills an assailant to protect herself from rape, she exercises a self-help remedy that the law has long viewed as appropriate—at least in theory—to the situation. Because law enforcement officials cannot be everywhere at once, the permissibility of deadly self-help in the face of a rapist reflects the seriousness with which the law takes the predicament of a potential rape victim. Unlike a person who threatens to take a person's wallet, in other words, an attempted rapist threatens to inflict sufficient harm to justify the use of deadly force in response.

A very different question arises, however, when the police have apprehended a rapist, after the fact, and a jury finds him guilty of the crime beyond any reasonable doubt. The State may now inflict punishment on the rapist, and for a long time, many state criminal laws included the possibility of a death sentence for such offenders. The Supreme Court ruled in 1977, however, that death is a disproportionately severe penalty for a rape that does not take the life of its victim. The Court left open the question of whether executing rapists of children and of men is similarly disproportionate.

The next chapter considers the implications of permitting the execution of child molesters while holding that rapists of adult women have not committed a serious enough offense to justify capital punishment.

·16·

Are Rapists Too Good for the Death Penalty?

In August 2003, in Louisiana, Patrick O. Kennedy was sentenced to death for the rape of an eight-year-old child. The state law under which he was sentenced, passed in 1995, permits the death penalty for the rape of a child under the age of twelve.

If the sentence withstands appellate challenges in state court, the U.S. Supreme Court may eventually grant review,[1] because the issue presented is both important and relatively untested within our federal jurisprudence: Does the Eighth Amendment's ban on cruel and unusual punishments permit the execution of those whose crimes do not take a victim's life?

In 1977, the U.S. Supreme Court ruled in *Coker v. Georgia* that the government may not constitutionally punish the rape of an adult woman with death. A plurality of the Court reasoned that such a punishment would be "grossly disproportionate" to the crime of rape, because the rapist does not take the life of his victim. The opinion explained that "[l]ife is over for the victim of the murderer; for the rape victim, life may not be nearly so happy as it was, but it is not over and normally is not beyond repair."[2]

By specifying the question presented as revolving around the "rape of an adult woman," the Court left open at least two questions: May a state execute the rapist of a child (of either sex)? And, might death be a constitutional penalty for the rapist of an adult *man?*

The Louisiana child rape case plainly raises the first question. But it also implicitly invites us to reconsider the *Coker* decision regarding the execution of rapists more generally, in light of the way the Court there explicitly singled out the suffering of "adult women" relative to all other potential victims.

WHY RECONSIDER *COKER*?

At this point, readers might be wondering why I would propose revisiting *Coker*, when the Supreme Court could simply leave that decision in place and limit itself to answering the questions left open there.

One reason to reconsider *Coker* is that nothing about the Court's arguments there provides convincing grounds for distinguishing between rapists based on the age or identity of their victims. If the death penalty is excessive because adult rape victims survive their victimization, then the very same logic should hold true in the case of child rape (or any other crime not resulting in death). People might view one crime as worse than the other, but neither, by hypothesis, entails a victim's death.

It is arbitrary, moreover, to treat child rape as *qualitatively* more heinous than the "rape of an adult woman," for death penalty purposes. To do so minimizes the devastation of rape for women, because it suggests that although the rape of some category of people might be bad enough to call for execution, adult women do not qualify—as a matter of constitutional law—for inclusion within that category.

Put another way, predators of adult female victims—by contrast to predators of children—can claim that what they did is not really bad enough to merit death, that death is actually "grossly disproportionate" to rapes against *these* victims.

Even more disturbingly, it is not only the rape of adults, but the rape of *women* in particular, that *Coker* specially exempts from qualification for the death penalty. None of the Justices in *Coker* explicitly mentioned male victims of rape. One wonders, however, whether the homophobia that animated Justice Byron White's later opinion in *Bowers v. Hardwick*[3] might have led him to conclude that male-on-male, but not male-on-female, rape could merit death. After all, why would the Justices in *Coker* have emphasized the sex of a victim, if not to imply that it might carry some significance?

Imagine, for illustrative purposes, an opinion in which the Court identified the question it faced as whether the death penalty is grossly disproportionate punishment for the rape of white Mormons, or of black Baptists, and declared that it was limiting its discussion to that issue alone. It is difficult, in the twenty-first century, even to imagine the Court framing the issues in these ways.

THE ROLE OF RACE IN *COKER*

For another reason to revisit *Coker*, consider the role that race played in that decision. Without ever mentioning the word "race" explicitly, the main opinion is widely regarded as a response to the toxic history of interracial rape accusations in this country. Lynch mobs, for example, often cited, in defense of their atrocities, the need to protect the "purity" of white women from black rapists, real or imagined.

False accusations of black-on-white rape abounded during the post-Civil War era, with often-deadly results for the black men accused. And men convicted of rape and sentenced to death were typically black, and their victims white.

The Court, in identifying a purportedly "gross disproportion" in the imposition of penalties for rape, could have responded to the stunning disparity between the criminal justice system's response to black-on-white rape, on the one hand, and to all other instances of rape, on the other. Due to such differential treatment, the image of punishing a black man for raping a white woman has come to exemplify white supremacy in the United States.

The history of racism in accusations and punishments for rape is sordid and shameful. It calls for serious introspection on the part of our nation and our courts. The opinions in *Coker*, however, do not address that history at all. The plurality fixates instead on how much less serious the rape of an adult woman is than murder. By doing so, it effectively attempts to remedy racist injustice by trivializing misogynist violence.

To similar effect, during his confirmation hearings for the post of Associate Justice on the United States Supreme Court, then-Judge Clarence Thomas accused the U.S. Senate of engaging in a "high-tech lynching" for calling him to task in connection with his alleged sexual harassment of Anita Hill. Thomas testified that he did not even listen to Hill's testimony describing his conduct, thereby suggesting that for the Senate even to consider such an allegation, when leveled at a black man, would itself constitute racism. As readers may recall, the accusation had its intended effect, and the arch-conservative Justice Thomas was subsequently confirmed by a Senate dominated by Democrats who might otherwise have been inclined to oppose him.

THE ROLE OF RACE IN THE DEATH PENALTY MORE GENERALLY

It is, of course, not exclusively in cases of rape that the death penalty has been disproportionately visited upon African-American defendants for interracial crimes. As studies have demonstrated, defendants convicted of black-on-white murder have also suffered the disproportionate imposition of capital punishment.

Notwithstanding this disparity, however, the Supreme Court has not declared the death penalty unconstitutional under all circumstances. Unless the Court is prepared to do so across the board, it is therefore not appropriate to try to protect one vulnerable group (African-Americans) by minimizing the outrages committed against another (adult females of all races). It is not, in other words, inherently racist to execute rapists, any more than it is inherently racist to execute murderers. Because the Court failed to speak openly of race, however, it was impossible for the Justices to engage this argument on the merits.

The imposition of criminal penalties across the board may, of course, reflect the racial biases of our population. Harvard Law Professor Randall Kennedy has persuasively argued, for instance, that jurors selectively empathize with victims of their own race.[4] But this problem transcends the crime of rape, and thus its consideration must similarly extend beyond and leave behind this country's history of trivializing misogynist violence and female subordination.

PROPORTIONALITY: IS DEATH ALWAYS TOO GREAT A PUNISHMENT FOR RAPE?

So far, I have focused on potentially dubious distinctions that the *Coker* plurality implicitly draws and on the potentially flawed displacement of the majority's proper outrage about racial injustice onto the improper target of punishment for the crime of rape. But on the merits, how strong is the argument that death is too harsh a punishment for a crime of rape that does not result in a death?

Perhaps the retributive philosophy of "an eye for an eye" precludes the taking of a life for a rape. The disproportion between rape and death, however, is by no means self-evident. As the dissent in *Coker* explains, moreover, a punishment that is no more severe than the crime it punishes often has little power to deter the crime in question, because many criminals count on avoiding apprehension. "For example," argues the dissent, "hardly any thief would be deterred from stealing if the only punishment upon being caught were return of the money stolen."[5]

On the particular facts at issue in *Coker*, the defendant was already serving a term of life imprisonment when he escaped and raped the sixteen-year-old Mrs. Carver (the "adult woman" in question). Coker had previously been convicted of murder, rape, kidnapping, and aggravated assault. Short of executing him, it is hard to imagine either deterring or incapacitating this man from further violent behavior. Without a death penalty, in fact, the State was not in a position to impose *any* punishment upon Coker at all.

One might, of course, take the view that proportionality in sentencing trumps the need to serve instrumental objectives such as deterrence and incapacitation. Even on the basic question of retributive justice, however, murder is not necessarily the only or even the most heinous crime that one person might commit against another. Many consider torture, for example, to be worse than murder. For that reason, U.S. law rejects physically brutal but nonlethal penalties such as limb amputation, even as it permits the death penalty.[6]

Like torture, the harm of rape can leave its survivors with irreparable psychiatric injury that sometimes leads to suicide. Though alive, what rape victims have lost could therefore arguably merit the most serious punishment that the law has to offer.

LIFE VERSUS DEATH: THE STRANGE EIGHTH AMENDMENT DIVIDE

Last, but not least among the arguments for reconsidering *Coker* is the peculiar divide between Eighth Amendment precedents regarding death, on the one hand, and life imprisonment, on the other.

The Supreme Court has embraced an Eighth Amendment proportionality principle, for both capital and noncapital offenses, which says that the punishment must fit the crime. Yet the same Court has upheld a penalty of mandatory life imprisonment without parole for possession of 672 grams of cocaine. It has similarly upheld a life sentence imposed upon a person convicted of fraudulently obtaining money and property totaling under $250. And most recently, in *Lockyer v. Andrade*, it upheld two consecutive terms of twenty-five years to life imprisonment, imposed under three strikes legislation, against a person whose two triggering "strikes" were the theft of videotapes from K-mart, totaling under $160 in value.[7]

Whatever one thinks of execution for rape, it seems a far less disproportionate penalty than a lifetime of confinement in a prison cell, for nonviolent, petty property crimes against a corporate entity. If the Court is serious about proportionality review, it should perhaps begin by applying that review to something other than the severity of penalties for rape and other violent crimes. Its failure to do so discredits the entire enterprise, along with its claims about gross disproportion with respect to rape and the death penalty.

TARGETING RAPE FOR TRIVIALIZATION

As I have proposed, there are many arguments for reconsidering and overruling *Coker*. I am sympathetic, however, with the view that the death penalty should be abolished, regardless of how undeserving of solicitude the typical person subject to execution might be.

Nonetheless, opposition to the death penalty is not necessarily a reason to embrace or leave standing the decision in *Coker v. Georgia*. The *Coker* opinion does not simply condemn a neutral subset of executions. It makes a value judgment about the rape of adult women and deems this crime to be insufficiently serious to call for the ultimate punishment. This judgment trivializes the suffering of rape.

Perhaps it is time for the Supreme Court—one that generally defers (to an arguably alarming extent) to legislative judgments about retributive justice—to reconsider whether it is appropriate to continue to single out the rape of an adult woman as the one intentional, violent crime to be explicitly and uniquely shielded from the most severe penalty.

POSTSCRIPT

In March of 2006, South Carolina Attorney General Henry McMaster advised a state Senate Panel to propose legislation that would qualify child rapists, those who have raped children under eleven at least twice, for capital punishment. If passed, such legislation would make South Carolina the second state, after Louisiana, to subject child rapists to a potential sentence of death.

Once the Supreme Court declares a subset of crimes or criminals off-limits to capital punishment, it is unlikely to turn back. For better or for worse, the Court tends to view the contraction of death-eligible crimes as "progress." Because rape is so typically associated with female victims, however, the marginalization of this crime cannot, under any circumstances, be characterized as progressive. And the Court in *Coker*, of course, specifically singled out the rape of an adult *woman*, leaving open the possibility that the rape of a *man* by another man might inspire the outrage that justifies a capital sentence.

To understand the majority opinion in this light is to recognize that it is a sexist opinion even as it spares the lives of capital defendants. For women to have a full and equal place in our world, the sexual violation of women must be understood as a devastating crime, comparable in its impact to torture and murder. To kill a person who violates the sanctity of a woman's body is not, as the plurality wrongly concluded, "grossly disproportionate" to the offense. Like the body of a man, that of a woman is entitled to its boundaries.

Whether or not a convicted rapist faces possible execution, of course, he is likely to spend years in prison if his crime involved the rape of a stranger. In such cases, at least in modern times, a jury is generally sympathetic to the plight of the victim and accordingly angry at the offender. When the victim complains, however, that she (or he) suffered rape at the hands of a man whom she (or he) knew, something very different happens.

Many jurors (and members of the public generally) wonder whether "date rape" is truly a serious offense. Along with such skepticism over the gravity of the crime comes an unusual amount of skepticism about the sincerity of the complaining witness. The next two chapters address the source and propriety of such skepticism toward the credibility of the complaining witness as well as toward the seriousness of the crime itself.

·17·

Date Rape and the Presumption of Innocence

When it comes to the presumption of innocence, misconceptions abound. One of these misconceptions surfaced during the extremely controversial Kobe Bryant rape prosecution. As that drama unfolded, some suggested that the presumption of innocence, in a case like Bryant's, amounts to a presumption that the accuser is lying.

WHAT THE PRESUMPTION OF INNOCENCE DOES, AND DOES NOT, MEAN

Many nonlawyers (and even some lawyers) mistakenly hold the following view of the presumption of innocence: unless and until the prosecution has proved a defendant guilty beyond a reasonable doubt, to the satisfaction of a jury, the defendant remains factually innocent. To believe otherwise, on this flawed (and even preposterous) view of the law, is positively un-American, not to mention unconstitutional.

Taken seriously, this view would bar members of the public from believing that a defendant charged with a crime is guilty of it, unless and until a jury has so concluded. In truth, every one of us is free, both factually and legally, to think whatever we wish about the guilt or innocence of a defendant, regardless of what a jury has said or will say on the matter. Indeed, the First Amendment positively protects our freedom of thought in this regard.

The presumption of innocence applies *only to the members of a jury in a criminal trial.* Even as to them, moreover, the presumption does not dictate a juror's thoughts. Instead, it simply obligates them to select "not guilty" as their verdict if the prosecution fails to produce sufficient evidence to persuade them of a defendant's guilt beyond a reasonable doubt.

Members of criminal juries that ultimately acquit may and often do conclude, based on the evidence, that the defendant really was guilty of the crime for which they acquitted him or her. That evidentiary reality is both unobjectionable and statistically inevitable, given the weighty burden that the prosecution bears.

WHAT THE PRESUMPTION REQUIRES OF JURORS IN DIFFERENT KINDS OF RAPE CASES

A related notion regarding the presumption of innocence is that it obligates jurors and potential jurors to believe at the outset that a rape complainant is probably lying when she accuses a defendant of date rape.

Though "date rape" is not a technical legal term, I use it here to distinguish rapes in which the victim and perpetrator are acquainted with each other prior to the crime, from "stranger rapes," in which the victim first encounters her attacker at the time of the sexual assault. Because there is virtually no risk of mistaken identification in cases of date rape, it follows that a conclusion that the defendant *did not* rape the complainant almost always carries with it the implication that the accuser has leveled a false (insincere) accusation against the defendant.

Consider why this implication is almost inescapable at date rape trials. In a stranger rape case, the accuser has ordinarily selected the defendant out of a lineup or mug book as the perpetrator. To believe that the defendant is innocent in such a case accordingly does not require anyone to think ill of the complaining witness. The defendant's supporters, on the contrary, may (and most often do) believe the victim's account of having been raped but believe at the same time that she is *mistaken* about who committed the crime.

Making an honest mistake is no crime, and it is therefore possible to view the defendant as innocent without viewing the victim as anything other than a sincere person and an actual victim (albeit of a different perpetrator), who deserves justice. If the presumption of innocence demands that jurors experience skepticism about the prosecutor's case, then, such skepticism does not involve thinking any less of the complainant's character in stranger rape cases.

Contrast this state of affairs with the date rape context. Here, the complaining witness and the defense typically agree that intercourse occurred between the defendant and his accuser. The main dispute revolves around whether the defendant acted with or without the accuser's consent. That was the case in the Kobe Bryant prosecution.

Because the difference between rape and consensual sex is almost certainly going to be a memorable one for any victim, the defense is unlikely to propose that the complainant is simply *mistaken* in her recollection of what occurred between her and the defendant. The defense is far more apt to suggest that any discrepancy between the defendant's and the complainant's versions of what occurred reflects dishonest testimony on the part of the latter.

There is naturally no polite or sympathetic way to suggest that an accuser is making a false rape accusation. People make "honest" mistakes, but they do not tell "honest" lies implicating innocent people in criminal conduct. For that reason, a juror who interprets the presumption of innocence as requiring an attitude of skepticism and incredulity in the face of the prosecutor's evidence will necessarily adopt an unflattering and even hostile view of the complaining witness at a date rape trial.

Some believe, in keeping with this reasoning, that it is incumbent upon jurors in date rape cases to approach the evidence with the assumption that the person who says she is a victim is actually a false complainant.[1] If that were the law that applied to jurors, then no one could be blamed for regarding Kobe Bryant's accuser with suspicion and disbelief.

HOW THE PRESUMPTION ALLOWS JURORS TO COME TO THEIR OWN CONCLUSIONS

As it turns out, the presumption of innocence requires no such thing of jurors. It does not tell the jury to assume that prosecution witnesses are either mistaken or lying. Like members of the public at large, the judge does not instruct jurors in a criminal case on what they should think. Jurors properly instructed on the law are consequently free to accept any witness's story, as they see fit.

In determining whether to believe a witness, jurors can accordingly rely on the witness's demeanor, his ability to respond to questions on cross-examination, and the overall plausibility of his account of the events in question. They can also take into consideration any systematic (or particular) biases that a witness brings to the proceedings. For example, jurors could permissibly consider—in weighing Kobe Bryant's testimony—the fact that he has an incentive to say that he is innocent, regardless of the truth; his freedom and successful career hang in the balance.

In other words, the presumption of innocence does not require jurors to be any more skeptical of the prosecutor's witnesses than they are of the defendant's. They should instead approach all of the evidence with an open mind and bring their insight to bear in processing the testimony and evidentiary exhibits that they consider.

The presumption of innocence governs only the jury's answer to the verdict question. The jury must find the defendant "not guilty" if a fair and impartial consideration of the evidence leads the jury to conclude that guilt has not been proved beyond a reasonable doubt. When the prosecution presents witnesses in a stranger rape case, the jury does not have to presume that the prosecution witnesses are mistaken (although it may certainly conclude that they are). And when the prosecution offers testimony in a date rape case, the jury is likewise not required to presume that the accuser is lying.

The reflexive hostility that some of Kobe Bryant's defenders have shown toward his accuser therefore exhibits no fidelity to the presumption of innocence. It instead prejudges the case before the evidence has been presented.

Of course, members of the public are free to prejudge the case on the basis of their emotional investments and blink at reality, as they wish. But the one thing that a *jury* must never do is decide in advance to reject testimony and evidence that it has not yet heard. And for any juror to presume that Kobe Bryant's accuser is lying is to do exactly that.

POSTSCRIPT

This case against Kobe Bryant was dismissed September 1, 2004, after the accuser decided that she was unable to go forward with the trial.[2] The two parties also reached a settlement in the civil action filed by the accuser. The judge had ruled evidence of the accuser's relations with another man after the alleged rape by Kobe admissible.[3]

Often, the denial that a particular hate crime has occurred at all goes hand in hand with an underestimation (or even embrace) of the harm that such a crime inflicts. Holocaust deniers, for example, tend to be fans of Adolph Hitler and of the very agenda that they deny he carried out.[4] This tendency—to deny and devalue simultaneously—appears to characterize attitudes toward date rape as well. In chapter 17, we saw the "denial" phenomenon, along with the misconstruction of the presumption of innocence in the service of that denial. In the next chapter, we examine more closely the devaluation process at work.

• 18 •

What's Wrong with Date Rape?

In my first-year criminal law class at Rutgers, I teach a unit on rape. Because the subject implicates the roles of gender and sexuality in a free society, it poses distinct challenges in the classroom.

Law professor Susan Estrich—the author of the book *Real Rape*[1]—observed in 1986 that "[t]o examine rape within the criminal law tradition is to expose fully the sexism of the law."[2] Though she wrote these words more than two decades ago, attitudes have not evolved as much as one might have hoped. In particular, mainstream perceptions of acquaintance rape, or "date rape," remain extremely troubling.

DATE RAPE PORTRAYED AS A TRIVIAL OFFENSE

A half-dozen years ago, I picked up the "Weekend" section of the *New York Times*. I thought it would be pleasant to read about something other than war and terror. I chose a review of a movie called "Tape," directed by Richard Linklater. The review was positive, and the movie sounded intriguing. As a professor teaching rape law and as a woman, however, I found the article quite disturbing.

"Tape," according to the review, is a movie about two former high school classmates, both male, and the girl they used to love. During the course of a tension-filled verbal power struggle between the men, it emerges that one of them raped the girl they had both dated.

Though the reviewer enjoyed the film, he identifies what he sees as a flaw in the narrative: "As incisive as 'Tape' is," he observes, "it is ultimately limited by the moral weight of the deed under consideration and the sexual politics swirling around the subject. This wasn't a murder, after all, but sex forced on a woman who admits she was in love with the man who took advantage of her. . . . To put it bluntly, it is very small potatoes."[3]

Reading this movie review reminded me that many mainstream moviegoers remain unconvinced that the rape of an acquaintance—what some call "date rape"—is a serious offense. Such a perspective poses a serious problem, because most rapes in the real world fall into the "date rape" category.

According to the United States Department of Justice, three out of four victims of sexual assault have had a prior relationship with their respective attackers.[4] If having had a relationship vitiates the severity of the offense, then the overwhelming majority of rape crimes are "small potatoes."

The movie reviewer in question was a man, but men are not the only people who take the view he expresses. Generation-X author Katie Roiphe became famous for writing that much of what prudish feminists call "rape" is not actually rape at all but just "bad sex" that women regret after the fact. Other writers like Camille Paglia have suggested that resistance to a man's sexual advances does not convert his subsequent behavior into rape; it is all just part of the erotic game.[5]

DATE RAPE PERCEIVED AS A "VICTIMLESS" CRIME

Rape is not unique among crimes in triggering controversy as to whether (in certain circumstances) it should qualify as a serious offense at all. Many have criticized laws that ban drug possession and prostitution, for example, and there are organizations dedicated to the repeal of these laws.

The difference, though, is that proponents of legalizing drug possession and prostitution can plausibly claim that these are "victimless" crimes, and that prosecuting them therefore does far more harm than the crimes themselves. Rape, by contrast, is never victimless. Those who perceive the crime as "small potatoes" thus demonstrate a profound failure of empathy.

The kind of rape that most people take seriously involves a man who attacks a woman he neither knows nor has reason to believe has any interest in him. When the discussion turns to date rape, however, people are skeptical of victims' allegations and dubious about the weight of the offense, even if it did occur.

The reason for such skepticism and doubt is the possibility that the victim might have liked her assailant and found him attractive. If she did, some believe, then his forcing himself on her could not have been that bad.

As the movie reviewer described it, the rapist under such circumstances would have only "taken advantage" of his victim—the sort of manners offense that an eager salesperson might commit against a customer who really would have preferred, after the fact, not to have bought the most expensive suit on the rack.

THE REALITY OF DATE RAPE

This view of rape, however, bears no relation to the reality of the crime. The very types of attacks that people minimize may have the most devastating consequences for their victims.

Studies have shown that rape victims who previously knew their attackers take even longer to recover from the psychological trauma of the crime than those who were raped by strangers.[6]

Now that we live in an age of terrorism, this phenomenon should not surprise anyone. The closer we are to a familiar environment when tragedy strikes, the less safe we feel in what was previously "home." What is true for the physical spaces of our lives can be just as true for our relationships.

This is one reason why many consider incest against children a worse offense than child molestation by a stranger. The law normally recognizes that the people in whom you place your trust bear an added responsibility not to betray it.

When someone you love, someone in whom you trust, hurts you, it is uniquely damaging, because it shakes the foundations of your sense of security. When you would normally retreat to the familiar for comfort, it is the familiar that frightens you most.

You also come to doubt your ability to distinguish between friend and foe, between safety and danger—because after all, you were the one who chose the company of your own enemy. (This further aggravates the insidious tendency of women to blame themselves for their own date rapes, on the logic that they should have known better than to date such a man, or dress provocatively, and so on.)

The movie reviewer was right that rape "after all" is not murder. As we discussed in chapter 16, the Supreme Court held in *Coker v. Georgia* that capital punishment is an excessive penalty for rape, because the rape victim survives.[7] But the fact that rape is not murder does not diminish the gravity of the crime to "small potatoes" either.

Like survivors of any disaster, rape victims continue to suffer long after the physical ordeal has passed. As one of my students said in analyzing *Coker*, rape is arguably worse than murder, because the attacker has, in some sense, both killed his victim and made a survivor out of her.

TEACHING RAPE AMIDST CONTROVERSY

A former colleague of mine once told me that he chooses not to teach rape law at all, because it is the one crime of which he is sure there will be survivors in the classroom who might become upset by the material.

This is a real concern and one that I do not take lightly. I nonetheless resolve the matter in favor of teaching this material, because I worry that cutting it out of the syllabus communicates to students that this crime—one that alters forever the lives of its victims—does not "count" as much as manslaughter and robbery do.

By covering the law of rape, in all of its complexity and controversy, I hope to convey to students that the crime is neither invisible nor insignificant. Rather, it is important and worthy of our attention, both as attorneys and attorneys-to-be and as members of a civilized society that aspires to equality for women.

POSTSCRIPT

A person's attitudes toward date rape are very revealing of his (or her) overall view of women as a group. A woman who accuses a man of date rape has, necessarily, asserted that she has the right to control her body, no matter who wants to have sex with her and no matter what his relationship with her might be. Unlike a stranger-rape, in which a man violates all norms of sexual intimacy, a date-rapist takes out the woman he desires on a date. For her to say "no" to him therefore disappoints an expectation that he might have rationally formed on the basis of her willingness to go out with him. According to some people, she has therefore acted as a "tease." A tease is thought to deserve what she gets or at least to lack the moral high ground to complain about what has occurred. I have, on more than one occasion, had students announce in class that although date rape may be wrong, it is not "the really bad kind" of rape.

In a world where women are truly valued as full persons, equal to men, sex will not be something that men are entitled to "expect" from women when they have played along with the "dinner and a movie first" script. It will be something in which people engage by mutual consent. No matter what a man's relationship with a woman might be, he commits a hate crime against women when he forces her to have sex against her will.

The hostility and peculiar reactions that date rape victims encounter in court reflect the reality that many people do not fully accept the criminality of date rape. They believe that a woman who agrees to go out on a date with a man may implicitly agree to have intercourse with him as well. In a related phenomenon, there are those who believe that once admittedly consensual sex has begun, a woman may not legitimately change her mind and ask her partner to stop. The next chapter explores the implications of the latter view—which follows logically from the first—and analyzes its rejection in the State of California.

·19·

Can a Woman Say "No" If She Has Already Said "Yes"?

In January 2003, the Supreme Court of California confronted a somewhat novel issue about how rape should be defined under the law. In *People v. John Z.*, the court held that a woman who initially consents to sexual intercourse does not thereby give up her right to end the encounter at whatever point she chooses.[1] In other words, when a woman tells her partner to stop, and he forces her to continue, he is guilty of rape.

One could imagine difficult factual variations, in which the woman's communication is ambiguous or her partner's compliance is almost, but not quite, immediate. The basic ruling, however, should not be controversial. If a woman (or a man) is clear in conveying the desire to end a sexual interaction, then a decision forcibly to disregard that desire is an instance of rape.

Of greater interest than the California court's decision itself, is the fact that the court took the case in order to resolve a lower court split over the issue. According to at least one court in the state of California, for purposes of rape law, consent to penetration—once given—*may not be withdrawn during* the encounter in question. And courts in other states have held the same.[2]

Such a position rests on outdated ideas about the harm of rape and the biological imperatives of men who are engaged in sexual intercourse.

AN OLD VIEW OF THE HARM OF RAPE

In *People v. Vela*—one of the cases the California Supreme Court overruled with its recent decision—a California appellate court held that as long as an alleged victim gave consent prior to penetration, no rape occurred, despite the withdrawal of consent during intercourse.[3]

The *Vela* court cited precedents from Maryland and North Carolina as persuasive authority. The majority reasoned that "the essence of the crime of rape is the outrage to the person and feelings of the female resulting from the nonconsensual violation of her womanhood. . . . If [, after consenting to penetration,] she withdraws consent during the act of sexual intercourse and the male forcibly continues the act without interruption . . . the sense of outrage to her person and feelings could hardly be of the same magnitude [as would the disregard of an initial refusal]. . . ."[4]

Though the court speaks of the woman's person and feelings, its use of the words "violation of her womanhood" evokes an earlier century—a time when a woman who was no longer "intact" would have much less cause to feel violated by rape than her purer sister. The court's argument, then, suggests a continuum of harms, one in which sex without consent is in some instances very bad; in some, not so bad; and in some, perfectly fine, depending on the woman's sexual status.

Consider the greatest "outrage" along the *Vela* court's implicit scale. The virgin who has saved herself for her wedding night has the strongest interest in avoiding unwanted intercourse. Her purity as a maiden hangs in the balance, and any man who would disregard that purity commits a grave offense against her and her family. Indeed, in the Bible, a man who rapes a virgin is said to owe her father damages and is expected to marry his victim.[5] In that way, presumably, he can ensure that her reduced market value does not eliminate her prospects for marriage and a family.

ANOTHER ANTIQUATED VIEW: "PROMISCUOUS" WOMEN SUFFER LESS FROM RAPE

In modern secular cultures, by contrast, nonvirgins also have a right not to be raped. And a rapist cannot avoid liability for his crime through marriage.

Nonetheless, juries today remain skeptical about a woman's claims of rape if she is "promiscuous"—a vestige of the notion that a woman has one opportunity to decide whether she will be a good girl who waits until she is married or a bad girl who does not. As soon as she says "yes" once, she's "that kind of girl" forever, available for the taking.

The crime of rape, on this account, has more to do with a victim's character or "virtue"—her status, that is—than it does with her right to bodily integrity against all manner of sexual intrusion.

THE MARITAL RAPE EXEMPTION: ANOTHER RELIC

Another facet of the status view of rape is that with respect to any particular man, one might believe that a woman who says "yes" to him forfeits her right to say no forever after. This is the perspective of the marital rape exemption. Only a few decades ago, such exemptions permitted men in much of the country to force their wives to have intercourse without incurring criminal liability for rape. Many jurisdictions, moreover, continue to treat marital rape as less serious than the rape of a stranger, in a variety of ways.[6]

A progenitor of the marital rape exemption in this country was Sir Matthew Hale, a notable eighteenth-century Chief Justice in England. When British practices were imported to the United States, Hale's view on marital rape came along. Hale had famously said that "the husband cannot be guilty of a rape committed by himself upon his lawful wife, for by their mutual matrimonial consent and contract the wife hath given up herself in this kind unto her husband, which she cannot retract."[7]

Some even argued in the late twentieth century for extension of the marital rape exemption to cohabitants. The argument for such an extension was that limiting the rape license to married men was unfair to unmarried men who have undertaken committed, monogamous relationships that should entitle them to the same unfettered sexual access to *their* women as married men have to theirs. A number of states—including Connecticut, Kentucky, and Pennsylvania—apparently found such reasoning convincing, for they embodied it in their own laws.

On this theory of rape, a woman may decide which men have and do not have consent, but once that initial decision is made, she cannot pick and choose on which occasions those men may exercise their prerogative. Consent thus becomes something like an unrestricted train pass on Amtrak.

Under such a view, the logic of the *Vela* decision is unassailable. A woman who not only has chosen to consent to a particular man but has consented to him *in the very same encounter* has necessarily given up any right to stop him. She may still be able to decide to say no to some men (and perhaps even to decide on any given day whether to say yes *again* to a man with whom she has been intimate before). But if consensual penetration has already taken place, she must live with her decision, a variation on the expression, "You have made your bed. Now lie in it."

AN ALTERNATIVE, MODERN CONCEPTION OF THE HARM OF RAPE

We could, however, understand the harm of rape very differently. On this alternative understanding, rape is wrong because it compels a person to be subjected to sexual intercourse, when she has specifically and clearly indicated that she does not want to be.

She may choose to say "stop it" for any of a variety of reasons. Perhaps the particular man is unattractive to her, or she is not in the mood to have sex, or maybe she has an infection that unexpectedly renders the particular experience physically painful. Regardless of her reasons, though, the consent is hers to give or take away, on any particular occasion, as she so chooses, because her body belongs to her, just as a man's body belongs to him.

This view takes account of an emotional reality: Regardless of what motivates a particular woman to refuse a man, his deliberate, forcible disregard of that refusal is a brutal, traumatizing, and humiliating experience for her. A rape inflicts great harm because it takes a decision about the most intimate, personal, and vulnerable matters in her life out of a woman's hands.

The harm of rape, then, lies in forcibly depriving a person of her right of bodily integrity. The marital rapist—or any rapist who has once received consent—still violates the woman, because he treats her earlier consent as a transfer of dominion instead of an expression of desire that—to be freely given—must be freely revocable as well.

THE PROBLEM WITH A "WAIVER" APPROACH TO CONSENT

Not only does the *Vela* approach to sexual consent reflect a regressive view of women's sexuality, but it is also troubling for a second reason: It treats consent as the moral equivalent of "waiver."

In legal parlance, waiver refers to a situation in which a person voluntarily decides to give up a right that he holds. A defendant charged with a crime, for example, has the right to a trial. If he pleads guilty, he waives that right and thereby foregoes the benefits that a trial might have accorded him. He cannot later, after sentencing, decide that he would like to exercise his right to a trial after all.

Similarly, a defendant who goes to trial has a Fifth Amendment right to refuse to take the witness stand. She may decide nonetheless to testify in her own behalf. By doing so, however, she waives her Fifth Amendment right not to be compelled to answer a prosecutor's questions (at least those that fall within the scope of her answers on direct examination). She cannot "plead the Fifth" in response to legitimate cross-examination, once she has chosen to open that door.

In these situations, the person has waived her rights and has thereby given them up, along with the ability to reassert them later, on reflection. The waiver, in other words, is irrevocable. The giving of *consent*, however, should not be.

Almost by definition, an assertion that "I don't want to do this anymore" negates an earlier consent. The reason that waivers are not always revocable is that the party who has obtained the waiver may develop an interest in relying on the waiver, because that party has reciprocally given up something valuable as well.

When a defendant takes the witness stand and waives her Fifth Amendment rights, for example, she provides the jury with evidence that the prosecutor now has an interest in rebutting, an interest that was not present prior to the defendant's having testified. It would accordingly be unfair to deny the prosecutor an opportunity for cross-examination under these circumstances.

THE MYTH OF THE UNSTOPPABLE MALE

Should consent to sexual intercourse be treated as an irrevocable waiver? Those who argue in the affirmative believe that a man who has received consent will properly allow his biological urges to take over in a way that makes it unfair and unreasonable to demand of him that he stop. He has, in other words, relinquished his obligation to exercise self-control, in response to a woman's invitation.

As the brief in support of the defendant in *John Z.* put it, "[b]y essence of the act of sexual intercourse, a male's primal urge to reproduce is aroused. It is therefore unreasonable for a female and the law to expect a male to cease having sexual intercourse immediately upon her withdrawal of consent."[8]

Giving legal protection to a male's unstoppable "primal urge" treats the man's sexual desire as a bullet that—once fired—cannot physically be stopped. This view and the reality that it presumes have significant implications for women's safety and liberty.

Taken to its logical conclusion, such an approach requires women to restrict their behavior in all sorts of ways—including how they dress and whether they appear in public unescorted—if they are to avoid being sexually assaulted. The approach removes male accountability for sexual assault and instead places responsibility upon a female victim to prove that she took all possible steps to avoid awakening the man's unstoppable primal urge.

Like the status definition of the harm of rape (which suggests that rape only counts when it happens to virtuous women), the myth of the unstoppable male effectively regulates women in the guise of defining sexual assault. In fact, it may be precisely the desire to dominate and punish a woman who has behaved like a "tease" that motivates a man to force her to continue to have sex after consent has been unambiguously withdrawn. In that sense, the sexual act that proceeds after a woman's withdrawal of consent is no longer truly the "same" act as that which took place while her partner still had her consent.

The law thus has a choice to make about whom to discipline: It will either punish men who inflict forcible intercourse or condone the violent punishment of fickle women who frustrate the "primal urge."

NO MEANS NO, WHENEVER AND TO WHOMEVER IT IS SAID

Many of us are loath to regulate intimacy. Some readers may even remember the infamous Antioch Code, in which male college students were expected to ask female companions' permission for each advancing stage of intimacy in a sexual encounter.[9] Comedians had a field day with the Antioch Code, including sketches in which a male would say such things as, "May I now escalate our level of intimacy by moving my lips from your neck to your ear?"

In a democracy, it would seem, consenting adults should generally be free to engage in sexual relationships without government oversight or instructions on how to escalate intimacy. No one wants to hear Miranda Warnings before intercourse. That being said, however, the reality of consent is a crucial precondition to such sexual freedom. The liberty to harm another is not, and should not be, protected.

Freedom thus requires that consent be neither presumed nor irrevocable—but actual and true. To permit women to decide whether or not to have (or to continue to have) sex, then, free men must be capable of resisting primal urges, no matter how strong or at what point they emerge. Those men who cannot or will not do so are sexual predators and should be legally recognized as such.

POSTSCRIPT

Both Illinois and Kentucky have followed California's lead in defining rape to include incidents in which a victim withdraws consent during sexual intercourse. In *State v. Bunyard*,[10] the Court of Appeals in Kentucky held that if a woman withdraws consent after penetration, continued sexual intercourse, even for five or ten minutes more, constitutes rape. Illinois had addressed the issue statutorily and passed the "No Means No" bill in July of 2003. The statute states that when an individual initially consents to sexual intercourse but later withdraws consent, that individual has not consented to any sexual intercourse that occurs after the withdrawal of consent.

What does the withdrawal of consent have to do with sex-discrimination? The answer turns on the perspective that one takes in assessing the question itself. If one takes the aroused man's perspective, it seems like a difficult issue: once a man begins the act of intercourse, it is difficult and very unpleasant for him to stop. His strong urge is to "keep going" until the point of ejaculation. If he has arrived at this state with the consent of his partner, it might seem to many men utterly unfair to ask that he stop just because she has decided that she does not want to go through with it.

From a woman's perspective, however, the moment that she asks a man to stop having sex with her—no matter what her reason might be for doing so—his refusal to honor her request converts an act of consensual sex into violence. However aroused a man feels, in other words, he does not have the right to occupy another person's body without her continuing participation (or at least acquiescence). If a man wants intercourse with a woman to stop, he can make it stop. To say that he must stop if it is the woman who tells him to stop is to give her the same rights that he has to exercise power over his own body.

In prosecuting crimes such as rape, even when properly defined, a prosecutor confronts a variety of obstacles. The prosecutor must find the perpetrator and assemble a strong case against him to leave the jury without any reasonable doubts regarding his guilt. But sometimes, the evidence might be extremely powerful, and the prosecutor is nonetheless unable to bring that case. This happens when the statute of limitations has run. The chapter that follows considers a proposal to abolish the statute of limitations for rape.

•20•

The Rapist Who Got Away: The Injustice of Statutes of Limitations

In the summer of 2005, New York City District Attorney Robert Morgenthau announced his desire to see a change in the law of rape, specifically, the repeal of the statute of limitations. In the context of the criminal law, a statute of limitations provides for a limited period of time after the commission of a crime during which the government may charge a person with that crime. The statute of limitations period begins to run when an offense is committed.

The D.A.'s announcement came on the heels of the arrest of Fletcher A. Worrell. Worrell's DNA reportedly linked him to at least twenty-five rapes over three decades.

Morgenthau's proposal raises important questions about statutes of limitations in general and the crime of rape in particular.

WHY ARE THERE STATUTES OF LIMITATIONS?

In defending statutes of limitations, people invoke three primary rationales: the diminishing value of evidence over time, the need for diligence by law enforcement, and the importance of closure.

Let us consider first the diminishing value of evidence. After an event takes place, with the passage of time, memories fade and physical evidence may disappear. As a result, delay in prosecuting an offense may compromise the strength of a prosecutor's case against a defendant.

The longer a prosecutor waits to charge a defendant with a crime, therefore, the less likely a jury or judge will have sufficient evidence to conclude, beyond any reasonable doubt, that the defendant is guilty of that crime. The statute of limitations acknowledges this reality by categorically barring the pursuit of what may well have turned out to be the weakest and least compelling prosecutions.

Second, consider the argument for police diligence. Ideally, law enforcement officers should be investigating and handing matters over to prosecutors with speed and efficiency, in part because evidence *can* degrade over time. A statute of limitations, from this perspective, serves to light a fire under the police and remind them that justice delayed is justice denied.

If police fail to act quickly, then they have failed the public and are unlikely to find a culprit many years later, even if, theoretically, they might have done so. Like the act of setting an artificial deadline generally, the statute of limitations dramatizes this reality by eliminating the—largely theoretical—possibility that the police might find the perpetrator at a later date. It also, and for similar reasons, permits an innocent defendant to exculpate himself with fresh evidence, if it exists.

Third, people contend that statutes of limitations provide closure and relief for those who might be falsely accused of an offense. When a crime occurs, there is always a possibility that the authorities will identify the wrong person as the culprit and attempt to build a case against him. Though witnesses and police ordinarily try their best to identify the guilty party correctly, people do on occasion lie or make mistakes. When these things happen, an innocent person can find herself defending against a false accusation.

The burden of this position can cause great anxiety and expense that may increase over time, as evidence and memories of the truth disappear, while accusations hang over the heads of the wrongly accused. A statute of limitations, for such people, can serve to release them from that purgatory.

Once the statute runs, the possibility of being charged and convicted on false accusations expires, and this expiration permits closure for the target of an unscrupulous or simply erroneous focus. And even for the guilty defendant, the statute provides repose after a period of time.

SO WHY REPEAL THE STATUTE OF LIMITATIONS FOR RAPE?

These three arguments are substantial, so why would the New York District Attorney urge the repeal of the statute of limitations for rape?

In so proposing, Robert Morgenthau was responding to the developing power of DNA analysis to identify a perpetrator from a small quantity of human tissue left at the scene of a crime. And this response makes a great deal of sense.

First, in the past, when a man (the usual perpetrator of such crimes) committed a rape against a stranger, and his victim reported it, the most likely path to discovering the attacker's identity was through eyewitness identification. Typically, the victim would look at a book of arrest photographs and identify her assailant. That feature of rape investigation has changed with the routine collection and analysis of DNA evidence.

When a rape occurs, the attacker generally cannot avoid leaving some of his tissue on the victim. And once he does so, that DNA can be traced to him if, at an earlier point, the police had occasion to collect his DNA.

The fact that memories fade over time is now far less significant in a rape prosecution, for the victim's ability to recognize the rapist is no longer crucial. Indeed, the fact that none of the defendant's DNA is found on a victim may lead to an acquittal even when the victim is confident in her identification. And likewise, a victim's inability to recognize the perpetrator will not necessarily undermine a positive DNA identification.

A second reason for abolishing the rape statute of limitations is that the police are generally motivated to investigate stranger rapes because they are acknowledged to be violent, frightening offenses that can terrorize the population. The fact that law enforcement has not identified a rapist in five years, the length of the statute of limitations for rape in New York, is therefore more likely to result from the perpetrator's evasive action than from police neglect.

Repeal of the statute of limitations for rape is thus unlikely to lead to a sudden onset of lethargy in police investigations of this crime.

And third, there is the matter of closure. In this area too, the advent of highly sophisticated DNA identification technology greatly reduces the likelihood of error. In the past, chances were substantial that a witness would make a mistake years after the fact (or even shortly after the fact) when examining a book of mug shots or observing a lineup. The less we must rely on eyewitness identification, however, the less relevant the passage of time becomes to the accuracy of a trial and its outcome.

VICTIMS DESERVE CLOSURE: THE INJUSTICE OF A PROVEN RAPE THAT CANNOT BE PROSECUTED

There is also, finally, an affirmative reason to repeal the statute of limitations on rape, and that is closure for victims.

Rape remains a highly underreported crime, because of the stigma that still attaches to its victims, even to this day. At the same time, the crime of rape causes devastating trauma to its victims, from which they do not easily or always recover.

As with the crime of murder—for which no state has a statute of limitations—a crime as serious as rape merits investigation and prosecution, no matter how much time has passed. The victim and other potential victims of the same predator deserve as much.

In sum, the arguments for the rape statute of limitations have become less persuasive, given the nature of the crime and the advent of DNA evidence. In this context, these last affirmative reasons for its repeal—closure for past victims, and the protection of possible future victims—should carry the day.

For these reasons, New York State should abolish its statute of limitations for rape, just as the New York District Attorney has proposed.

POSTSCRIPT

In June 2006, New York State Governor George Pataki signed a bill repealing the statute of limitations for rape.[1]

In discussing the impact of sexual assault on women's equality, we consistently confront the question of what ought to "count" or "qualify" as rape. We have seen that a broad definition in general reflects a greater respect for women's autonomy and bodily integrity, regardless of what her relationship with the perpetrator might be. In the language of feminist rallies, "however we dress, wherever we go, yes means yes and no means no." But what happens when the definition is so broad that "yes" no longer means "yes"? We turn now to the area of statutory rape, in which consent is no defense to the charge.

• 21 •

Jailbait: When "Yes" Means "No"

A few years ago, the Georgia Supreme Court heard arguments in *Dixon v. State*.[1] The case involved the conviction of Marcus Dwayne Dixon for statutory rape and aggravated child molestation. (Dixon was acquitted of rape and several other charges.)

Statutory rape is sex between an adult and a minor, while aggravated child molestation also involves an injury. At the time of his offense, Dixon was an eighteen-year-old high school football player who had sex with a fifteen-year-old female classmate. The aggravated child molestation statute mandates a ten-year minimum sentence, and Dixon challenged the harshness of the resulting penalty.

The case attracted claims of racism, because the victim was a white girl and the convict an outstanding African-American student with a football scholarship to Vanderbilt.

One provocative underlying (if unstated) question that contributed to the notoriety of this case was whether the law should be able to send teenagers to prison for having sex with other teenagers, in the absence of force. Because every state has a statutory rape law in some form, this case presents a challenge to a long and continuing tradition of criminal laws that confine men for what could be consensual sex with minors who are close to the age of majority.

Such liability is controversial in a number of ways, but it also has some benefits that are often overlooked by critics, thus leaving us with a difficult dilemma that admits of no easy answers.

THE UNSAVORY ORIGINS OF STATUTORY RAPE LAWS

Statutory rape laws have a checkered past. A primary purpose of these laws was to guard the virginity of young maidens against seduction by unscrupulous cads. To give up one's "virtue" to a man who was unwilling to pay with his hand in marriage was foolish and presumptively a product of youthful, poor judgment.

Such laws accordingly had more to do with preserving female virginity than with the force and violence that define rape. One sign of this is the fact that a man could defend himself against statutory rape charges by proving that his victim was already sexually experienced prior to their encounter (and thus not subject to being corrupted by the defendant).[2]

MODERN JUSTIFICATIONS FOR STATUTORY RAPE LAWS

Despite their unsavory beginnings, however, some feminists have favored these laws. Progressive women support such statutes mainly as measures to help combat the sexual abuse of young girls.

Though a statutory rape charge does not require proof of force or coercion, young girls were (and may continue to be) especially vulnerable to being raped by the adults in their lives. In one study, for example, seventy-four percent of women who had intercourse before the age of fourteen and sixty percent of those who had sex before the age of fifteen reported having had a forced sexual experience.

In addition, prosecutors attempting to prove rape in court have historically faced significant burdens, such as corroboration requirements premised on the complaining witness's presumptive lack of credibility.

For many years, legal thinkers like eighteenth-century British jurist Sir Matthew Hale were convinced that rape "is an accusation easily to be made and hard to be proved, and harder to be defended by the party accused, though never so innocent." Thus, rape law did not provide a reliable or efficacious vehicle for addressing most sexual violence, and it continues to be of limited utility for acquaintance rapes, as I discussed in chapter 18.

For this reason too, feminists might view statutory rape laws as a potential godsend. As long as there was sexual intercourse and an underage victim, the jury could convict. And more importantly, that possibility itself might deter real sexual abuse.

BURDENS OF PROOF: IS STATUTORY RAPE JUST RAPE WITHOUT PROOF OF ONE ELEMENT?

Viewing statutory rape laws as salutary in this way does raise a serious problem, however. In *In Re Winship*,[3] the U.S. Supreme Court required that prosecutors prove every element of a crime beyond a reasonable doubt before a conviction could be constitutionally valid.[4] Removing the "force" element of rape and leaving only intercourse and age might seem to amount, from one perspective, to a presumption that the force element of rape is established, without the prosecutor's having to prove it and without the defense even having the option of affirmatively disproving it.

Such a presumption would allow for the possibility that a fully consensual sexual encounter would be openly prosecuted and punished as rape. Some might understandably believe that this possibility unfairly subjects essentially innocent men to unduly harsh treatment, simply in the name of deterring other, unrelated men from engaging in very different and far more culpable sorts of conduct.

RESPONSES TO CONCERNS ABOUT PROSECUTING CONSENSUAL SEX

There are two potential responses to this legitimate concern. First, at some level, we might have doubts about the competence of a minor to "consent," in a meaningful way, to sexual activity. Because of her youth, the minor might not fully appreciate the full physical and emotional implications of her decision (including the possibility of offspring for which she will likely have little means of support).

Of course, many adults might also fall into this category, and the decision to treat intercourse as distinctive in this way might simply represent a revival of the old view that maidens should be protected from the corruption of their virtue. Why, otherwise, should girls who are sexually attracted to men be considered the men's victims rather than participants in arguably unwise and socially costly but mutually gratifying activity?

Another response to the concern for innocent men is more in keeping with a rejection of sex-role stereotypes and discrimination. It is that when sexual activity with a minor is truly consensual, the activity is unlikely, at least in modern times, to be prosecuted. In other words, to the extent that statutory rape is truly a consensual and therefore victimless crime in a particular case, it is highly unlikely to generate a criminal action.

In the Dixon case, for example, the fifteen-year-old victim claimed that the defendant "tracked her down in a classroom trailer that she was cleaning as part of her duties in an after-school job, asked if she was a virgin, grabbed her arms, unbuttoned her pants and raped her on a table." This description renders the statutory rape and aggravated child molestation prosecution something quite different from the state targeting consensual activity for unduly harsh punishment.

Though Dixon was acquitted on the rape charge, that fact does not rule out the possibility of sexual assault. It means only that the jury was not convinced beyond a reasonable doubt that Dixon forced the fifteen-year-old girl to have sex against her will. The statutory rape prosecution therefore, perhaps, reduces the burden of persuasion but still focuses primarily on forced rather than consensual encounters. A conviction, on this view, might reflect the conclusion that the defendant probably forced the minor to have sex.

The normative question, then, becomes this: Is the possibility that consensual sex will be punished with imprisonment sufficient to override the benefits of statutory rape legislation in facilitating the fight against actual sexual abuse of young adults?

LEGAL SHORTCUTS: IS EVEN A SLIM POSSIBILITY OF CONVICTING IN THE ABSENCE OF FORCE UNACCEPTABLE?

One reaction to this question is that even the theoretical possibility of convicting in a case of consensual sex is unacceptable and unconstitutional. Prosecutors and juries, on this reasoning, should not have the options, respectively, of prosecuting and of finding a person guilty in the absence of force, regardless of how unlikely they are to exercise that option. Consensual sex is not criminal, period.

The assumptions underlying this reaction, however, though understandable, are at odds with other areas of the criminal law. Consider drug laws. Possession of a large quantity of narcotics is regularly treated as a far more serious offense than possession of a smaller quantity. One reason for this distinction is that the first is viewed as possession with the intent to distribute (that is, drug dealing), while the second is thought to be consistent with personal use. Since legislators and others view dealing as much more harmful than mere personal possession, the penalties are accordingly more severe.

Yet possession of a large quantity of drugs, though highly suggestive, is not *necessarily* accompanied by any intent to distribute. A person might, for example, possess large amounts of drugs to avoid having to risk apprehension or sources drying out, through repeated purchases. Like suburban homeowners who shop at Costco, this person might enjoy buying in bulk.

Suppose the drug statute *did* require proof of intent to distribute. If so, then the judge would, on request, have to instruct the jury that the bare fact of quantity alone is enough for a conviction only if the jury draws the inference, beyond a reasonable doubt, that the defendant intended distribution. Without such a separate finding of intent, the jury would have to acquit.

With a statute providing instead that quantity is the sole element, however, intent becomes legally irrelevant. As a result, even the prosecutor and jury who believe that the defendant is simply saving up for an anticipated heroin shortage rather than planning to deal drugs, can, respectively, prosecute and convict the defendant of the more serious felony without giving rise to any grounds for appeal.

By crafting a statute without an "intent to distribute" element, in other words, legislators target distribution without requiring its proof (or even allowing for its disproof as a defense). One might characterize this as an end-run around the constitutional requisite of proving every element of guilt beyond a reasonable doubt, particularly given the relative infrequency of authentic possession prosecutions.

The same "end run" accusation can be leveled against statutory rape laws. Young girls may represent a substantial portion of rape victims, perhaps because they are vulnerable and have not yet become sufficiently suspicious of the people around them. In most cases, though, a truly consensual encounter with a minor will probably not be brought to a prosecutor's attention or trigger the prosecutorial will to punish.

As with large-quantity drug possession laws, then, the omission of a requirement that would pose proof problems might generally serve the interests of justice, despite appearances to the contrary.

CONSENSUAL SEX WITH MINORS IS NOT A FUNDAMENTAL RIGHT

What permits legislatures the discretion to enact such laws, ultimately, is the fact that, like plain drug possession, consensual sex with minors is not a constitutionally protected activity. Even if it is victimless, sex with a minor may be criminalized and punished severely without resort to a force requirement. Indeed, it once was punished routinely in this way, because of misogynist concerns about preserving female purity.

In modern times, though, when consensual sex among teenagers is generally understood to be both common and profoundly different from the crime of rape, there still might be a role for statutory rape laws in protecting young girls from actual rapists, through deterrence and the real possibility of retribution.

DISCRIMINATION CONCERNS: THE RACISM WORRY RAISED IN THE DIXON CASE

A remaining concern is the worry about racism specifically, and discrimination more generally, that arises whenever officials are vested with the discretion to prosecute conduct that could be completely innocent. In Dixon's case, one witness testified that the victim had told the witness that the sexual intercourse in question was consensual but that she chose to claim it was rape in order to avoid the wrath of her violent, racist father. This testimony might have given rise to reasonable doubt in the jury on the rape charges.

By easing the burden of proof at trial by eliminating the requirement of proving force, then, the law does permit unscrupulous prosecutors and complainants to bring charges on the basis of what is truly victimless behavior.

One does wonder, though, why a girl would choose to tell a violent and racist father about her consensual sexual encounter with a black man—falsely characterizing it as rape—in the first place, rather than simply keeping the information from him, if the encounter were actually consensual.

AMBIVALENCE: ARE STATUTORY RAPE LAWS WORTH THEIR COST?

In short, the criminalization of statutory rape may have originated from repressive and misogynist conceptions of sexuality. Nonetheless, it has (and may always have had) some redeeming characteristics, taking into account the realities of prosecuting rape and of women's equality. It makes it easier, for example, to prosecute and thus deter real rapists who count on jury skepticism about acquaintance rape allegations.

Still, reducing burdens of proof relies a great deal on trust—in victims and in prosecutors—that the omitted element will truly be present when cases come to trial. If and when that trust is misplaced, as it may or may not have been in the case of Marcus Dwayne Dixon, a grave injustice can result.

POSTSCRIPT

The Georgia Supreme Court heard arguments on January 1, 2004, and reversed the lower court ruling on May 3, 2004, finding that where conflicting statutes apply, the more recent one prevails, and here the 1996 statute characterized sex between teenagers less than three years apart in age as a misdemeanor and not a felony. In its discussion, the court also analyzed the rule of lenity, which provides that a court should err on the side of leniency when applying and interpreting an ambiguous criminal statute.

Up until now, this Part has dealt exclusively with the subject of rape. The final chapter in this Part, however, is not, strictly speaking, about rape. It is about security officials performing frisks of travelers at the airport. Because of how people, including security officials, view women's bodies, however, even a search for implements of terrorism can come to look a lot like a sexual assault. When this happens, the question becomes whether the payoff for such investigation is sufficient to offset the harm to women's privacy and safety. The next chapter takes up that question.

• 22 •

When Cops Cop a Feel: National Security and Women's Privacy

In mid-September 2004, the Transportation Safety Administration (TSA) put into place a policy that provided for the physical frisking of selected airline passengers prior to boarding. The purpose of the new policy was to detect nonmetallic explosives of the sort that apparently were used by two Chechen women in terrorist attacks that destroyed two planes and killed ninety airline passengers in Russia earlier that year. The theory behind the policy was that the electronic equipment and wands used at airports could miss nonmetallic explosives carried on one's person.

Women passengers were especially unhappy about the new policy and made numerous complaints. In addition, there was reason to believe that the numbers of complaints understated the true scope of the problem, because—as with sexual assaults generally—women's distress at being fondled by airline security personnel might have been underreported.

The policy led to severe invasions of privacy—and, at the same time, may not even have been effective at locating nonmetallic explosives.

SPECIFIC EXAMPLES: INTRUSIVE APPLICATIONS OF THE NEW POLICY

In late November 2004, the *New York Times* provided accounts by several women who had been physically frisked at the airport.[1] Singer and actress Patti LuPone reported that an airline security screener had demanded that LuPone remove her shirt. After protesting, LuPone did so, revealing a thin, see-through camisole. According to the singer, the screener then "was all over me with her hands," touching areas including her groin and breasts.

An advertising executive complained that "[r]outinely, my breasts are being cupped, my behind is being felt, and I feel I can't fight it. If I were to say anything, I picture myself being shipped off to Guantánamo."

According to the *Times*, another female executive "reluctantly agreed to a search by a male security officer when a woman was not available. After he gave her a full body pat-down, she said, 'he lifted my shirt and looked down the back of my pants.'" A seventy-one-year-old woman who walked with a cane was also subjected to a breast patdown at the airport.

When LuPone asked why she had to undergo this invasive search procedure, one screener responded that "[w]e don't want another Russia to happen." Whatever indignity the women were suffering, in other words, was preferable to a lethal terrorist attack. The truth, however, is that frisking may not even be effective at protecting the country from terrorism.

WHY FRISKING MAY BE INEFFECTIVE

But isn't it obvious, the reader might wonder, that if airline security personnel frisk lots of passengers, the odds of a Chechen-like terrorist attack will diminish? Not necessarily.

There are at least three problems embedded in the conclusion that frisks will help protect the country against terrorists. First, as the *New York Times* reported, we do not have any evidence that the Chechen suicide bombers—the inspiration for the security measures in question—were carrying explosives on their persons, as opposed to in their carry-on luggage. We simply do not know. Therefore, it is not even clear that frisks would have done anything to prevent the tragic deaths in Russia that motivated the policy in the first place.

Second, even if we suppose that the Chechen bombers did carry the explosives on their persons, we do not have evidence that a frisk policy of the sort the TSA adopted would have detected those explosives. The frisks applied only to selected passengers—chosen at the screener's discretion. Thus, to be effective, the person carrying out the searches would have to be skilled at deciding whom to stop and knowing how to distinguish those who pose a threat from those who do not.

It is hard to be optimistic about the employees' skill in this regard, however, after learning that so many women—and in particular, Patti LuPone, elderly women, and female business executives—were among those selected. Unlike in Israel, where avoiding hijackings and terrorism is also a high priority, airport security employees in this country are not well paid. Thus, on the whole, they may not be especially skilled or talented.

Third, and finally, even if the frisk policy would have detected the explosives used in Russia, it does not follow that the policy will detect explosives in future terrorist attempts. Terrorists, unfortunately, can adapt fairly quickly to new circumstances. If a terrorist knows that he might be frisked, he can place a nonmetal explosive in a location that will not be disclosed by a frisk.

The terrorist might, for example, swallow or surgically implant the explosive (thus necessitating an x-ray for detection). Or a group of terrorists could simply travel in sufficient numbers to make it unlikely that every one of them would undergo a frisk.

After Richard Reid's 2001 attempt to blow up a plane with bombs placed inside his shoes, airport security began focusing on passengers' shoes. But this approach echoed France's decision to construct the famed Maginot Line following World War I. That decision assumed—incorrectly, of course—that the next German invasion would follow the precise pattern of the previous one. Measures that fight yesterday's battles are likely to fail in tomorrow's wars.

INVASION OF PRIVACY AND DIGNITY: THE FOURTH AMENDMENT AND AIRPORT SEARCHES

The Fourth Amendment guarantees the people a right against unreasonable searches and seizures. But because of the special risks that attend flight, and because people have the option of not flying, our courts have relaxed Fourth Amendment requirements in reviewing blanket searches and seizures at airports.

Lower courts have accordingly approved the use of metal detectors on every person, and the use of x-ray machines on carry-on luggage, as consistent with the Fourth Amendment. And the Supreme Court, though it has not ruled directly on the issue, has suggested its agreement. In *Chandler v. Miller*, for example, the Court noted that "where the risk to public safety is substantial and real, blanket suspicionless searches calibrated to the risk may rank as 'reasonable'—for example, searches now routine at airports and at entrances to courts and other official buildings."[2]

Once these relatively unobtrusive and universal search methods yield an articulable ground for suspecting particular individuals, moreover, officials can subject these individuals to more invasive physical searches, under familiar principles.

But the frisk policy of which Patti LuPone and others complained went well beyond blanket x-rays of luggage and the use of metal detectors on every person. It singled out particular people (thus heightening stigma and humiliation) without any articulable basis for suspecting them of wrongdoing. And when this happens, the people chosen must suffer bodily groping, sometimes by a member of the opposite sex (if they hope to make their scheduled flight and no same-sex groper is available).

The hunches of security personnel (the reliability of which is nowhere evident) were, for the duration of this policy, enough to authorize subjecting people to what would otherwise constitute a sexual assault, that is, a nonconsensual touching of breasts and/or groin, as a condition for innocent nonsuspects to travel freely around the country and internationally.

Given the lack of evidence to suggest that these searches would yield any positive benefit in terms of security, it would seem "unreasonable"—and thus, contrary to the Fourth Amendment—to inflict them upon passengers. As people sometimes forget, it is quite possible to diminish our privacy without thereby enhancing our safety. It seems that in adopting the frisk measure at issue, the TSA may have done exactly that.

POSTSCRIPT

A disgruntled female traveler responded to being frisked by grabbing the breasts of a TSA employee and was later found guilty of assault on a federal employee. The woman was sentenced to one-year probation, $2,000 in fines and 100 hours of community service. Due to outrage over the screening procedures, the TSA amended its policy in December 2004 and limited screeners to the "chest perimeter."[3]

III

WHAT IS SEX DISCRIMINATION?

We saw in Part I that to be female is to have some relationship to pregnancy, whether it is in the past, present, or future, and whether it is a relationship that one seeks to escape or a relationship that one pursues and treasures deeply. The uniquely female reality of pregnancy, as illustrated in the first chapters of this book, has important consequences for how the law should and should not be structured when the object of regulation is a pregnant woman's body.

In Part II, we examined rape, a phenomenon that—although theoretically a threat to both women and men—in fact uniquely plagues women in most contexts. This reality both results from and results in a distorted vision of rape as either a less serious harm than it truly is or as a harm that is mitigated by a woman's generating expectations—through turning tricks, dating or initially consenting to a man—that she later rebuffs. Part II developed the idea that rape is truly harmful in all of its incarnations and that the law and its agents hurt women who say they were raped by treating them as presumptive liars.

In this third and last Part of this book, we confront the question of what is and what is not sex discrimination. The question is a deceptively simple one. To discriminate on the basis of sex is to treat a woman differently from a man because she is a woman. But answering this question is much more difficult than it seems, because—as we have seen in the first two Parts—ignoring differences can at times do as much mischief as attending too closely to them. There are differences between men and women, and these differences sometimes matter, as in the case of a pregnant woman who is accused of harming her unborn child. So how, in the light of this complexity, does one avoid discriminating?

Courts have not done a great job of finding the solution to this conundrum. As we will see in Part III, moreover, they have often failed to protect women even when it should be *obvious*—without much subtle analysis—that they have suffered invidious discrimination. The problem arises in part from the fact that beyond actual maleness and femaleness and the reproductive realities that characterize each, employers and others ordinarily expect and demand many of the stereotypically masculine and feminine qualities that characterize a gendered world. When a person fails to live up to such expectations and demands, others become uncomfortable and may not even realize exactly what has caused the discomfort.

To provide an outlandish example, imagine how people would react to a pregnant man. To blatantly violate people's expectations is necessarily to attract attention and confusion. Discrimination will often, and predictably, follow such attention and confusion.

In this Part, I will attempt to unpack and articulate some of the implicit and often unconscious ideas that drive most if not all of us to treat women differently from men, even when we do not mean to do so.

In addition to drawing a clearer picture of what ought to count as discrimination against women, this Part will also explore the matter of anti-male discrimination. The right to be free from discrimination on the basis of sex is, after all, a right that cuts both ways. And just as pregnancy places special burdens and needs on the shoulders of women, the male role in reproduction places him in a uniquely vulnerable position as well, one in which he can at times do little to control (or even know about) how many of his biological offspring populate the world.

Chapter 23 addresses the claim by one employer that forcing female workers alone to wear makeup is not sex discrimination. The chapter explains how and why forcing women to conform to gender stereotypes—by acting "feminine," by wearing makeup, or by otherwise sustaining the connection between biological femaleness and feminine attributes—is indeed sex discrimination. Chapter 24 takes up the validity of sex discrimination claims by transsexuals who want to be treated just like other, biologically born, members of their sex. In some ways hostile to common stereotyping claims, the transsexual says that she should be able to select her sex so that it lines up better with her other attributes, even as opponents of stereotyping want to challenge the notion that being a woman or a man necessarily entails any particular characteristics. The chapter grapples with this contradiction and proposes a response to it.

Chapter 25 explores a third dimension of sex-based rules of behavior: sexual orientation discrimination. In this chapter, I explain why punishing a woman for choosing to love a woman (or a man for choosing to love a man) derives from the same, invidious, stereotyping impulse as a makeup requirement does. It compels women to do what is (wrongly) perceived as coming naturally to all women—acting feminine, loving men, and otherwise acting out their proper role without complaint. For this reason, it follows, sexual orientation discrimination is sex discrimination, pure and simple.

Chapters 26 through 30 comprise the portion of Part III that addresses some of the ways in which law and custom might regulate women's ability to "cheat" mother nature—by limiting reproductive technology to married couples, by refusing to provide insurance coverage for birth control pills, by creating or protecting obstacles to women seeking emergency contraception, and by prohibiting sex-selection abortions. In each of these cases, one vision of morality comes into direct conflict with the autonomy of particular women. In each case as well, women suffer disproportionately when forced to let nature take its course. And that suffering often reflects the reality that pregnancy is a uniquely female event in reproductive life.

Chapters 31 through 35 take up the problem of anti-male sex discrimination. Chapter 31 explores the strange case of a man who claimed that a woman had compelled him to become a father by using sperm collected during oral sex to impregnate herself. I discuss here the pervasive question of how fair it is for the law to allow women complete control over pregnancy, when men's lives and futures are very much at stake as well. In keeping with that theme, chapter 32 asks whether men have the right to what some have called a "financial abortion"—the ability to cut off financial support to one's unwanted offspring. Chapter 33 discusses a very different case, in which a man who fails to pay child support is ordered—as a condition of probation—not to have any more children. The right to procreate, like the right not to procreate, is far from a sex-neutral right. Once again, men have less biological and legal control, and these chapters consider the possibility that men *perhaps* should have accordingly fewer responsibilities, at least in some cases.

Chapter 34 talks directly about why "reverse discrimination" against men seems often to harm women as well as men, while "reverse discrimination" against white people rarely appears to have a parallel bilateral impact. Chapter 35 explores the question of whether male circumcision is an abusive practice that should encounter some of the same regulations and concerns as female genital mutilation. And Chapter 36 discusses the sad case of a young man who used a baseball bat, at his girlfriend's request, to terminate her pregnancy. The young man subsequently faced the threat of prosecution, and I raise the possibility that it is invidious sex discrimination to treat the boyfriend any differently from the girlfriend, given that he is acting at her behest.

• 23 •

Bartenders without Blush

In 2004, in *Jespersen v. Harrah's Operating Company*, a three-judge panel of the U.S. Court of Appeals for the Ninth Circuit held that an employer could legally terminate a female employee for her failure to wear makeup.[1] According to the court, the employer's imposition of makeup requirements on female workers did not run afoul of federal antidiscrimination law. The court made a serious mistake in ruling as it did—a mistake that a larger panel of judges failed to correct when it decided the case two years later.[2]

THE FACTS OF THE CASE: A MODEL EMPLOYEE WHO REFUSED TO WEAR MAKEUP

Darlene Jespersen, the plaintiff in the case, worked for almost twenty years as a bartender at a sports bar in the defendant's casino. Jespersen received consistently outstanding work evaluations from supervisors and customers alike, who found her highly effective and excellent.

In February 2000, Harrah's instituted a set of mandatory "appearance standards" for employees in guest services, including bartenders, and the defendant soon modified the standards to require that women wear makeup.

The amended policy specifically stated that "[m]ake up (foundation/concealer and/or face powder, as well as blush and mascara) must be worn and applied neatly in complimentary colors," and that "[l]ip color must be worn at all times." In addition, women had to have their hair "teased, curled, or styled every day," in addition to wearing stockings and nail polish.

In contrast, the men's appearance rules, among other things, *prohibited* male service employees from wearing makeup or nail color. Under the standards, men also had to keep their hair short and their fingernails clean and neatly trimmed.

Throughout the 1980s and 1990s, Harrah's had encouraged but not required its female employees to wear makeup. Though Jespersen had never liked makeup in the past, she tried for a period to follow the recommendation. She found, however, that wearing makeup made her feel "forced to be feminine" and "dolled up" like a sexual object.

Perhaps more importantly, Jespersen believed that appearing in makeup interfered with her effectiveness at her job, a position that sometimes required her to manage unruly and intoxicated customers. After a few weeks, Jespersen stopped wearing makeup and ultimately refused to comply with the mandate once it went into effect.

In the summer of 2000, Harrah's terminated Jespersen for her refusal to wear makeup.

THE RULING: WHY THE COURT REJECTED JESPERSEN'S SEX DISCRIMINATION CLAIMS

Jespersen argued that she was a victim of sex discrimination on two separate grounds. First, she said, the requirement that women wear makeup creates a burdensome expense that only women, and not men, must absorb. Second, she argued, makeup requirements demand conformity with sex-role stereotypes that subordinate women to men in violation of the law.

To the first (expense-based) discrimination claim, the Ninth Circuit responded that the plaintiff had produced no evidence that would allow a jury to conclude that, taken together, the Harrah's appearance requirements imposed a greater financial burden on women than on men. To the second (stereotyping) contention, the court simply asserted, in part based on prior circuit precedents, that imposing a different appearance standard for women than for men does not illegally discriminate on the basis of sex.

The court said that as long as no one sexually harassed the person who failed to conform to a sexual stereotype and as long as the distinction between what is required of men and what is required of women does not disproportionately burden either sex, the different appearance requirements are acceptable.

CONTRARY TO THE COURT'S RULING, WOMEN PLAINLY PAID MORE UNDER THE POLICY

As Judge Sidney Thomas's dissent pointed out, common sense and everyday lay knowledge could allow a jury to conclude that compliance with the neatness standards required of men by Harrah's (including short hair and clean and short nails) would cost less money than compliance with the female grooming standards (including hair, makeup, and nail polish requirements), even in the absence of specific evidence offered of expense differences among Harrah's particular employees.

In a future action, of course, a plaintiff could gather and introduce affidavits demonstrating the unequal financial burden of being a female employee at Harrah's. As a matter of precedent, then, the far more important error in the Ninth Circuit's majority opinion was the decision to reject the plaintiff's stereotyping claim.

THE SIGNIFICANT BURDEN OF STEREOTYPING

Let us more closely examine the distinction between the financial expense of makeup and the stereotyping burden that the plaintiff alleged.

Imagine that instead of requiring women to wear makeup and men to refrain from wearing makeup, Harrah's had required men to wear a gold bracelet with the word "Harrah's" on their right hands, and had required women to wear a platinum bracelet (of the same size) with the word "Harrah's" on their right hands. This set of rules would represent disparate treatment on the basis of sex, and the requirement would impose a greater financial burden on women, because platinum is a more expensive metal than gold. Therefore, in that case, the women of Harrah's could sue their employer under Title VII—the main federal statute prohibiting discrimination in conditions of employment.

Nothing about the distinction between gold and platinum, however, would lend Harrah's imprimatur to outdated and offensive traditional gender role assignments.

Imagine, now, that instead of a metal bracelet, Harrah's required each service employee to wear a sign, provided by the management, that included the server's name. For men, the sign would read: "I am [name], your gentleman server for the evening." For women, the sign would say, "I am [name], your sex object for the evening."

This gender-based requirement would not demand any financial outlay by employees, because Harrah's itself would provide the signs. Nonetheless, a court would likely find that Harrah's in this example had discriminated on the basis of sex in setting the conditions of employment, because it had assigned a humiliating sign to women on the job, but not to men.

WHY FORCING WOMEN TO WEAR MAKEUP AS A JOB REQUIREMENT IS SUBORDINATING

The reader might object here that few women would voluntarily wear a sign calling herself a customer's "sex object," whereas millions of women voluntarily wear makeup to work every day. Upon closer scrutiny, however, the distinction is largely illusory.

Women who voluntarily wear makeup to work are, of course, distinct from women who wear the hypothetical sign. Different women wear makeup for different reasons. Some wish to hide what they view as facial flaws, others to accentuate what they see as attractive attributes. Still others want to look pretty to men (or to other women) at the office. And yet others find that makeup relieves the monotony of their daily routine (in the way that colorful ties might do for men).

The important thing, however, is that women who choose to wear makeup could decide to stop altogether or to wear more or less makeup, depending on their goals and their sense of fit between those goals and makeup. The Harrah's rules, by contrast, specified that women *had to* wear makeup, regardless of their own preferences, and that the makeup *had to* include lip color, blush, concealer/foundation or face powder, and mascara.

Because women do not all look alike, the presumption that they all should be wearing each of these kinds of makeup carries with it the implication that there is a particular way that women—all women—are supposed to look. This implication is especially powerful when coupled with the prohibition against men wearing any makeup at all. For women who do not want to look "feminine," or conform to the view of women as eye candy, such a requirement serves to put them in their place. Women are to be decorated; men may not be.

When one's job includes the need to discipline rowdy and potentially violent male customers who have been drinking, moreover, the painted face that one must wear can also communicate a message of ineffectuality and a lack of seriousness that may be as destructive to the self-perception of the person who wears the face as it is to the image she projects to her customers.

To deny women a choice in the matter permits no escape from the sex-object role that was once required in the service professions.

THE DISSENT'S DISCUSSION OF SUPREME COURT PRECEDENT IS PERSUASIVE

To challenge the court's view that Harrah's did not discriminate against Jespersen, Judge Thomas's dissent cited the leading Supreme Court case of *Price Waterhouse v. Hopkins*.

In *Price Waterhouse*, the plaintiff was denied a partnership at the accounting firm where she had been working.[3] The evidence indicated that the basis for that denial was the view that the candidate was too "macho" and not sufficiently feminine—that is, she did not wear makeup, have her hair styled, or wear jewelry, as Harrah's explicitly required its female employees to do. The U.S. Supreme Court found that the plaintiff had made out a valid claim of sex discrimination, even though she was not denied partnership on the basis of her femaleness itself but rather, because of her failure to conform to sex-role stereotypes.

To defend its decision denying Jespersen a cause of action, the appeals court attempted to distinguish *Price Waterhouse*, saying that the Ninth Circuit had only applied that ruling to cases of *sexual harassment* and that no one had presented any evidence of sexual harassment in *Jespersen*. This argument, however, makes no sense at all.

The Supreme Court, and not the Ninth Circuit, has the power to define the relevance of stereotyping to a Title VII claim, and nothing about the distinction between termination and sexual harassment bears on the judgment by the highest Court in the land that sex stereotyping is sex discrimination. In fact, *Price Waterhouse itself* was not a sexual harassment case.

As Judge Thomas's dissent suggests, one unfortunate effect of this unprincipled decision will be to allow employers in blue-collar service industries to engage in the sort of sex-role stereotyping as a condition of employment that has long been prohibited in white collar employment contexts.

Because the power difference between employer and employee may be that much greater in the service industries, this decision takes the law of Title VII in exactly the wrong direction. One can only hope that the U.S. Supreme Court will eventually see fit to review this ill-considered judgment.

POSTSCRIPT

The Ninth Circuit Court of Appeals granted a motion for en banc review, brought by Jespersen, in May 2005, and heard argument on June 22, 2005. The Ninth Circuit en banc panel affirmed the lower court's decision in favor of Harrah's.[4]

If sex-role stereotyping raises the thorny questions that we have examined, in applying the laws against sex-discrimination, the class of people whose very membership in one or the other sex is itself contested faces what are potentially even more serious obstacles to prevailing in court. The next chapter takes up the rights of transsexual individuals under the antidiscrimination law.

•24•

And Ain't I a Woman?

On November 7, 2005, the U.S. Supreme Court denied review in the case of *Barnes v. City of Cincinnati*. The case raised the issue of whether transsexuals may invoke federal antidiscrimination law to address their mistreatment at the workplace.

The Court's decision was a victory of sorts for Philecia Barnes, born Phillip Barnes. Barnes had sued the Cincinnati Police Department alleging that her failure to obtain the rank of police sergeant resulted from hostility to her inability—as a transsexual—to conform to sex stereotypes. A jury found in Barnes's favor, and the U.S. Court of Appeals for the Sixth Circuit upheld the jury's finding.[1]

The issue of whether federal law[2] indeed protects transsexuals, presents an important opportunity to consider competing visions of what antidiscrimination law is supposed to accomplish and what a desirable freedom from sex discrimination at work (and in general) might look like.

THE RACE MODEL: IS SEX DISCRIMINATION THE SAME AS RACE DISCRIMINATION?

One approach to sex discrimination is to say that it is just like race discrimination. In both cases, a person comes into the world with a race and a sex that are not easily altered. But in spite of real differences in physical appearance between people of different racial groups or people of different genders, much of what constitutes the "difference" between people has more to do with socially constructed modes of behavior and dress than it does with biology.

In almost every instance, moreover, a decision about whether an employee should be fired or promoted at work should not turn at all on that person's race or sex. In other words, whatever biological facts might distinguish people of distinct races or genders should rarely, if ever, affect an employer's treatment of an employee.

DEPARTING FROM THE RACE MODEL: IS SEX DISCRIMINATION LESS INVIDIOUS?

A competing approach to sex discrimination is to suggest that it is quite different from race discrimination. The difference, on this account, is that people belonging to distinct racial groups are not in fact distinct from one another in any biologically significant way.

People of African descent, for example, are as different from each other as any one of them is from a random person of European descent. To speak of different races, then, is to engage in a culturally meaningful but biologically vacuous discourse.

The sexes, by contrast, truly are meaningfully different from each other, anatomically and chemically, and these differences might sometimes justify differential treatment that would be inappropriate in the case of race. Under this model, there is greater room for legitimate sex discrimination than there is for legitimate race discrimination.

AN EXAMPLE: SEX-SEGREGATED RESTROOMS

One example that illustrates the difference between the two approaches outlined above is that of segregated restrooms. In the case of race, virtually everyone would agree that an employer who required employees of different racial groups to use different restrooms would be engaged in blatantly illegal (and morally outrageous) conduct. In the case of sex, however, most employers continue to provide separate restrooms to their employees, a practice that does not generally raise many eyebrows.

The "sex is just like race" approach would find separate restrooms objectionable. It would hold that as a society, we have come to accept separate restrooms for men and women only because we buy into sex stereotypes that are, in fact, destructive and frequently false. Proponents of this view would suggest that separate restrooms can unfairly disadvantage women.

One could observe, for instance, that because men and women use separate restrooms, and because men are provided with urinals, women are much more likely to have to wait in line to use the restroom. As a result, women's accommodations at work are arguably inferior to those of men. This is certainly true at the theater, where the lines to the women's room prevent many a female customer from being able to use the bathroom and return to her seat before the end of intermission.

At work, moreover, people regularly discuss business in the restroom, and, to that extent, women are shut out of that component of networking with their male counterparts. The common response that women prefer a separate restroom for privacy and safety reasons assumes, perhaps wrongly, that a unisex bathroom could not be built to accommodate privacy and safety and that once people overcame the initial unfamiliarity of it, a common restroom might not serve women better.

In support of the "sex is like race" view of restrooms, there is nothing about a woman's anatomy or physiology that requires that she use a bathroom limited to members of her own sex. The same could be said of modes of dress—there is nothing inherent in the fact of being a woman or the fact of being a man that should dictate that some clothing is off limits to one or the other.

Such differences are instead cultural, and because much of what is culturally "feminine" corresponds historically to second-class citizenship and the denial of equal status, we should presume that gendered clothing requirements are invidious, as are separate restrooms.

THE CASE OF THE TRANSSEXUAL: THE PLAINTIFF SEES SEX AS ESSENTIAL, BUT SHOULD THE LAW?

This brings us to the case of the transsexual, a case that is inherently challenging in at least one sense. The transsexual—almost by definition—accepts the notion that there are important differences between men and women. A person who seeks sexual reassignment surgery and hormone treatment ordinarily does not believe that one's sex is either entirely or largely irrelevant to the way one lives one's life. Instead, the transsexual tends to embrace the idea that women and men really are very different. It is because of this difference that a person who experiences himself or herself as "truly" being of the opposite sex will remain unhappy until he or she can physically *become* that sex.

In this respect, a transsexual can be very "essentialist" about gender. While many feminists contest the true centrality of biological sex—except in maintaining cultural hierarchy—transsexuals tend to feel that there is, indeed, a fundamental divide between masculinity and femininity, and they wish to relocate to the other side of that divide. Rather than blurring or challenging the lines between men and women, transsexuals thus affirm those lines and seek out surgery designed to cross them.

The gender essentialism of the transsexual is challenging, because a more radical view of gender—as almost entirely irrelevant—offers the most promise to him or her of freedom from sex discrimination. If everyone has the right to use the same bathroom, for example, then the transsexual will not have to face a battle over whether a person who was born a biological male should be able to use the ladies' room. And if everyone can dress in as masculine or feminine a manner as he or she pleases, then the male-to-female transsexual's preference for women's clothing will not generate complaints.

The punitive events likely to confront the transsexual at work, in other words, result from the very essentialism—the view that "girls were girls and men were men" articulated by the Archie Bunker character in "All in the Family"—that transsexuals may sometimes uncritically adopt. And the legal position that males should be masculine and females, feminine—which transsexuals might share—could have the paradoxical effect of excluding them from the coverage of antidiscrimination law, by virtue of their "incorrect" sexual identification.

I once attended an academic conference at which a male-to-female transsexual scholar presented a paper. This scholar wore a lot of makeup and very stereotypically feminine clothing. As I listened to other women at the conference speak in private settings, I kept hearing the same complaint: this transsexual thinks of womanhood as an exaggerated caricature of feminine characteristics. She does not understand that what makes us "women" is having been treated as women by other women and by men all of our lives. Sexual reassignment surgery, on this view, could never turn a man into a woman, because gendered life experience, and not biology, makes us who we are.

My reaction was to share the skepticism about the ability of surgery to make a grown man into a woman. Nonetheless, I felt very sad for the transsexual scholar, because she so badly wanted to be included in our midst and seemed to be facing the very sort of rejection that might have convinced her to become a woman in the first place.

THE BETTER VIEW: TRANSSEXUALS MAY SUE UNDER TITLE VII

There are tensions, then, between a transsexual's view of gender and the resistance to stereotypes that a robust view of Title VII entails. Notwithstanding those tensions, however, I would propose that the correct way to resolve the dilemma is to allow a transsexual to sue under Title VII.

Every one of us has some choice about how strongly we wish to identify with the stereotypes that define our sex. If I enjoy wearing high heels, long hair, makeup, and dresses, I should be able to act accordingly without jeopardizing a promotion at my job. And likewise, if I prefer to wear androgynous clothing and cut my hair short, then those preferences should similarly engender no retaliatory treatment at work.

The transsexual may police gender lines in himself or herself just as rigidly as does the misogynist who persecutes the transsexual. The difference, however, is that the law should not regulate how we view ourselves, but it must regulate how we treat others. A man who does not fit a "macho" stereotype might punish himself for that failure, but that inability to liberate himself from gender's cultural mandates does not justify an employer's coercive imposition of these mandates on the employee.

Part of what it means to avoid discriminating on the basis of gender is a willingness to allow employees to sort out their own gender identifications without the threat of job consequences. And that is, in essence, what the Supreme Court said in *Price Waterhouse*.[3] If a woman cannot be denied partnership at her firm on account of masculine characteristics, then a history of having previously been a man and a failure currently to conform to gendered expectations should not preclude a promotion either.

In sum, the Sixth Circuit Court of Appeals was right to decide the case as it did, and when the Supreme Court some day addresses this issue, it should affirm the freedom of transsexuals and others to explore and define their own gender identity.

POSTSCRIPT

A different court recently followed the *Barnes* decision in *Mitchell v. Axcan Scandipharm, Inc.*[4] There, a male employee alleged that he was fired after he announced his intention to undergo a sex change operation. The defendant moved to dismiss the suit, but the court denied the motion, finding that if the facts alleged were proved, Mitchell would have a valid cause of action under Title VII.

The notion that transsexuals have a right against discrimination may be jarring to some readers. Indeed, many people have a visceral reaction even to the notion that people ought to have a right to engage in what some would characterize as genital self-mutilation. If an Asian person were to seek surgery to make his eyes appear Caucasian, many would view such a case as a sad sign of how much work our society must do to provide equality to people of all races. We would not, moreover, want to encourage a surgeon to take on such surgery. A person ought to be able to thrive as a member of his or her own race or sex. Indeed, it is the perceived *immutability* of race and sex that justifies special laws protecting people from race and sex discrimination.

When it comes to sex, however, segregation continues to govern people's lives. Though the provision of separate bathrooms for white people and black people has long violated both the law and most sensibilities, the provision of separate restrooms for men and for women has not. People raise their male and female children differently, and our culture (and virtually every culture) makes distinct (and often decidedly unequal) demands of each sex.

Though such practices are frequently unfair and ought to trigger the application of sex-discrimination law, they often do not, as we saw in chapter 23. Given these realities, there will inevitably be some people who not only *wish* they were members of the opposite sex but experience themselves as actually *being* members of the opposite sex already. Their own sense of who they are, in other words, matches up better with the very distinct set of expectations that face the opposite sex than with those that face their own.

Given the reality that one's sex is *not* irrelevant to one's identity, a number of people will decide to alter that physiological sex to correspond to their own experience of who they truly are. When they undergo sexual reassignment surgery, they have made apparent their dissatisfaction with the sex to which they were born. For an employer to discriminate against them is to confirm that "biology is destiny," and nothing could be further from the aspiration that sex become irrelevant to one's life prospects.

Some day, the cultures of femininity and masculinity may die, and the notion of wanting surgery to "become" a man or a woman may seem incoherent. As long as it is possible to feel a chasm between the identity that one experiences internally and the identity that the external world expects, however, it is the job of the law to prohibit discrimination on the basis of that chasm. Short of healing the chasm and making it disappear, that is the least the law can do.

For many readers, one of the things that essentially define gender identity may be a romantic attraction to members of the opposite sex. At the same time, however, a person can experience an attraction without acting on it. The division of one's attractions and one's actions forms the basis for an important debate about the rights of gay men and lesbians. The next chapter enters this debate on whether or not sexual orientation discrimination is, in fact, sex discrimination.

•25•

Why Gay-Bashing Is Sex Discrimination

At the end of 2002, the Supreme Court granted review in *Lawrence v. Texas*, an appeal of two convictions for consensual, homosexual sodomy. The case invited the Court to revisit the breadth of constitutionally protected privacy and the status of homosexuality in our legal system. It also confronted our judiciary with an instance of sex discrimination that has yet to be recognized as such.

As of the Court's decision to grant review, Texas, like three other states in the United States, specifically made it a crime for two people *of the same sex* to engage in "deviate sexual intercourse."[1] Under a state statute, "deviate sexual intercourse," known to many as "sodomy," occurs when there is "any contact between any part of the genitals of one person and the mouth or anus of another person; or . . . the penetration of the genitals or the anus of another person with an object."[2]

In the Texas case before the Court, police officers went to a residence in response to a neighbor's false complaint of a weapons disturbance. Upon arrival, the police found no weapons but did observe intimate activities between two men.

Both men were charged with violating the Texas criminal sodomy law and were convicted after offering a plea of no contest. Having been fined for their conduct, the men brought a challenge to the constitutionality of the law, on both privacy and equality grounds.

BOWERS V. HARDWICK: THE COURT'S EARLIER SODOMY CASE

To longtime Court watchers, these facts probably triggered a sense of déjà vu. The last time the Supreme Court had considered the validity of laws criminalizing homosexual conduct was in the 1986 case of *Bowers v. Hardwick*.[3]

There, the Court held that because of our country's long tradition of criminalizing homosexuality, it would be "at best, facetious" to maintain that the Constitution protects a privacy right to engage in such behavior.

The Georgia statute challenged in *Hardwick*, unlike the Texas law later before the Court, was gender neutral on its face—it prohibited enumerated sexual acts regardless of whether the partners were of the same or the opposite sex. A majority of our Supreme Court, however, nonetheless treated *Hardwick* as a case about gay sex.

The Court said specifically in *Hardwick* that "[t]he only claim properly before the Court . . . is Hardwick's challenge to the Georgia statute *as applied to consensual homosexual sodomy*. We express no opinion on the constitutionality of the Georgia statute as applied to other acts of sodomy."[4]

Thus, the de facto discriminatory enforcement of the Georgia statute against gay couples might actually have contributed to its survival in *Bowers v. Hardwick*. (De facto discrimination occurs when the government disproportionately applies a law, neutral on its face, to members of a particular group.)

THE STATUTE PLAINLY DISCRIMINATES ON THE BASIS OF SEXUAL ORIENTATION

It is readily apparent that the Texas statute discriminated against gay men and lesbians. In the past, Texas had prohibited all "deviate sexual intercourse," just as nine states did at the time of this case. In 1973, however, Texas amended its deviate intercourse law to limit criminal status to *same-sex* practitioners of sodomy.

Rather than prohibit private, consensual sexual behavior between all consenting adults, Texas thus decided that it would now leave heterosexual partners free of government scrutiny in the bedroom and visit that indignity on homosexuals alone.

The Texas Supreme Court roundly rejected the petitioners' discrimination arguments. Under U.S. Supreme Court precedent, the majority pointed out, sexual orientation is not a "suspect classification" like race or national origin—and therefore does not trigger searching judicial review.

Instead, the highest court of Texas asserted, a legal distinction drawn between heterosexuals and homosexuals only needed to be minimally rational. Because the law in question furthered the State's power to "preserve and protect morality," the court found the statute valid, despite its patent sexual orientation discrimination.

THE STATUTE ALSO DISCRIMINATES ON THE BASIS OF SEX

The defendants raised another argument in favor of striking down the statute: the statute represented not only sexual orientation discrimination, but sex discrimination as well, something for which the Constitution ordinarily demands an "exceedingly persuasive justification."[5]

The highest court of Texas dismissed this argument out of hand but should not have done so. To see the strength of the argument, consider a decision that is often (correctly) cited as the proper analogue in the area of race discrimination.

In the 1967 case of *Loving v. Virginia*, the U.S. Supreme Court struck down a statute prohibiting interracial marriage.[6] It thereby recognized that a law limiting the universe of people from whom an individual may choose a spouse, on the basis of race, represents race discrimination in violation of the Fourteenth Amendment.

Many commentators since then observed that the same principle applies to laws that limit the universe of people with whom a person can have sexual relations, on the basis of sex.

In both cases, the race or sex of the individual charged with a crime counts as an element of the offense. The Texas statute at issue in *Lawrence*, in other words, discriminated on the basis of sex, because in prosecuting the crime, one had to identify the sex of the defendant. If the crime is sodomy with a man, for example, the prosecution cannot prevail unless it shows that the defendant is a man.

NOT JUST SUPERFICIAL SEX DISCRIMINATION

The sex discrimination involved, moreover, goes deeper than this formal analysis would suggest. Sex discrimination—like race discrimination—is a phenomenon that reflects the belief that different classes of people, defined by sex or by race, should occupy distinct spheres of life.

Historically, men were people of the public sphere who could carry on political activities, provide material sustenance to their wives and children, and run the household. Women, on the other hand, were people of the private sphere who could raise children, provide refuge for their men from the cold world out there, and obey the wise dictates of their benevolent husbands. Women who wished to deviate from the assigned feminine role—either within or outside of marriage—were treated with suspicion or worse.

Much has changed—at least in this country—since the time when women were denied the vote and men were permitted to rape their wives with the law's blessing. But sex discrimination has not disappeared. Gay bashing—whether in the form of violence in front of a gay bar or the passage of a statute that differentially permits the arrest and prosecution of gay people for engaging in the same acts as straight people do—makes that plain.

HOMOSEXUALITY AS SEX ROLE REJECTION

Persecution of gay men and lesbians in American society amounts to a vestigial directive about the proper roles of women and men. In addition to being nurturing and soft, a woman is supposed to yearn for and cultivate a sexual relationship with a man. In addition to being strong and competent and earning more money than women, a man is expected to feel sexual desire for women.

One indication that homosexuality violates traditional male and female role assignment rules is the fact that people raise their eyebrows about male nurses and hairdressers in much the same way as they do about gay men generally.

And just as professions are gender-typed (and thus sometimes receive an adjective when held by the "wrong" gender, like "male nurse"), so are the categories of people whom one is supposed to find sexually attractive.

The persecution of interracial couples was always about more than sex. It served the purpose of keeping people of each race in their proper "place." The "place" of whites was to be dominant and of blacks to be subordinate, and any coupling between the two could potentially threaten the apparent inevitability of that division as the natural order of things.

Discrimination against gay men and lesbians has likewise been about more than a specified contact between genitals and orifices. Men must be dominant, women subordinate, and homosexuality potentially threatens that division.

People have, over time, become more comfortable with men and women holding jobs and carrying out activities that traditionally belonged to the other's sphere. But that comfort is precarious, a reality that is still apparent in reactions to homosexuality.

Children at school continue to stigmatize each other by using slurs for gay men and lesbians. Even tolerant parents report observing such behavior, as they attempt to teach their children that bigotry is wrong. (I remember hearing slurs of this sort as a child in the 1970s, for example, before I even knew what "sodomy" was.) The hatred reflected in the slurs enforced gender norms then and continues to do so now, albeit with less ferocity and greater subtlety.

THE LAW AND VESTIGIAL SEX DISCRIMINATION

What gave the hatred continuing strength and legitimacy was the prerogative of states like Texas to authorize police, prosecutors, and judges to arrest, condemn, and punish people for choosing a partner who is "morally" reserved to members of the opposite sex.

Accordingly, it was high time that the U.S. Supreme Court put a stop to legalized sex discrimination in the form of gay-bashing.

POSTSCRIPT

The U.S. Supreme Court decided *Lawrence v. Texas* on June 26, 2003, holding that the Texas sodomy statute violated the Due Process Clause of the Fourteenth Amendment ("Due Process") and thus overruling *Bowers v. Hardwick*.[7] Concurring in the judgment, Justice Sandra Day O'Connor found that the Court did not need to overrule *Hardwick*, because the Texas statute violated the Equal Protection Clause of the Fourteenth Amendment ("Equal Protection"). The reason the statute violated Equal Protection is that it did not treat homosexual persons as equal under the law, and even under a deferential, rational basis standard of review, moral disapproval in and of itself does not qualify as a legitimate state interest justifying the discriminatory ban.

Though the Court did not adopt the Equal Protection rationale, the Due Process approach represented the broader ground for the decision, suggesting as it did that expanding the antisodomy law to cover straight people too would not "cure" the constitutional infirmity. The decision therefore still represented an important victory for equality—between gay and straight people and between men and women as well.

The offending statute remains on the books in Texas, as in the three other states that banned homosexual sodomy, although the statutes are no longer valid, after *Lawrence*.

Now that the Court has overturned *Bowers v. Hardwick* and thereby blocked the application of the criminal law to sodomy, the next frontier, for gay men, lesbians, and others who fail to embrace the norm of heterosexual married union, is family law. How easy or difficult will it be for people to form families in ways that differ from the "traditional"? One area in which this question has already arisen is in the use of reproductive technologies. For people who want to have biological children but cannot do so without third-party assistance, such technologies can be crucial. The next chapter explores the implications of legal restrictions that at least one state has attempted to place on unmarried people's use of assisted reproduction.

·26·

Single People Seeking Babies: Can the Law Ban Them from Assisted Reproduction?

Early October 2005, the State of Indiana was on its way to considering a statute that would have confined the use of assisted reproduction to married couples.[1] Sponsored by State Senator Patricia Miller of Indianapolis, the law would have required people who wished to utilize assisted reproduction to obtain licensing and would have denied such licensing to unmarried people. In addition, criminal penalties would have followed for the "unlicensed" reproducer.

Miller withdrew the bill after a firestorm of controversy. Yet this law, or one like it, might be coming soon to a legislature near you.

The proposed bill raises important and novel questions about what the Constitution has to say about the use of new technologies in procreation.

WHAT IS ASSISTED REPRODUCTION?

What exactly is at stake when the government regulates "assisted reproduction"?

In the proposed Indiana law, "assisted reproduction" referred to hi-tech methods of procreating, such as intrauterine insemination, in vitro fertilization, egg donation, and intracytoplasmic sperm injection.

What unifies all of these techniques is that they allow for the conception of children without sexual intercourse. Users of such technology could also become parents without genetically contributing to their children's existence.

WHO WOULD SUFFER IF SUCH A LAW PASSED?

Under the proposed law, a person would have to be part of a married couple to qualify for a license to use assisted reproduction.

The people most likely to suffer the consequences of such a law would accordingly have been single people who wished to conceive children on their own, and lesbian and gay couples (in the overwhelming majority of states that prohibit gay marriage) that wanted at least one member of the couple to have a biological relationship to the children.

How might this group of affected individuals have gone about challenging the constitutionality of such a law?

THE RIGHTS TO CONTRACEPTION, ABORTION, AND AVOIDING STERILIZATION

The U.S. Supreme Court has long protected an individual's right to decide not to have children, under the rubric of "privacy" protection within what is called "substantive" Due Process. This right includes contraception and, with various caveats, abortion as well. The Court has also prohibited the use of sterilization as a criminal penalty.[2]

How do the cases announcing these principles bear on the proposed Indiana law?

First, the Court has developed the right not to procreate as a fundamental entitlement of every person to decide *whether or not* to bear or beget children. Because having children is such an important and life-altering undertaking, the Court has said, the government must not interfere with a person's privacy in this realm.

The actual cases, in their factual settings, protected the decision *not to* have children. However, the Court's recognition of a right to *choose* whether or not to procreate necessarily precludes governmental interference with the private decision *to* procreate as well as not to. If one can have an abortion without government interference, in other words, then one can presumably take a pregnancy to term without government penalty as well.

Second, in *Skinner v. Oklahoma*, the Court grappled more directly with the right to *have* (rather than not to have) children.[3] In *Skinner*, a majority invalidated a provision of Oklahoma law that allowed sterilization as a penalty for some, but not other, criminal offenses. Though the petitioner in *Skinner* succeeded in a Fourteenth Amendment Equal Protection challenge to the legislation at issue, the reason that the Court applied as exacting a test as it did in evaluating the law, is that the Justices deemed the interest implicated by the sterilization penalty—in being able to have children—a fundamental one.

It followed accordingly that denying the interest in procreating to some but not all convicts would trigger what would now be called the fundamental rights prong of "Equal Protection strict scrutiny."[4] And when a fundamental right is at stake, the government may not discriminate in denying it, unless such discrimination is necessary to serving a compelling government interest.

The Court has subsequently cited *Skinner* for its recognition that procreation is a fundamental right.[5]

There is thus a history in this country of recognizing that people have the right to become parents. But does that right extend to unmarried people? Other Supreme Court precedents indicate that the answer is yes.

UNMARRIED PEOPLE HAVE THE RIGHT TO DECIDE WHETHER TO HAVE CHILDREN

In *Eisenstadt v. Baird*,[6] the Supreme Court held that just as married couples have the right to use contraception, recognized in *Griswold v. Connecticut*,[7] single people have that right as well, as a matter of equality. Again, because the analysis behind access to contraception involves a general right to *decide* whether or not to have children, rather than simply to avoid having children, this extension to unmarried people of the privacy right to prevent pregnancy would appear to entail a right *not to* prevent pregnancy (i.e., to pursue pregnancy) as well.

In *Skinner*, moreover, the Court in no way suggested that the unacceptability of the sterilization penalty turned on the target's present or future marital status.

Thus, we have several indications that every person has the right to have children, and that the decision not to marry does nothing to alter that right. But what about when the person intends to have children in an unconventional way?

THE CONSTITUTIONAL STATUS OF ASSISTED REPRODUCTION

The proposed Indiana law would have regulated assisted but not "unassisted" reproduction. Therefore, if two people—regardless of marital status—were to have sex with each other, and a pregnancy resulted, Indiana would not have required any special licensing of the parents. Rather, it is only if a couple were unable or unwilling to conceive a child in the usual way that the proposed Indiana law might have applied. Only people who wished to go to a fertility clinic to reproduce, in other words, would have had to contend with the proposed Indiana restrictions on procreation.

Should that fact make a difference in our assessment of the validity of the legislation under consideration? The short answer is "perhaps."

All of the older cases protecting the right to control one's reproductive life involved reproduction through sexual intercourse in which the intending parents were also the genetic parents of the resulting child. A court could therefore conclude, consistent with the precedents, that once a third party—that is, the genetic parent who contributes sperm or eggs—becomes involved in the process, regulation might be acceptable and appropriate.

Furthermore, one could read precedents permitting the denial of Medicaid funding for abortion as drawing a legal line between exercising rights on one's own, on the one hand, and exercising rights with assistance, on the other.

The problem in drawing the line between assisted and unassisted reproduction, however, is that contraception and abortion *also* involve third parties. Among the parties who brought the case of *Griswold* to the Supreme Court, in fact, were people who distributed contraceptives to others and were worried about the law criminalizing that distribution. If couples are to have protected access to contraception, the Court held, then the government may not prohibit their distribution *or* use.

When the Court protects abortion, moreover, it often does so by invalidating laws that target doctors and other providers rather than the women whose right it is to terminate their pregnancies. To protect the right to abortion, then, is to permit third parties to assist in its exercise, without legal sanction. Though the government may be allowed to refuse to subsidize abortions (or, for that matter, assisted reproduction), it would appear not to follow from this allowance that the government may bar *private* third parties from providing that subsidy or from acting as facilitators.

ADOPTION AND ASSISTED REPRODUCTION

One area that might have provided the precedent that Indiana needed for regulating assisted reproduction is, ironically, its low-tech alternative—adoption. When people have a difficult time conceiving a child in the privacy of their own home, they often consider two alternative routes to parenthood: utilizing the services of a fertility clinic, and adopting. When a couple or a single person decides to adopt a child, the government typically plays a role in regulating and approving the process, a role quite similar to that set out for intending parents in the Indiana proposed statute.

Before being allowed to adopt, a prospective parent must satisfy a social worker or other government official that he or she will provide a good home for the child to be adopted, a home that might include a specified amount of space and worldly possessions. Unlike a couple conceiving a child through intercourse—presumed fit unless and until proven otherwise—the adopting parent thus operates under a de facto presumption of unfitness that he or she must effectively rebut before legally becoming a parent.

Scholars and commentators have raised questions about why those who adopt a child should have to confront such challenges, when their biological counterparts do not.[8] The reason, whether compelling or not, is that people tend to view the entitlement of parents to keep the children they conceive "naturally" as fundamental and sacred, quite independently of what the law happens to say. People expect that under the law, then, officials will recognize what is prior to the law—that a biological mother and father are entitled to have and to raise their child.

Adoption, by contrast, involves the placement of an orphan into one home rather than another. The family that wishes to adopt thus has no greater entitlement to a particular, biologically unrelated child, than another hopeful family does. The government may therefore, *in loco parentis*, decide who does and does not qualify for the privilege of adopting a child who might otherwise find a home elsewhere. One's potential shortcomings as a parent—though not relevant for a biological mother or father—may therefore legitimately register with the government when it is choosing, at least in theory, between a variety of possible placements.

Does assisted reproduction work in the same way?

That is ultimately the question that the proposed Indiana law squarely presents. When a child's parentage is unclear, the government may step in and assign status. This means, in the case of adoption, that John and Jane Doe are not constitutionally entitled to become Lucy's mother and father—that their ability to do so successfully is a privilege rather than a right.

In assisted reproduction too, parentage—as we ordinarily conceive of it—is subject to debate. While a biological mother is usually both an "egg donor" and a gestational parent, arrangements such as gestational surrogacy and third-party egg donation call that confluence into question, as chapter 12 discusses.[9] Similarly, though a father is usually the same person as the "sperm donor," the practices of intrauterine insemination and in vitro fertilization permit departure from that norm as well.

This is where, perhaps, the government may step in. Once people disaggregate pregnancy from the contribution of an egg, or insemination from fatherhood, the government can say who the "real" mother or father is. And Indiana could thus say that if a person using assisted reproduction wanted to ensure that he or she would be the legal parent, the only way to do so would be through government authorization.

Without a license, a person might risk criminal penalties and the loss of her child to a government-designated parent, just as she would do by taking custody of a child without formal adoption approval and authorization.

SOME BURDENS MIGHT BE SENSIBLE

It is difficult to argue that when a variety of people claim (or could claim) parentage, the government should have nothing to say about resolving the conflict. After all, when a child is at issue, a purely contractual resolution of her family situation—based on the wishes of the adults at the time of conception—might not be in the *child's* best interests.

Once it is possible for several people plausibly to claim that "he is not the parent; I am," it thus seems appropriate for society to intervene and find the right home for the sought-after child. Even if each party agreed at the outset to give the child to the intending parent or parents, moreover, the potential for disputes may justify government regulation of some sort.

IRRATIONAL DISCRIMINATION

The question for Indiana, however, was whether the decision to discriminate absolutely in favor of married couples and against singles and unmarried (typically gay or lesbian) couples when resolving parental disputes comported with the Constitution. The answer to that question is, and ought to be, no.

The Constitution does not allow for arbitrary discrimination. Though married couples may, on the whole, make very good parents, they often do not. More importantly, for our purposes, single and gay and lesbian parents often do an excellent job of parenting. The proposed Indiana statute did not simply say that marital status is a permissible *factor* in the government's deciding whether to issue a parental license to a particular person taking advantage of assisted reproduction. It said instead that *any* unmarried individual who used assisted reproduction to create a child would be a *criminal*, not legally protected in his or her status as parent.

Such a statement is utterly irrational and accordingly violates the Equal Protection Clause of the Fourteenth Amendment. As the Supreme Court said in *Romer v. Evans*[10] and *Lawrence v. Texas*,[11] the government may not take a group of people and place them and their family lives outside the protection of the law.

The increasing number of single individuals and gay and lesbian couples who have made nurturing and happy homes for their children is testament to the foolishness of the assumptions underlying Indiana's proposed legislation.

LESS A MATTER OF PROCREATION THAN OF EQUALITY

Whether through adoption or through the use of reproductive technologies, it has for some time been possible for people to become parents without having sex with coparents. In response to this possibility, the law will predictably speak, because one's status as mother or father might otherwise be contested.

The law could possibly say, in answer to our "Brave New World," that reproductive technologies such as in vitro fertilization are undesirable and therefore illegal. To support such a position, one could point out that the world is sufficiently populated without extra babies, that medical resources might be better directed at treating and curing illness, and that until every child has a home that he can call his own, assisted reproduction—as a direct competitor—could be harmful to orphans, existing children to whom the government has an obligation.

But the proposed Indiana law did not stand for these plausible arguments. It embraced instead a bigoted vision of the ideal venue for child-rearing—however underinclusive—to govern the lives of its population. Unlike most adoption laws, in other words, the Indiana statute disqualified an entire group of people from undertaking the status of parent, without any good reason for doing so.

In such a case, the greater power to prohibit the use of technology altogether should not include the lesser power to dictate by fiat which kinds of families can and cannot take advantage of it. In this sense, the right against discrimination in the freedom to form families may be more important than the right to use assisted reproductive technologies in forming them. An outright prohibition, in other words, could be less offensive than a discriminatory one that affected fewer people.

It is accordingly fortunate that its sponsor withdrew the Indiana bill under consideration, and we can only hope that similar legislation does not emerge elsewhere.

POSTSCRIPT

In the law of discrimination, there is a concept called "disparate impact." It stands for the straightforward proposition that a policy or practice may seem "neutral with respect" to sex or race on its surface but actually operate, in the real world, to harm members of a disadvantaged group. One example is the height rule for firefighters. Though the requirement that firefighters be at least six feet tall is not explicitly based on sex (and would, in fact, allow some aspiring female applicants to meet the standard), it would have a dramatic effect on the gender composition of the workforce, if put into effect.

Regulation of access to fertility treatments will have a more subtle but equally significant disparate impact on women. Women are far more likely to seek parenthood outside the context of traditional marriage than are men. Though this is changing somewhat, it is still the case that the overwhelming majority of single parents are female.[12] Perhaps because the culture of femininity encourages women to aspire to motherhood, regardless of her circumstances, single women adopt or try to conceive children in far greater numbers than single men do.[13] The same is true for lesbian couples, as compared to gay male couples.[14] A law that limited reproductive technology to married couples would therefore frustrate the wishes of women to a far greater extent than it would the wishes of men. And therefore, in the absence of persuasive justification, we should condemn such a law as the sex discrimination that it is.

Just as many people desperately want to have biological children and hope to utilize third parties and technology to do so, others (and sometimes the same people, at different points in their lives) want very much to avoid biological parenthood. The latter group relies on third parties as well, though their reliance is of a different sort. Heterosexual individuals who want to be sexually active without having children rely on contraception. And for people who depend on employer-provided health insurance, the failure to reimburse for the cost of birth control can be decisive. The next chapter discusses a ruling that such failure to cover contraception also amounts to illegal sex discrimination.

•27•

A Woman's Right to Birth Control Coverage

In late 2000, the Equal Employment Opportunity Commission (EEOC) ruled that when an employer provides its employees with a prescription drug benefit plan that fails to cover birth control, it may be unlawfully discriminating on the basis of sex.[1] This was welcome news for female employees. Birth control is expensive, and many women sensibly believe that it should fall well within the scope of any reasonably comprehensive health plan.

The fight for coverage as a matter of gender equality has been a difficult one, however. The challenge has been in finding the appropriate analogy to women's birth control in men's repertoire of medical needs.

An analogy is necessary because benefit plans do not literally deny women coverage for the same prescription that they cover for men. In other words, if a doctor were to prescribe birth control pills for a male employee, the benefit plan in question would not cover that either. The policy is thus formally gender-blind: Anyone who needs birth control pills is denied coverage.

Nonetheless, this formal gender blindness only thinly veils an obvious gender difference as to who, in practice, receives coverage. And just as a plan covering treatments for testicular cancer but not ovarian cancer would represent sex discrimination, the failure to cover birth control for women may also represent sex discrimination if an analogous prescription for men is covered. But what "male" prescription might be considered analogous?

EMPLOYER INSURANCE COMPANIES' ANALOGY TO MALE BIRTH CONTROL

For obvious reasons, the analogy that most appeals to employers is that of male birth control. Since employee benefit plans do not reimburse men for the cost of condoms or of (presently nonexistent) male prescription contraceptives, employers argue, they treat women equally in denying them coverage too—whether for the so-called female condom, for the diaphragm, or for birth control pills.

The problem with this argument is that women bear the biological consequences of pregnancy in a way that men do not. Legal doctrine has recognized this practical reality as well.

In the 1981 case of *Michael M. v. Superior Court*, for example, then-Justice William Rehnquist embraced this principle when he explained, on behalf of a plurality of the Supreme Court, why statutory rape laws may fairly target men alone without violating the Equal Protection Clause.[2] Rehnquist, and the plurality, reasoned as follows: "Because virtually all of the significant harmful and inescapably identifiable consequences of teenage pregnancy fall on the young female, a legislature acts well within its authority when it elects to punish only the participant who, by nature, suffers few of the consequences of his conduct."[3]

Viewed from this perspective, one that takes into account the uniquely female experience of pregnancy, the failure to cover the cost of contraception does not have the same medical implications for men as it does for women. If the lack of coverage contributes to a pregnancy, the woman suffers more.

THE EEOC'S ANALOGY TO PREVENTABLE MEDICAL CONDITIONS

Pregnancy is a physically burdensome, risky, and potentially painful condition that many women choose (and have the right to choose) to avoid. But is preventive medicine really the proper analogy to contraception?

Unlike hypertension, as employers were quick to argue to the EEOC, pregnancy is not an abnormal or pathological condition. While no one would choose to have high blood pressure or the flu, people do choose to become pregnant and sometimes go to considerable expense for fertility treatments that allow them to do so. To treat pregnancy as a preventable illness therefore seems to miss an important feature of pregnancy that distinguishes it from other conditions that send people to the pharmacy.

The analogy to preventive medicine—such as vaccinations—is flawed for a second reason as well. In addition to treating pregnancy as pathology, it assumes that in the absence of birth control, women would become pregnant, just as some men and women would become hypertensive without preventive medication. But of course, that is not necessarily the case.

Women faced with the risk of an unwanted pregnancy could choose to abstain from sex. Indeed, the possibility of this choice is what drove Rehnquist to say in the statutory rape case that "the risk of pregnancy itself constitutes a substantial deterrence to young females. No similar natural sanctions deter males. A criminal sanction imposed solely on males thus serves to roughly 'equalize' the deterrents on the sexes." The goal, in other words, is to motivate girls and boys alike to avoid pregnancy through abstinence.

THE ANALOGY TO VIAGRA AND SIMILAR DRUGS

If we understand sexual intercourse as an activity that women might choose to forego, then it becomes clear that what birth control primarily does is to facilitate sexual activity for women rather than to prevent pregnancy.

This notion—that denying women birth control is more akin to denying them sexual agency than to forcing pregnancy upon them—is actually a familiar one. It is the reason that many women's groups expressed outrage when employee insurers that would not cover contraception decided nonetheless to provide coverage for Viagra, a pill that helps men overcome sexual impotence (or "erectile dysfunction").

Though birth control does not literally make sexual intercourse possible, in the way Viagra does, it is nonetheless similar to Viagra in that it gives women access to this activity even when they wish to avoid pregnancy. The failure to cover birth control has, for this reason, signified for many a hostility to women's sexuality.

A willingness to provide coverage for Viagra but not birth control touched a nerve precisely because it seemed to capture the sexist double standard: the failure to view women's sexuality as a normal part of women's lives that ought to be supported, accommodated, and even celebrated, to the same extent that men's sexuality is.

The EEOC has chosen, however, to compare birth control to blood-pressure medicine—not to Viagra. Because that analogy will help provide the coverage that so many women seek, it should be applauded.

At the risk of looking a gift-horse in the mouth, however, I would suggest that at a theoretical level, it might make better sense for the EEOC to view contraception as analogous to Viagra and other treatments for male sexual dysfunction—as a medication that can facilitate women's chosen sexual relationships with their male partners.

This analogy would resonate better with women's own perception of what they do when they purchase birth control, and because it comports better with women's experience, it might be more likely to survive judicial scrutiny.

Classifying birth control as a medicine for facilitating sex for women would also have the added benefit of conveying a liberating message about women's lives. The message would be this: Not only is it legitimate to choose not to become pregnant, but it is also legitimate to seek nonprocreative sexual fulfillment without facing the threat of an unwanted pregnancy—a threat that Rehnquist aptly described in his statutory rape opinion as comparable in deterrent effect to that of a prison sentence.

POSTSCRIPT

In subsequent cases, such as *Erickson v. Bartell Drug Co.* and *EEOC v. UPS*, courts have held that even if an employer health plan denies prescription drug coverage for erectile dysfunction medication like Viagra, denying coverage for contraceptives still constitutes a form of illegal sex discrimination.[4]

While the EEOC has classified denial of contraceptive coverage as sex discrimination, the FDA (the Food and Drug Administration) has taken a very different approach to contraception. In particular, it has resisted approval for over-the-counter access to emergency contraception—also known as the "morning-after pill" (so named because it is taken *after* unprotected intercourse). At the same time, a variety of states have introduced legislation that would protect the rights of pharmacists with moral qualms about emergency contraception to refuse to dispense the medicine, even when patients have a prescription. The next two chapters discuss these developments and offer a point of view on the validity of the underlying claims.

•28•

FDA Resistance to Over-the-Counter Emergency Contraception

A few years ago, the Food and Drug Administration (FDA) announced a three-month delay in its planned decision on whether to approve the "morning-after pill" for over-the-counter (OTC) distribution. Those awaiting the FDA's decision were forced to remain in suspense for reasons that had nothing to do with the safety or efficacy of emergency contraception.

A woman can take the morning-after pill (which also has various brand names) within seventy-two hours of unprotected or inadequately protected intercourse to prevent pregnancy from occurring. Estimates of the drug's efficacy range from seventy-five to ninety-nine percent.

The FDA denied that politics played any role in the delay. Nonetheless, the FDA faced pressure from conservative Republicans who said that OTC availability of the morning-after pill could be "disastrous" to teenagers.[1]

Upon closer analysis, however, the arguments against the pill emerge as disingenuous attempts to impose an extremist and undesirable religious agenda on America.

WHAT DOES SCIENCE HAVE TO SAY?

The FDA drug chief, Dr. Steven Galson, has asserted that the delay in an approval decision on the morning-after pill is "totally based on scientific issues and questions." These questions appear to involve the gathering of information about sixteen- and seventeen-year-olds who have used the medication.

The scientists on the FDA Advisory Committee, by contrast, have overwhelmingly endorsed sale of the pills without a prescription, calling them a safe and important way to decrease the number of abortions. So what might account for the opposition?

DO MORNING-AFTER PILLS ENCOURAGE UNSAFE SEX?

A group of conservatives led by Representative Dave Weldon (R-Florida) have argued that the ready availability of the morning-after pill would encourage people, especially teenagers, to engage in unsafe sex. It is, of course, refreshing to learn of conservative Republicans joining their ideological adversaries in opposing unsafe sex among our youth. The "abstinence only" programs that conservatives ordinarily promote fail to draw any distinction based on the relative "safety" of sex, even implying, on occasion, that condoms are useless in preventing the spread of HIV infection.[2]

However, though admirable in its implied support for safer sex, the argument that an OTC morning-after pill will encourage unprotected intercourse has one small flaw: It makes no sense.

Almost by definition, a person who finds herself in need of emergency contraception did not plan to be in that situation. If she had, she would have either used birth control herself or asked her partner to do so.

If, on the other hand, she was either not thinking about the possibility of conception or did not consent to intercourse, then the availability of the morning-after pill would not appear to have made any difference in her behavior.

FAMILIAR MYTHS ABOUT CONTRACEPTION GROUND MORNING-AFTER PILL OPPOSITION

One striking aspect of the "morning-after pill encourages unsafe sex" argument is how similar it is to moral arguments opposing contraception generally. Opponents of condom distribution in schools, for example, say that it will motivate teenagers to have more sex. Along related lines, Representative Weldon's coalition of conservative lawmakers has argued that it is inconsistent for the Bush administration to advocate sexual abstinence and then approve the morning-after pill. That claim, however, is unpersuasive.[3]

Presumably, even the current White House has nothing against married couples engaging in sexual intercourse. Given that attitude of tolerance, it follows that a married couple that forgets to use contraception, or whose method of contraception proves defective (for example, when a condom breaks), could potentially find itself in need of the morning-after pill.

In addition, a woman who is raped, and thus had no abstinence option at her disposal, might wish with some urgency to minimize the chances that she will conceive and bear a child with her attacker's sperm.

OTC availability of the morning-after pill would allow these two groups of people—who may be the very religious Christians whose life choices find approval among conservative Republicans—to go to a drug store and buy what they need, without having to try to schedule an appointment with a doctor within seventy-two hours of intercourse.

SIMILAR MYTHS ABOUT ABORTION SHOW THE SAME FLAWED LOGIC

But what about those irresponsible teenagers? Isn't the FDA sacrificing the potential deterrent value of unwanted pregnancy on teenage sex?

That question corresponds to the argument that the morning-after pill could encourage teenagers to have unsafe sex. The implicit suggestion resembles the claims that are often made about women who have an abortion—that is, that they use it as a form of birth control. The idea is that women have sex without thinking about the consequences, because they know that they can always resort to "abortion on demand" in the event that they become pregnant.

It may be true that some people use abortion as their method of birth control, but the claim that such behavior is widespread seems more of a slur against women who have abortions than an accurate portrayal of what that choice might ordinarily signify.

In any event, however, the way in which the morning-after pill works simply does not permit the sort of "wait and see" attitude that supposedly animates the women who rely on abortion to avoid having children. Any woman who actually had this attitude would not use the OTC morning-after pill.

Why not? Because there is no way for anyone to know within seventy-two hours of intercourse—the time period within which the pill must be used—whether a pregnancy would otherwise have occurred.

All one knows about conception in the first three days after intercourse was already known at the time of intercourse itself. Therefore, the person who will choose to purchase the morning-after pill is ordinarily going to be someone who would have used (or did use) *birth control itself*—not abortion—as a form of birth control.

The morning-after pill is accordingly not a means of terminating a discovered pregnancy that a woman did not bother to prevent, because there can be no discovery in the first seventy-two hours.

HOW DOES THE MORNING-AFTER PILL WORK?

Some people might wonder how a pill can prevent pregnancy after intercourse has already taken place. It sounds a bit like closing the barn door after the horse has escaped.

The morning-after pill works, however, by altering hormone levels in a woman's bloodstream. If intercourse occurs before a woman ovulates, then sperm can remain viable inside the woman's body for several days, waiting for an egg to appear. While the sperm wait, the morning-after pill can prevent the woman's ovaries from releasing an egg. Without an egg, there can be no pregnancy.

If, on the other hand, a woman has already ovulated by the time of intercourse, the hormones can prevent the egg and sperm from uniting to form a zygote. Though a man releases about five hundred million sperm cells with each ejaculation, the odds of one of those sperm cells fertilizing a woman's egg—even if she ovulates around that time—are relatively slim; hormone alterations can reduce those odds to close to zero.

Finally, if the egg and sperm have already formed a zygote before the woman ingests the morning-after pill, then the hormones that she takes can prevent her uterus from permitting implantation of the embryo, an implantation that medically defines pregnancy.

In each of these cases, then, the morning-after pill resembles other forms of birth control in that it prevents rather than terminates a pregnancy. Hostility to the morning-after pill therefore represents, in an important sense, opposition to contraception.

And that equation—between contraception and the morning-after pill—takes us to the most plausible reading of current efforts to block OTC distribution of the morning-after pill. The morning-after pill is a kind of birth control, and opponents do not want people to have direct access to birth control.

More insidiously, however, the morning-after pill is the kind of birth control that people use only *after* they have already had sex. To deny a person access to the morning-after pill is thus to say—whether to an adult woman or to a frightened teenage girl—"you have made your bed; now lie in it."

When a person decides that she wants to take the morning-after pill, it is, in other words, too late to undo the fact of intercourse, no matter how ill-advised. Only one of the potential consequences might be avoided, and opponents labor to make that consequence (that is, unwanted pregnancy) more rather than less likely to occur.

PREGNANCY AS A PUNISHMENT FOR SEX?

If the morning-after pill does not encourage sex or undermine abstinence, then why is the FDA (and those whose political views appear to drive most of our current administration's agencies) delaying its OTC availability?

The answer appears to be the view that pregnancies represent the divinely ordained punishment for sex. To allow a woman to take the morning-after pill (or to permit condom distribution) is to treat unwanted pregnancy and the spread of HIV and other sexually transmitted diseases as simply undesirable. But the moralizing minority may be somewhat ambivalent about that. What is undesirable from one perspective might represent "just deserts" from another.

No matter how much most of us would like to discourage teenagers from having sex, and however much President Bush would like to discourage everyone other than married, heterosexual couples from having sex, we all recognize the reality that many people who fall outside the approved group—however broad or narrow—will nonetheless have sex sometimes.

In refusing to stop unwanted pregnancy, then, at a stage at which even abortion opponents would have a difficult time crying "murder," those who oppose the morning-after pill and contraception in general declare their affinity for a view of pregnancies and sexually transmitted diseases as the rightful wages of sin.

This is an intolerant, punitive, and extremist view that has no place in a democracy whose Constitution prohibits the government from establishing a state religion. It also has no place in a politics of compassion, conservative or otherwise.

POSTSCRIPT

The Government Accountability Office (GAO) issued a report on November 14, 2005, detailing the Emergency Contraceptive Plan B OTC application process.[4] The GAO report described the FDA's procedure for denying approval of Plan B's application as "unusual." The GAO concluded that top officials at the FDA had already decided not to award Plan B OTC status even before the FDA had completed its safety review in April of 2004. Furthermore, FDA officials had evidently overruled the Scientific Advisory Committee's decision in favor of approval, for the first time in sixty-seven OTC applications. The report also found that FDA Drug Chief Dr. Steven Galson had given a "novel rationale" for denying approval, namely, the concern that the ready availability of emergency contraceptives would encourage younger teenagers to increase their sexual activity.

After the FDA denied OTC status to Plan B, Plan B filed another application in July of 2004, to address Dr. Galson's concerns. This time, the application specified that Plan B would only be available OTC for adults and teenagers sixteen years old and older and that teenagers under sixteen would still need a prescription. The FDA's original deadline of July 2005 for a decision was extended to September 1 of 2005, and in August of 2005 the FDA announced another delay. On August 24, 2006, the FDA approved over-the-counter access to Plan B for women 18 and older.[5]

Dr. Susan F. Wood resigned as director of the Office of Women's health in September of 2005 in protest of the FDA's delays in deciding whether to award Plan B OTC status.

·29·

Do Pharmacists Have a Right to "Choose" Not to Fill Prescriptions?

In 2005, fifteen states introduced bills that would protect the right of a pharmacist to choose not to fill prescriptions, based on his or her own personal, moral, or religious beliefs.[1] Some of the bills explicitly referred to prescriptions for emergency contraception (the morning-after pill), while others applied more generally.

Such laws present fascinating questions about how the reproductive choices of women do, and should, intersect with the moral choices of providers such as pharmacists. They force both the pro-life and the pro-choice thinker to articulate the scope and meaning of the rights that each embraces.

A HYPOTHETICAL PRO-LIFE PHARMACIST'S VIEWPOINT

Though I am not a pro-life pharmacist, I will here take on the persona of such an individual and defend my right not to distribute morning-after pills.

I believe that life begins at the moment of conception. For that reason, once an egg and a sperm unite to form one living cell, that cell is a human being entitled to all of the respect that we extend to a newborn baby. And just as a newborn baby cannot survive without food, warmth, and oxygen, a growing embryo cannot survive without attaching to a uterus.

Women take the so-called morning-after pill with the goal of preventing either fertilization of her egg or, if fertilization has already occurred, implantation of the resulting embryo in her uterus. In the latter situation, the hormones in the pill interfere with the natural process by which a woman's uterus becomes a hospitable place for an embryo to survive after ovulation. The pill accordingly causes the death of the embryo, just as surely as leaving a newborn baby naked on a freezing cold mountain would cause the death of that baby.

After the Supreme Court decided *Roe v. Wade*,[2] my approach to embryos became a dissenting view. I accept that reality, although I am not happy about it. I remain hopeful that some of the new legal minds joining the highest Court will revisit the abortion issue with greater sympathy for the unborn than previous ones have shown. In the meantime, however, I cannot accept the notion that I have to participate in the killing process by dispensing a pill that I consider an abortifacient.

I believe that preventing implantation is tantamount to abortion, because it kills a living embryo, and that abortion is the moral equivalent of murder. I should therefore have the right to avoid facilitating such an act. If I can be forced—at the risk of losing my job—to provide morning-after pills, then "freedom of choice" is truly just a slogan, and the only "choice" the law protects is that of people who find the killing of unborn children morally unobjectionable.

There is precedent in my favor, even under existing case law. The Supreme Court said in *Maher v. Roe* that the right to an abortion does not include entitlement to federal funding to pay for that abortion.[3] Why would the Court say that? Plainly to announce that just because one has a "privacy" right to something that many people consider immoral does *not* mean that other people must pay for it with our tax money.

Those who oppose abortion have rights too, even after *Roe*. A doctor should not have to participate in an abortion if she believes that abortion is wrong, and a pharmacist like me should not have to participate in one either. Lawyers, for example, can decide not to represent tobacco companies or accused rapists, without legal consequence. I too should be allowed to choose to opt out of the violence perpetrated in the name of choice.

ANALYZING WHAT THE HYPOTHETICAL PHARMACIST SAID

Let us now examine the argument of our hypothetical pharmacist. First, we note that she acknowledges—as this issue forces her to do—that she is opposed not simply to late- or midterm abortions.

Pharmacists who dispense morning-after pills do not participate in procedures that destroy an entity that looks remotely like a baby, in terms of shape, body structures or functions. To oppose the morning-after pill as murder, then, is to claim that one human cell has a moral entitlement—*against the contrary wishes of a woman who might have been raped (as many users of emergency contraception have been)*—to implant inside that woman's body, unimpeded.

Second, we should observe that the pharmacist characterizes as a *penalty* the consequences that her employer might choose to impose following the refusal to fill a morning-after-pill prescription. That is, the pharmacist—in the name of choice—wants the law to force employers to exempt her and other pharmacists who oppose morning-after pills from the otherwise generally applicable job requirement that they make every effort to fill all legal prescriptions that customers bring to them.

But how much is really asked of the pharmacist here? The lawyer who refuses tobacco litigation or rape defense is different from a person who wishes to dispense medicines selectively. The profession of law necessarily involves an intensive level of work, commitment and identification with a client; that simply does not hold true in the profession of pharmacy, in which every client must be equally welcome.

I shall now return again to the hypothetical pharmacist's persona to address these and a few other points.

OUR HYPOTHETICAL PHARMACIST'S REPLY

I do admit my view—of which I am not ashamed—that a fertilized egg cell is entitled to live. Rape is a horrific crime, and I in no way condone or excuse the actions of a rapist when I say that the rapist's innocent child should not have to pay for his father's offense. In the same vein, no one would argue that the mother of a two-year-old child, a child conceived in rape, may choose to kill that child.

The law should punish a rapist severely for his crime. But the rapist's child did nothing blameworthy and does not deserve to die for his father's violence. No matter what the circumstances of his conception might have been, once conceived, he is equal to all other human beings on this earth.

In response to the second point, I do believe that firing me for failing to fill a prescription for morning-after pills is a penalty. If I do my job well and simply refrain from filling a particular, morally objectionable prescription, then I do not deserve to be terminated, any more than a pharmacist who misses work one day because his child is sick deserves to lose his job.

To provide another analogy, what if the law protected a right of terminal patients to take poison and end their lives? And what if pharmacies began stocking a particularly "humane" cocktail of poisons that a doctor could prescribe for eligible patients? When a patient walked into a pharmacy to fill that prescription, many pharmacists (including me) would decline, believing that handing poison to a suicidal person is tantamount to murder. The law should never compel people to participate in murder, even if the law allows that murder to occur without interference, for whatever reason.

A FURTHER RESPONSE TO THE HYPOTHETICAL PHARMACIST

To step out of the persona once again, I believe that the above argument is persuasive and yet simultaneously devastating to the pharmacist's position. One could envision many different sorts of medications to which a pharmacist might have a moral objection. Some pharmacists probably believe—as the Pope does—that birth control is wrong and would therefore refuse to dispense birth control pills. (Indeed, several of the proposed bills under consideration allow pharmacists to refuse to dispense "artificial birth control.") Or, because birth control pills may be used at high doses as morning-after pills, the very same pharmacist we encountered earlier might not wish to dispense them for that reason.

Other pharmacists might oppose fertility drugs because they interfere with natural processes and might ultimately entail selective abortion if too many children are conceived. Still others might believe that antidepressant medication is morally wrong, because it is a mood-altering drug and therefore resembles heroin and cocaine. People should improve their moods through good works, some might claim.

And what about Viagra? One could plausibly argue that erectile dysfunction is often just a normal part of aging and that medicines to fix the problem are inappropriate and unnatural.

It is true that every individual—including the pharmacist—should be able to chart her own moral life and to avoid engaging in conduct that she considers wrong. But in choosing a service profession, one agrees to serve people who, on occasion, will do something one considers wrong. Pharmaceuticals in particular generate a great deal of debate, because they necessarily alter "natural" processes, and there are people who view each one of those natural processes as sacred in some way.

In the absence of medication, some people would become quite ill and die early. As a result of medicines prolonging their lives, they might instead have children who carry genes for illnesses that could cause great suffering and "should have" died out. Because of the availability of potentially lethal medication, some people will take an overdose and die when less risky alternatives might have worked. And also because of medication, some people will terminate the life of a human embryo before it can implant inside a woman's uterus.

But it is the people taking the medication who bear ultimate responsibility for any morally questionable consequences. For the pharmacist to make the judgment that a patient should not have an "immoral" medicine is not the exercise of a "choice" at all but an abdication of her responsibility to fill prescriptions so that patients can make up their own minds.

POSTSCRIPT

It will come as no surprise to the reader that I consider the refusal to fill morning-after-pill prescriptions an invidious form of sex discrimination. For one thing, the morning-after pill is a medication that is specific to women—it disrupts the process of fertilization and implantation that might otherwise have led to an unwanted pregnancy, a condition that is uniquely female. For another, to refuse a woman emergency contraception is potentially to force her into a pregnancy that she might otherwise have avoided, a condition that places her squarely into the "pregnant" side of the "pregnant"/"not pregnant" divide in which women perpetually reside. And given the moral compunctions that so many men and women alike have about abortion, it could ultimately force her to remain on that side of the divide for nine months, against her will.

If a pharmacist believes that nonprocreative sex is a sin, then the pharmacist may choose to abstain from such activity. But to participate in placing women in a situation in which they must choose either to have an abortion or to take a pregnancy to term, when a third option was temporarily available, is to participate in the subordination of women as a class.

As of October of 2006, thirteen new states had introduced or considered bills to give pharmacists the right to raise moral objections to filling a prescription.[4] These states are Alabama, Illinois, Minnesota, Missouri, New Hampshire, New Jersey, New York, North Carolina, Pennsylvania, Rhode Island, Ohio, Oklahoma, and Washington.

In Massachusetts, Wal-Mart had refused to stock the morning-after pill in its pharmacies, a policy that it had adopted across the country.[5] Several women, however, brought a lawsuit, and the Massachusetts Board of Pharmacy ultimately ordered Wal-Mart to stock the drug in its pharmacies.[6] Wal-Mart nonetheless continues to permit its pharmacists, individually, to refuse to fill morning-after-pill prescriptions, though no state law compels it to do so.[7]

People who oppose abortion (however broadly defined) on moral grounds generally address their advocacy to the circumstances of two distinct groups of women who seek to terminate their pregnancies. One group consists of people who do not want to have a child at all right now. They may be poor and unable to afford more offspring, or perhaps they suffer from a health condition that makes the pregnancy dangerous. For whatever reason, they do not want to be pregnant, period.

The other group consists of people who do want to have a child but seek an abortion because they have learned something about the particular fetus developing inside their bodies. For some women, an amniocentesis or other diagnostic tool reveals a chromosomal anomaly that could lead to profound disabilities, mental and/or physical. And for others, it may be the fetus's sex that motivates an abortion.

In China, the combination of poverty, customary relationships between sons and their elderly parents, and a one-child-per-family policy conspire to lead many families to want a male rather than a female child. For some, this desire means abandoning a baby girl at birth. For others, it could mean a sex-selection abortion. Both of these practices are illegal in China. The next chapter takes up the question of whether the second practice—sex-selection abortion—ought to be illegal in the United States as well.

•30•

Killing a Fetus on Account of Her Sex

Chinese law prohibits sex-selection abortions—that is, abortions performed because the parents would prefer to have a child of the other sex. In China, moreover, it is virtually always a female fetus that is aborted. Chinese law also prohibits ultrasound scans to determine the sex of a fetus.

A few years ago, the Chinese government reportedly considered a plan to go further—and criminalize abortions and ultrasounds obtained for sex-selection purposes, in the hopes that criminalization would prove successful in curbing these practices. Ultimately, however, the country's legislature voted not to go ahead with this plan.[1]

Consideration of such criminal laws in China arises out of the country's particular population policies and the reactions of Chinese families to those policies. And though it is rational for individual families to want male children, the country suffers when there is a disproportionately high number of men relative to women.[2] The question of sex-selection abortion, however, is not unique to China, even if the particular context for the criminal law might be.

In the United States and elsewhere, there are those who would selectively abort a fetus of one sex or the other. What, if anything, should the law do about that?

CHINA: THE CULTURAL AND LEGAL CONTEXT FOR SEX-SELECTION ABORTION

China's one-child policy is an essential ingredient in any analysis of the proposed Chinese criminal law under discussion. For over twenty-five years, Chinese families have been limited to one baby each. This policy represents an effort by the country to cope with an alarming birth rate that threatens to produce a Malthusian nightmare of extreme poverty, widespread starvation, and ultimately, dangerously high death rates.

Pursuant to Chinese custom, men support their parents as they age, while women care for their husbands' parents. For this reason, the couple that may only have one child understandably wants that child to be male. As a result, a variety of practices have developed in China, including female infanticide (in which girl babies are killed at birth) and female child abandonment. With the wider availability of genetic testing prior to birth has come an additional practice—sex-selection abortion.

As a result of these varied reactions to the one-child policy, China's younger generations will have a disproportionate number of men, relative to women. Right now, there are about 120 male births for every 100 female births in China, and the ratio is 130 to 100 or higher in some provinces.

Unfortunately, the disparity appears only to be increasing over time. Some project that by the year 2020, there will be forty million unmarried men in mainland China. Historically, extreme violence—including war, kidnapping, and rape—have accompanied such a surplus of unmarried men. Perhaps partly for this reason, China has seen a sharp rise in violent crime over the past ten years.[3]

It would be no exaggeration to say that every one of these developments leading up to the planned criminalization of sex-selection abortions is tragic and extremely disturbing. Overpopulation, infanticide, child abandonment, sex-selection abortion, and serious disparities in sex ratios, *in China*, all reflect extreme circumstances, including a level of poverty that few people in the United States can even imagine.

Rather than attempt to judge the behavior that occurs under such circumstances, I will therefore turn my attention to the simpler dilemma of sex-selection abortion in the United States.

WHY THE SEX-SELECTION ABORTION DILEMMA MAY BE SIMPLER IN THE UNITED STATES

A few facts about this country change the equities when we assess sex-selection abortion in the United States. First, the United States does not systematically produce more (or fewer) men than women. For a variety of reasons—no doubt including the relative wealth here, the existence of a social safety net for the elderly in this country (at least for the moment), and the modern blurring of sex role differentiation—the people who are intent on having a girl seem to balance, numerically, the people whose hearts are set on a son.

As a result, the practice of sex-selection abortion does not threaten to destabilize the population here, as it does in China, even if it happens regularly.

In addition, U.S. law traditionally protects reproductive freedom. As our

Supreme Court precedents currently define it, that means that people have a legal right to have as many children as they physically can and want to have and to prevent or terminate as many pregnancies as they are able to prevent or terminate (at least prior to fetal viability). Because of this legal tradition, a criminal ban on sex-selection abortion would appear to violate basic legal norms in this country.

In short, it would seem that the case for prohibiting sex-selection abortions in the United States is quite weak. Such abortions do not pose a grave threat to the population as a whole, and a ban on the procedure would, on its face, limit reproductive choice.

IS THE ISSUE OF SEX-SELECTION ABORTION IN THE UNITED STATES REALLY AS SIMPLE AS IT SEEMS?

For many readers, however, even those who are pro-choice, the matter may not appear quite so simple. Two norms in the United States press *against* a right to sex-selection abortion: One is an equality norm—the notion that people should not discriminate against anyone, even a fetus, because of that someone's sex, and the other is the belief—shared by many who support abortion rights, along with those who do not—that terminating a pregnancy is a serious act that one should not undertake for affirmatively bad reasons.

From the perspective of these two sets of values, the absence in the United States of the population concerns that drive policymaking in China does not necessarily dictate a different result here as to the legitimacy of a criminal ban on sex-selection abortions.

Consider, first, the equality norm. In the United States, federal and state laws prohibit discrimination on the basis of a variety of attributes, including sex. The law of discrimination notably does not, however, govern one's intimate associations. And pregnancy is undoubtedly among the most physically intimate associations that two human beings can have with each other.

Nonetheless, our laws prohibiting discrimination *do* reflect a strong antipathy to the sort of decision necessarily involved in a sex-selection abortion: the choice to kill a developing child because he or she is not the "right" sex. To kill someone because of his or her sex is arguably a hate crime. And our criminal laws have recently tended to punish hate crimes more severely than others, though this practice has generated some interesting controversy.[4]

Furthermore, on a moral and philosophical level, the very foundation of reproductive freedom is in tension with the practice of sex-based abortion. One underlying reason that people have fought for reproductive choice is the wish to protect women from having the onerous and painful burdens of pregnancy forced upon *them alone*. The three-Justice plurality opinion said it well in *Planned Parenthood v. Casey*:

> The mother who carries a child to full term is subject to anxieties, to physical constraints, to pain that only she must bear. That these sacrifices have from the beginning of the human race been endured by woman with a pride that ennobles her in the eyes of others and gives to the infant a bond of love cannot alone be grounds for the State to insist she make the sacrifice. Her suffering is too intimate and personal for the State to insist, without more, upon its own vision of the woman's role, however dominant that vision has been in the course of our history and our culture. The destiny of the woman must be shaped to a large extent on her own conception of her spiritual imperatives and her place in society.[5]

Because sex-selection abortion is itself a species of sex discrimination, those who support reproductive choice as a matter of gender equality are not necessarily comfortable defending the practice of sex-selection abortion.

In addition to representing a particularly violent example of sex discrimination, moreover, sex-selection abortions in this country indulge the most trivial sort of preference at the cost of a developing being who would otherwise be welcome. Sex-selection abortion is, in other words, the sort of abortion that provides fodder for those who would outlaw the procedure altogether: an abortion for a very bad reason.

Given the various competing considerations, it is likely that existing and future bans on sex-selection abortions will provoke little opposition in the United States. Indeed, in *Planned Parenthood v. Casey*, the Supreme Court's 1992 decision reaffirming the core holding of *Roe v. Wade*,[6] the plaintiffs did not even challenge the provision of the Pennsylvania law that prohibited sex-selection abortion. They understandably expected that attacking such a provision would be politically costly, with little payoff.

Though sex-selection abortions may not destabilize the population, and though reproductive choice is a protected freedom in this country, the individual woman's interest at stake in a sex-selection abortion seems unimportant, while the countervailing harm appears substantial.

As in China, though for different reasons, a ban on sex-selection abortions thus might seem to strike a reasonable accommodation between the various interests—both weighty and weak—that appropriately make their way into this calculus.

THE PROBLEM WITH INVESTIGATING A WOMAN'S REASONS FOR ABORTION

As we have seen, most people can agree that there is no right to choose the sex of one's offspring and—accordingly—no right to sex-selection abortions.

Nonetheless, a criminal law prohibiting the procedure could still raise serious difficulties for reproductive freedom in this country.

Consider the enforcement of such a law. If police suspected a woman of having had a sex-selection abortion, they could subject her to the sort of interrogation that might ordinarily accompany a homicide investigation. Conversations that she might have had with friends about her hope for a girl or a boy would become subject to discovery. And the government could scrutinize her treatment of any existing children as well: Does she, for example, favor her daughters over her sons, or vice versa?

Even if a woman accused of wrongful abortion were found "innocent" after this investigation, the fact of her abortion would have become public knowledge, and she would have suffered the stigma that attaches to this procedure (even when obtained for medically sound reasons).

Also, because it may often be difficult for a person to establish her reasons for terminating a pregnancy, the prospect of a criminal accusation could place a serious chill on the exercise of the right to abortion, even for women who have no preference for one or the other sex among their offspring.

In the end, our moral instincts here may have to remain legally unenforceable. Morally, the decision to terminate a pregnancy on the basis of a baby's sex may be an ugly decision that deserves no protection. But the reality is that the reproductive rights of women who would never abort on the basis of sex depend on the government's staying out of the decision altogether.

If a woman has a right not to become pregnant and a right not to remain pregnant against her will, a consequence of those rights—if they are to be truly protected—is that the government may not pry into her reasons for an abortion. We must hope, instead, that women will prove worthy of the trust and responsibility that we place in their hands, even as we refrain from finding out whether that trust is warranted in a particular case.

POSTSCRIPT

What makes sex-selection abortion such a painful issue for any feminist is that it pits a woman's right to physical autonomy squarely against a baby's right against sex discrimination. What, after all, could be more discriminatory than terminating a life because that life is female? And to make matters worse, it is often precisely because the surrounding society devalues women's lives that an individual woman feels motivated to choose an abortion over the birth of a baby girl.

For good reason, however, laws against discrimination rarely apply to intimate relationships or contracts for personal service. We cannot, for example, demand that a man marry a particular woman, even if his only reason for choosing not to marry her is her race. The right to avoid unwanted physical intimacy must trump the right to be free from discrimination, as it does in all private areas of life. Sex-selection abortion is nonetheless indisputably a tragedy and a symbol of all the work that remains to be done in the fight against discrimination on the basis of sex.

Up until now, this book has dealt primarily with discrimination as a problem for women. And women as a group do undoubtedly suffer more than men from sex discrimination. But there are exceptions, and discrimination takes many different—and sometimes unpredictable—forms. In the next two chapters, we turn to an area in which women in the United States may have greater power than men—the area of reproductive rights. Chapters 31 and 32 address the right to avoid biological parenthood, which men apparently surrender the moment they part with their sperm, and chapter 33 discusses the loss of the right to become a biological father.

•31•

When Oral Sex Results in a Pregnancy: Can Men Ever Escape Paternity Obligations?

In a lawsuit against his ex-girlfriend, Richard O. Phillips alleged that approximately eight years earlier, he engaged in oral sex with her. Unbeknownst to Phillips, he said, his girlfriend, Sharon Irons, allegedly saved the resulting semen and used it to inseminate herself. A pregnancy resulted, Irons gave birth to a baby, and DNA tests proved Phillips to be the genetic father.

Though Phillips allegedly did not learn of either the pregnancy or the birth until some time later, a court nonetheless ordered him to pay approximately $800 a month in child support.[1]

Irons disputed Phillips's claims and asserted that she conceived her child in the ordinary way. For purposes of this chapter only, however, I will assume the truth of Philips's allegations, so that we can explore the legal consequences of such a situation, were it to arise.

Phillips's suit originally contained allegations of theft, fraud, and intentional infliction of emotional distress. An Illinois Appellate Court, however, dismissed the theft and fraud claims and allowed only the emotional distress action to go forward.

The facts of this case raise significant questions about the contours of a man's right—if any—to avoid any risk of paternity.

A WOMAN'S RIGHT TO CONTROL PATERNITY

When a woman becomes pregnant, the man who impregnated her has few legal rights with respect to that pregnancy. He cannot, for example, require the woman to remain pregnant if she chooses to have an abortion. Conversely, he cannot force her to have an abortion if she wants to remain pregnant and give birth.

Whether it is the right to become a parent or to avoid becoming a parent, then, the pregnant woman's choice trumps that of the father of the pregnancy. Furthermore, if the woman chooses to go to term with the pregnancy, the father is legally liable for child support.

All of this may seem quite unfair. If a man has no control over paternity, then why should he have to pay for the resulting child? Don't responsibilities ordinarily come with rights, and vice versa?

One reason for the inequity between women and men surrounding pregnancy is the disparate physical circumstances in which a pregnant woman and the man who impregnated her, respectively, find themselves. To grant a man a legal say in whether or not a woman stays pregnant and bears their child is effectively to give him dominion over his partner's body.

As the crucial three-Justice plurality opinion stated in *Planned Parenthood v. Casey*, the case in which the Supreme Court declined to overrule *Roe v. Wade* and accordingly struck down the husband-notification provision of a Pennsylvania statute, "it is an inescapable biological fact that state regulation with respect to the child a woman is carrying will have a far greater impact on the mother's liberty than on the father's. The effect of state regulation on a woman's protected liberty is doubly deserving of scrutiny in such a case, as the State has touched not only upon the private sphere of the family, but upon the very bodily integrity of the pregnant woman."[2]

Providing otherwise would give a man not simply a voice in whether or not he acquires the status of parent. It would authorize him to order the invasion of a woman's body, whether to destroy a pregnancy that she wants to continue, or to force her to sustain a pregnancy that she wishes to terminate.

As the Justices also said in *Casey*, "the Court today recognizes that, in the case of abortion, the liberty of the woman is at stake in a sense unique to the human condition and so unique to the law. The mother who carries a child to full term is subject to anxieties, to physical constraints, to pain that only she must bear."[3] The law accordingly gives her the right unilaterally to override the wishes of the man who impregnated her.

THE FINANCIAL IMPLICATIONS OF PATERNITY

Even accepting the unequal distribution of rights over a pregnancy, however, some argue that if a woman has complete control over whether or not to have a baby, then she should also bear the financial consequences if she chooses to remain pregnant.

In other words, if a woman can impose biological paternity on a man against his wishes, then that power should simultaneously relieve the man of his obligation to support the child that results, shouldn't it?

The answer that the law gives is no. When a baby comes into the world, both the man and the woman whose gametes led up to the child's existence are ordinarily responsible for the care of that baby, regardless of whether the child was "wanted" by both parents. Unless the two genetic parents decide to give up their baby for adoption, that responsibility continues until the child reaches the age of majority.

Men, in other words, can seemingly be conscripted into fatherhood against their will and then forced to take care of the child whom they never agreed to have.

Some say, in response, that the man, in effect, agreed to have the child when he had sex with a woman and thus risked such an outcome. On this view, a man who engages in sexual intercourse assumes the risk of becoming a father. If he wants to avoid paternity, he must abstain from sex or undergo sterilization. Because pregnancy as well as its termination have such physically intimate consequences for a woman, the man—physically separate from these experiences—loses control over paternity once he consents to having intercourse.

This argument, of course, is in some tension with the notion that a woman does not consent to maternity when she engages in intercourse. Such tension is not lost on disgruntled fathers.

But even if one accepts that intercourse equals consent to paternity, what happens when a man does not consent to intercourse? Does he still bear the risk of becoming a father? The case of Phillips and Irons—as described in Phillips's complaint—tests our intuitions about that very question.

INVOLUNTARY PATERNITY: EXAMPLES

When Phillips—according to his version of the facts—engaged in oral sex with Irons, did he truly assume the risk that he would have a child?

Let us examine a series of hypothetical examples and attempt, through them, to answer this question.

First, consider the case of Adam and Eve. Eve gives Adam the date rape drug GHB, and he becomes unconscious. She then uses a needle to extract sperm cells from his body. Eve promptly goes to a doctor with the sperm, and the doctor uses it to fertilize her egg, implanting the resulting zygote in her body.

If Eve gives birth, is the resulting child Adam's? Genetically yes, but it would nonetheless appear grossly unfair to require Adam to pay child support. He has done nothing, after all, to surrender his childless status.

Now take the case of Onan and Eve. Onan masturbates in his home and deposits the resulting semen in the garbage, located in his kitchen. Eve visits Onan's home shortly after his encounter with himself. When Onan leaves the room for a few minutes, Eve takes the opportunity to rummage through his garbage and retrieves the discarded semen. She makes a quick exit and proceeds to inseminate herself.

If Eve becomes pregnant and gives birth, should Onan have to pay her child support? Again, as in the case of Adam and Eve, it would seem unjust to impose financial obligations on Onan. Though less violently than in Adam's case, Eve has stolen semen that did not belong to her and has used it to make children that Onan had no way of predicting would come into being.

The case of Phillips and Irons, as narrated by Phillips, falls somewhere further down the line toward consensual fatherhood than these two cases do. As Irons asserted, and as the Illinois appellate court agreed, "when plaintiff 'delivered' his sperm, it was a gift—an absolute and irrevocable transfer of title to property from a donor to a donee. . . . There was no agreement that the original deposit would be returned upon request."[4]

Unlike Eve, Phillips—even on his own version of the relevant events—did consensually surrender his sperm to Irons. Should this fact make a difference?

DOES ORAL SEX ASSUME THE RISK OF PATERNITY?

In the earlier examples, it was only through nonconsensual wrongdoing that Eve came into possession of Adam's and Onan's sperm cells in the first place. That is, if Eve had respected Adam's bodily integrity and the privacy of Onan's garbage, then she would not have been able to become pregnant through these men.

In our real-life scenario too, Irons allegedly crossed a line that Phillips did not anticipate, but that crossing occurred *after* she legitimately (and with his consent) came into possession of his sperm cells. In other words, Phillips might have expected and hoped that Irons would discard the sperm rather than keeping and using it, but—unlike Adam and Onan—he did convey it to her of his own free will.

IS SECRETLY OMITTING BIRTH CONTROL DIFFERENT FROM SECRETLY USING SPERM?

To test our intuitions further, consider the case of the couple in which one member mistakenly believes that the other is using contraception. Is there a distinction between Phillips (on his version of the facts) and the man who has consensual intercourse with a woman he (mistakenly) believes is using birth control?

If so, the distinction would seem to turn on a vision of "natural" versus "artificial" conception. When a man has intercourse with a woman, however "protected" from pregnancy he believes himself and her to be, he initiates a process that—left to its own devices—will sometimes yield a pregnancy. As a result, we hold him to have assumed the risk of such a pregnancy occurring, even when the man thinks that he and/or his partner have taken adequate precautions.

When a man does not engage in intercourse at all, however, then "nature," left to its own devices, will never yield a pregnancy. It is only with the intervention of a third party (here, the woman with whom he allegedly engaged in oral sex) that the sperm will have the opportunity to fertilize an egg. In our real-life case, then, "but for" Irons's alleged intervention, the sperm cells were destined to die. In the language of torts and the criminal law, Irons's alleged actions rather than Phillips's were therefore the "proximate cause" of the child's existence.

Though a man may have no right to expect nature to go exactly as planned, he does perhaps have the right to expect that a human being will not affirmatively intervene and deliberately turn an act of "safe sex" into a pregnancy. Seen in this light, Irons's alleged use of artificial means to convert discarded semen into a pregnancy and ultimately a live birth appears to take Phillips out of the equation and to turn him into an unwilling sperm donor, just as Adam and Onan were.

But is the fact that Phillips surrendered his sperm voluntarily irrelevant? I would suggest that it is. To understand why, consider an analogy.

TRANSFORMING A GIFT INTO SOMETHING ELSE

Suppose John Doe invites a police officer to visit his home. The officer accepts the invitation and brings John a gift: a pottery vase. Without telling John, the policeman has placed a listening device into the vase. After leaving John's home, the officer is therefore able secretly to monitor the conversations and other activities that go on in John's apartment.

It is clear that on these facts, John—by inviting the officer to his home—has not assumed the risk of the police listening to his conversations or the activities in his home after the officer has left the premises. Indeed, the officer, through his behavior, has blatantly violated John's Fourth Amendment right against unreasonable searches and seizures.

The fact that John accepted the vase from the police officer has no Fourth Amendment significance, because what he accepted was a piece of pottery, a gift that in no way entails the acceptance of audio-monitoring. The vase-as-vase, in other words, is an entirely different entity from the vase-as-listening device.

Similarly, when Phillips surrendered his sperm to Irons, allegedly through oral sex, he agreed only to her gaining custody of the sperm-as-sperm. Absent preservation and fertilization, sperm cells die and become garbage. Phillips thus consensually surrendered nothing more than waste products to Irons, on his version of the story, and Phillips legitimately relied upon Irons to leave the status of that waste alone.

Instead, through insemination and pregnancy, Irons allegedly converted the surrendered sperm into something else entirely—a child.

WHAT ABOUT THE CHILD'S NEEDS?

In examining these issues, one last concern deserves our attention. Child support, as its name suggests, is not simply a monetary payment by a noncustodial parent to a custodial parent. It is—primarily, in fact—the fulfillment of an obligation by a parent to his child, the latter of whom is an innocent bystander in his or her own conception.

Though, on his account of the facts, Phillips did not consent to the creation of his child, the child may still feel entitled—like other children—to have two parents who share financial responsibility. The child, in other words, did nothing wrong to Phillips and seems to deserve no less than another child of a "surprised" father.

One response to this point is that every child deserves to have everything that he or she needs, and to have people called "parents" take care of him or her for the duration of childhood. But when a man does nothing that foreseeably risks a pregnancy, the genetic link between him and the resulting baby is of no greater significance than the link between two siblings who are wide apart in age. And the law does not demand child support of the older sibling, precisely because he or she did nothing to create the biological relationship with the younger one.

Even when he avoids intercourse and does nothing to donate sperm to a reproductive endeavor, a man can still be forced into factual biological parenthood. Irons's alleged actions demonstrate as much. Further, that reality may lead to great suffering, as the Illinois appellate court recognized by allowing Phillips's emotional distress claim to go forward.[5] That reality should not, however, necessarily carry financial ramifications along with the emotional ones.

At some point, a man's lack of actual responsibility for the creation of a child must absolve him of financial responsibility as well. The circumstances of Phillips and Irons—as claimed by Phillips—seem a sensible place to start.

The next chapter raises the question of what happens when the biological father undisputedly did have intercourse with the biological mother, but the mother had told the father that she could not conceive a child. If the mother chooses to go through with the pregnancy, without the blessing of the father, should the latter be able to opt out of paternity?

•32•

Should Men Have the Right to a "Financial Abortion"?

In 2005, in Michigan, Matt Dubay was ordered to pay $500 a month in child support to his ex-girlfriend, Lauren Wells, for their biological daughter, Elisabeth. When the couple was together, Dubay claims, Wells assured him that she was physically incapable of becoming pregnant. After the two had split up, however, she gave birth to a baby girl and sought support from him.

What makes this case special is that rather than pay the child support (or fail to pay, as often occurs), Dubay—represented by the National Center for Men—filed a lawsuit in federal court.[1] Dubay claimed the right under the Equal Protection Clause of Fourteenth Amendment, to cut off all ties to his unwanted biological child.

This suit reflects a growing sentiment among self-described members of the fathers' rights movement and ought to be taken seriously, even if it is unlikely to prevail in the near future.

MEN'S ANGER: WHY SHOULD WOMEN HAVE ALL THE CONTROL?

Many men are quite angry about how little control they currently exercise over their reproductive lives. When a man decides to have consensual sexual intercourse with a woman, he risks unwanted fatherhood: If the woman conceives, it is she, and she alone, who decides whether to terminate her pregnancy. And that is true even if the woman falsely claimed that she was using birth control, that she had been told by a doctor that she could not conceive, or that if she did conceive, she intended to obtain an abortion.

In short, the argument goes, a woman has the ability forcibly to place her unwitting partner or ex-partner in a position that he never wanted to occupy—that of a father—with all of the financial and emotional baggage that the status carries.

SHOULD MEN HAVE THE ABILITY TO FORCE ABORTION? AN UNPOPULAR VIEW

Some fathers' rights advocates feel so strongly about this reproductive inequity that they maintain that if either a man or a woman wants to terminate a pregnancy, against the wishes of the other partner, he or she should be able to do so. According to the *New York Times* magazine, Michael Newdow, for example, railed against "the imbalance in reproductive rights—women can choose to end a pregnancy but *men* can't. . . ."[2] Newdow then cut himself off, in order, he said, not to "alienate" the interviewer.

(As readers may recall, Newdow is the man who unsuccessfully sued to stop his daughter's school from having the children recite the Pledge of Allegiance. Possibly confirming Newdow's sense of how little control he exercises as a father, the U.S. Supreme Court denied Newdow standing to pursue the lawsuit, because of his status as the noncustodial parent, coupled with the Court's deference to California domestic law.)

It appears, however, that the belief in a man's right to compel a woman to have an abortion is not widely held—as least not publicly. And indeed, it seems plainly unreasonable. The primary basis for a woman's right to abortion is that no person should be forced, unwillingly, to sustain the assault on bodily integrity that pregnancy represents for a woman. Though the ability to avoid parenthood is a component of the rationale for this right, it is primarily a matter of physical integrity and would therefore preclude any entitlement on the part of a man (or anyone else) forcibly to terminate a wanted pregnancy. Indeed, one of the very few areas in which pro-life and pro-choice activists would tend to agree, is this one: A man should not have the right unilaterally to terminate the lives of his unborn offspring in utero.

ANOTHER STANCE: IF THE FATHER OPPOSES BIRTH, HE SHOULD NOT PAY CHILD SUPPORT

There is a less extreme version of the argument that men should be able to choose an abortion. The argument acknowledges that men and women may be differently situated with respect to gestation, so that women but not men have the right to terminate an unwanted pregnancy. But with rights come responsibilities, and a woman who gives birth without the biological father's blessing should not be able to collect child support from him. By failing to terminate her pregnancy in accord with the father's wishes, in other words, she should assume the risk of parenting the child alone.

Some have referred to this approach as the right of men to a "financial abortion."[3] If a man does not want his child brought into the world and lets his sexual partner know of his preference, they contend, then, if she nonetheless goes on to keep the child that she conceived with him, he should have the right to "choose" not to affiliate with that child and not to provide support. He should be entitled to opt out of the role of parent in the only way that he can, just as a woman may opt out absolutely by having an abortion.

This argument is less alarming than the one urging a male right to require an abortion. But there is a difficulty here as well. The problem derives from the reality that abortion is not a simple choice for most women, nor do most people in this country believe that it ought to be. Once an unwanted pregnancy begins, there are therefore consequences, for both the man and the woman, however much they would each wish it were otherwise.

The initiation of an unwanted pregnancy, moreover, is just as likely to be the result of a man's oversight (or "fault"), as it is to be the result of a woman's. Perhaps the couple decided together to risk unprotected sex because contraceptives were not readily available. Or perchance the man's condom broke during intercourse. Or maybe a medical professional incorrectly informed either the man or the woman that he or she would never be able to conceive.

However conception might have occurred, a woman faced with an unwanted pregnancy will not necessarily feel comfortable obtaining an abortion. Her hesitation may result from religious or moral convictions or from the sense that perhaps this pregnancy was "meant to be." In the Dubay case, for example, the ex-girlfriend reportedly believed that life begins at conception. Regardless of a woman's motivation, she faces a real dilemma once she learns that she is pregnant—she must either have the child or have an abortion, neither of which is a trivial matter.

No matter which choice a pregnant woman makes—a choice that is (currently) hers by virtue of its substantial physical implications for her body—the man who helped place her in the situation should not easily be able to wash his hands of the consequences. Barring extreme and utterly unforeseeable circumstances (such as those discussed in the last chapter), the availability of abortion should not relieve men of equal responsibility for the children they helped create, once those children do make their way into the world.

DUBAY'S STRONGEST ARGUMENT: MOTHERS CAN GIVE UP CHILDREN FOR ADOPTION

Dubay makes one argument that is far more difficult to rebut than the others. It is that after a woman has had a baby, in Michigan and elsewhere, she has the right to give up that baby for adoption. If she exercises that right, she cuts off her own financial accountability to the child, along with other parental rights and responsibilities. A man, by contrast, may not relinquish his financial responsibility for an unwanted child unless the biological mother shares his wish to give up the child for adoption.

Dubay asks: Why shouldn't men have the same right that women have? And doesn't the law engage in sex discrimination by offering one sex an option that the other lacks?

In considering these questions, we need to examine how the different approaches to adoption might have arisen in the first place. It is not difficult to imagine that sex-role stereotypes played a role. Traditionally, in the United States, the law made three assumptions about parenthood: the mother's proper role is that of nurturer; the father's proper role is that of "breadwinner"; and every child, if at all possible, should be part of a nuclear family. Under this set of assumptions, a number of conclusions would follow:

If a woman is unwilling to nurture (or "mother") her child, the law cannot force her to do so. A child in the custody of an uninterested mother is a child in danger of abuse or neglect. Therefore, if a woman gives birth to a child for whom she does not wish to care, the law would be doing the baby no favors by leaving him or her with the rejecting mother. Adoption would seem a mercy to both mother and baby.

A father unwilling to pay for his offspring *can*, however, safely be forced to pay nonetheless, just as he could be required to provide financial support for his wife or ex-wife, regardless of his wishes. Nothing about the money that he might pay is compromised by his desire not to spend it. Financial support—the "father's job"—can be an impersonal contribution in a way that care and nurturance—the "mother's job"—simply cannot be. It is therefore a "no-brainer," if one embraces these traditional assumptions, that if a man sires a child, he must do his duty by that child and pay money for its support.

Recall now the third assumption—that children should—if at all possible—grow up in two-parent male/female households. If we share this assumption, as the law has done in the past (and, to a lesser extent, continues to do), it follows that when a couple splits up before a baby is born, the baby is better off if the mother gives him up to a family containing two parents.

Adoption is thus a desirable turn of events and should not only be allowed but encouraged.[4]

Women, though, are often quite attached to their babies and prefer to keep them, regardless of where the father might be. In such a case, the child gains nothing, and loses much, if the father decides not to provide financial support for his biological baby. Given the three assumptions, then, the law properly encourages single women to give up their children for adoption but also properly forces men to support the babies of those single women who cannot part with their infants.

However such assumptions developed, they are no longer fair, and they rest on outmoded and discriminatory assignments of parental responsibility. Women currently participate in the workforce in overwhelming numbers, even if their wages continue to lag behind those of their male counterparts.[5] Furthermore, men participate in nurturing their children far more than they did in the past; indeed, there are a growing number of "stay-at-home" dads in this country, and their contribution to day-to-day caring for their babies is profound. Under these conditions, it would be as practical to require women who give up their babies to pay child support to custodial fathers, as it is to require men to do the converse.

As a practical matter, this issue may not arise very often. When a woman gives birth to a child whom she does not want to raise, it may be an infrequent occurrence for a man to hope to step into the void and raise the child of his ex-lover alone. When such a case arises, however, there is no good reason to relieve the mother of financial responsibility toward her biological offspring when the law does not do so for a similarly situated father.

Perhaps that should be the outcome of Dubay's lawsuit: The law should no longer permit women to relinquish financial ties to their biological children when the father seeks custody of them. The result would not do much to help Dubay, but it would assist the conscientious father who wants to be a single dad but cannot quite afford the expenses of his children's care. And though Dubay would still be in the same boat, under such a legal regime, he could at least console himself with the knowledge that some women might end up in that boat right there with him.

A PHILOSOPHICAL QUESTION: SHOULD WE BE TREATING CHILDREN LIKE INJURIES?

Even if we address the equality problem by forcing women to pay men support for unwanted children, a philosophical question remains: Do we truly want to treat men and women as negligent actors who must pay for their mistakes when they create unwanted babies? As long as a man like Dubay must pay child support for a baby whom he has renounced, are we not suggesting that the child is an injury brought upon society, and that the person who helped cause the injury must pay the price for his conduct?

Forcing men (or women) to pay child support may be the only way, in our world of diminishing governmental assistance, to ensure that more children do not descend into poverty. But if it were possible, it might be better for all of us, as a society, to undertake to ensure that every child has what she needs to survive and to thrive, regardless of how rich or poor her uninterested father (or mother) may be.

With an increasing number of single-parent families on the scene, it is perhaps high time that we embraced the idea that every one of us bears responsibility to protect every child. Until such a time as we do, however, biological fathers, and eventually mothers, will be—and probably should be—financially on the line for their offspring.

POSTSCRIPT

The concept of "financial abortion" is in some ways quite appealing to those who wish to even the score between men and women. Men, like women, should be able to walk away after conceiving a child they do not want. But the very attempt to analogize financial freedom with abortion demonstrates its failure as a descriptive account of reality. The reason that women have a right to abortion—to the extent that women do have such a right—is that pregnancy involves such intimacy between woman and child. Her right to terminate the intimate association is not a right to financial freedom, though financial considerations may animate her wish to abort. It is instead a right to physical autonomy, a right that men already have by virtue of their biological status as men.

Someday, however, it might be possible to remove a living embryo or fetus from a woman, at no additional risk to her health, and attach that embryo or fetus to an artificial womb. At that point, pro-life advocates will have a much stronger case against abortion—the right to be physically separate from another being will no longer necessitate anyone's death, and the status of the embryo or fetus will therefore rightly come to dominate the debate. At such a time, moreover, a woman will likely be financially responsible, just like her male partner, for the child who eventually develops from the embryo or fetus that she conceived. But until that time, the right to abortion is not a financial right; it is a physical one, and it is therefore one that only a woman—a person who can be physically as intimate with another human being as a pregnant woman is—should have a right to exercise.

Fathers, of course, have rights as well, not only by virtue of biology but under the law. Like women, they cannot be subject to discrimination on the basis of their sex. But what does that mean, when it comes to controlling their reproductive lives, if they truly *want* to conceive children that society believes they should not be allowed to conceive? The next chapter addresses that question.

•33•

Can a Judge Order a Deadbeat Dad to Stop Having Children?

On Tuesday, July 10, 2001, the Wisconsin Supreme Court issued a ruling upholding a lower court's sentence of a convicted "deadbeat dad"—a father of nine who had failed to pay child support—to prison, followed by probation.[1]

The ruling was important because the sentence of probation included an unusual condition: The convict was required to refrain from procreating, as long as he failed to support his existing offspring, and until he could show that he would support any future children he might create.

While courts' imposing conditions on probation (for example, that the convict remain drug-free) is the norm, this nonprocreation condition was highly controversial. By interfering with reproduction, it evoked images of Nazi Germany and eugenics—the "science" of "improving" the genetic composition of the population.

Should a court be able to tell a person that he may only beget children at the government's pleasure? Isn't procreation a fundamental right? These questions, while important, only begin our analysis of the Wisconsin ruling—which, upon closer inspection, turns out to be more defensible than it might first appear.

PRIVACY AND THE FAMILY

In a series of cases, the U.S. Supreme Court has granted fundamental rights status to personal decisions that concern the creation and raising of a family. The Court has invoked the Due Process Clause of the Fourteenth Amendment in support of these holdings. It has done so through the doctrine of "substantive due process."

The Due Process Clause normally requires what is called "procedural due process," the mandate that certain procedures (for example, notice and a hearing) occur before the government deprives a person of life, liberty, or property. "Substantive due process," by contrast, provides that, with respect to some deprivations, no amount of process is enough.

Privacy rights that have received protection under the "substantive due process" doctrine include contraception, abortion prior to viability, procreation, and important choices regarding the education of one's children—such as whether to send them to private school, whether to opt out of foreign language classes, and whether to provide home-based religious instruction until children reach a particular age.

SKINNER: THE SUPREME COURT'S CASE ABOUT FORCED STERILIZATION

Most of the cases announcing substantive privacy rights involved statutes that specifically prohibited activities that the Court later determined were constitutionally protected. One such statute, for example, mandated public (as opposed to private) schooling, and another banned the use or provision of contraceptives. The Supreme Court held these statutes unconstitutional, because the government had failed to demonstrate a compelling interest at stake that would necessitate the deprivation of a fundamental right.

One of the Court's decisions, however, did not concern a law that directly proscribed protected conduct. Instead, the statute at issue in that case—*Skinner v. Oklahoma*—provided for sterilization as a penalty for a particular category of crimes.[2] The defendant, Skinner, a recidivist thief, challenged the statute.

A law that ordered the sterilization of all citizens would be blatantly unconstitutional, under the line of privacy cases described above. But what about a statute like Oklahoma's, that required sterilization only of those citizens convicted of a crime?

The Supreme Court held that Oklahoma's sterilization penalty statute was unconstitutional: It violated the Fourteenth Amendment Equal Protection Clause, by unfairly depriving some, but not other, criminals of the fundamental right to procreate.

Rather than sterilize the defendant, of course, Oklahoma could have incarcerated Skinner for his crime. It was thus the penalty, rather than the underlying conduct at issue, that triggered Skinner's constitutional injury.

DISTINGUISHING *SKINNER*

Since the Supreme Court's interpretation of the Fourteenth Amendment binds Wisconsin's judiciary, the Wisconsin Supreme Court had to distinguish *Skinner* when it upheld the probation condition in question. In both cases, after all, a man was convicted of a crime and, following his conviction, was prevented from procreating. There are, however, significant differences between the two cases.

First, unlike Skinner, who was to be sterilized without alternative options, David W. Oakley, the Wisconsin defendant, was ordered not to procreate as a condition of probation. He thus remained free to procreate if he preferred prison to contraception. Alternatively, by paying child support to his children, as he was legally required to do in any event, and by showing a willingness to support any others who might come along, he could also resume procreating.

Unlike Skinner, in other words, Oakley had it within his power to exercise his right to procreate, either by violating probation or by changing his unlawful behavior. Moreover, in contrast to Skinner's permanent sterilization, Oakley's condition was temporary. Once he had served his sentence, he could continue to procreate regardless of what he had done (or failed to do) for his children in the intervening time.

PURPOSE MATTERS

Furthermore, the respective procreation restraints in Skinner's and Oakley's cases had very different rationales. Punishing a recidivist thief like Skinner with sterilization makes sense only on a eugenics rationale. But Oakley's probation condition likely had a very different purpose.

Turning first to *Skinner*, note that procreation had nothing to do with the crime in question, recidivist theft. Nor, for that matter, did this crime have anything to do with sex, such that there could have been a preventive rationale—for example, the wish to avoid a future pregnancy resulting from rape. Finally, there was no evidence that the particular crimes at issue in *Skinner* were more likely than other crimes to be committed as a means of feeding one's growing family.

In 1942, however, when *Skinner* was decided, theories that criminality was an inherited trait abounded. Many believed that criminals of various sorts should not be allowed to inflict their "defective" offspring—supposedly likely to become criminals too—upon the rest of society.

By 1942, in Europe, beliefs like these had become popular among scientists around the globe. The Court decided *Skinner* at the height of Nazi efforts to eliminate "unfit" members of the population through sterilization and extermination. The timing no doubt contributed to the Justices' sense that the Oklahoma scheme was offensive and dangerous.

ENFORCING PARENTAL RESPONSIBILITIES

The purpose of the circuit court in the Wisconsin case was apparently quite different from earlier eugenic programs. Under the law, parents are responsible for providing food and shelter for their children. The Wisconsin court seems simply to have been trying to make sure this responsibility would be carried out in Oakley's case.

Oakley had intentionally refused to meet his obligations to his children, thereby harming nine people to whose existence he had given rise. Since he had been duly convicted of this crime, he could have been imprisoned for eight years.

But lengthy imprisonment would have thwarted the very purpose of the law that Oakley had violated, thereby eliminating any possibility that he might satisfy his paternal obligations. Accordingly, the Wisconsin court ordered a shorter prison term, to be followed by probation, on the condition that Oakley stop creating more responsibilities until he evidenced a willingness to take care of those already in existence.

As in a civil contempt proceeding—in which the defendant is said to "hold the keys to his own jail cell," since he can go free as soon as he cooperates with a court order—Oakley, too, would hold the keys to his own liberty to procreate.

The court thus narrowly tailored the probation condition to the compelling interest at issue: nine children's need to receive proper support. As soon as David W. met that interest, David W. Oakley could happily resume populating Wisconsin with his offspring.

REEVALUATING *SKINNER*

Though we can distinguish the *Oakley* case from *Skinner*, it is useful to ask the larger question of whether it makes sense categorically to prohibit a court from limiting procreation as a response to crime.

In most cases, I suspect that the answer will be yes, for the very reason that makes us oppose eugenics policies. The state should not be dictating the makeup of our gene pool. Rather, the government must treat all people as equals. Any policies involving officially sponsored genetic selection would set a dangerous precedent.

The concern, however, is one of equality rather than any strict interest of all people (including criminals) in being able to procreate. Where it is possible to rule out a eugenics objective, the *Skinner* principle rests on far weaker ground.

Consider the Oakley case. If the defendant there were sentenced to a full eight years of prison instead of five years of probation, he would likely be unable to procreate during that period of time, since prisoners generally have access only to other people of the same sex. The Wisconsin majority pointed out this irony in its opinion.

Moreover, a prisoner must forfeit not only the right to procreate, as a practical matter, but also the fundamental right to freedom from physical confinement. A focus upon procreation in this case thus obscures the serious deprivation that incarceration itself represents.

The right to liberty from physical confinement has long received short shrift in our legal system. When a person has been convicted of a crime carrying a jail term, confinement is automatically authorized. This is true no matter how trivial and innocuous the offending conduct is, as long as it is not itself constitutionally protected.

Jaywalkers, litterbugs, and those who spit into the gutter may thus all be deprived of their freedom from incarceration for extended periods of time. Indeed, as we learned from the U.S. Supreme Court decision in *Atwater v. City of Lago Vista*,[3] even those who fail to buckle their seatbelts may be arrested and taken to jail.

LESSONS FROM *OAKLEY*

Of course, I do not suggest here that litterbugs ought to be sterilized, or even that prohibiting Oakley from procreating is necessarily a good idea. As various dissenters in *Oakley* suggested, enforcement of the probation condition at issue might prove complicated. This is because Oakley is prohibited from procreating, not from having sex, and it will be a woman—not Oakley—who will ultimately decide whether to give birth to any children conceived with him. We explored the importance of this division of power and responsibility in chapters 31 and 32.

Furthermore, as the concurring Justices argued, financial status should not play a role in determining who can have children. In this case, Oakley was convicted of intentionally refusing to pay child support. But some individuals might wish to pay child support and be unable to do so. It would be unfortunate if *Oakley* became a precedent for denying such people the right to procreate.

Nevertheless, in considering probation conditions like Oakley's, we should keep in mind the importance of finding alternatives to prison. What is often forgotten is that for many crimes, particularly those that do not involve violence, the lengthy prison sentences routinely imposed do not receive (nor would they survive) any demanding substantive constitutional scrutiny. This is true even though prison often undermines the very interests it is employed to protect—with nonviolent perpetrators being incarcerated in penitentiaries that are "schools for crime," with little chance of a normal life when they finally return to society.

Incarceration represents a serious deprivation of a right that is at least as fundamental as the right to procreate. If the Wisconsin decision provokes us to rethink our unquestioning reliance on incarceration to solve our crime problems, it will have been worthwhile indeed.

POSTSCRIPT

The U.S. Supreme Court declined to hear the Oakley case on October 7, 2002.

Similar orders have issued elsewhere. In upstate New York, for example, a family court judge told a couple not to procreate until they could care for their offspring, who were placed into foster care.[4]

In Ohio, a judge ordered Sean Talty to use reasonable efforts not to procreate, but the Ohio Supreme Court ruled that the condition was improper because Talty could not escape the ruling even by paying his past-due child support.[5] In Kentucky, Luther Crawford signed a plea agreement in which one condition of probation was that he could not have sex. A reviewing judge rejected the plea, not because of the provision, but because the judge did not think Luther was an appropriate candidate for probation. In an interesting twist, Jeffrey DeWayne Ashby, a Kentucky man, got a vasectomy, and the prosecution agreed to probation for the deadbeat dad, in part because of the vasectomy.[6]

Some time ago, courts attempted to address child abuse and other criminal conduct by women with demands (or probation conditions) of Norplant, a surgically implanted form of reversible birth control for women.[7] Courts rejected these conditions on the same grounds that we have examined in this chapter. Apparently, though, there were courts that took the view that if men rather than women were targeted, the outcome should be different. Some might describe this view as "reverse discrimination."

When we speak of reverse discrimination, we tend to conjure up images of disgruntled white people opposed to affirmative action. In the case of sex discrimination, however, men sometimes suffer (and can claim reverse discrimination) even when traditional, and therefore presumptively "pro-male," bias manifests itself. For example, a nursing school that admits only women harms men and simultaneously makes sex-stereotyped assumptions about men occupying the dominant role of doctor while women occupy the subordinate role of nurse.[8] The next chapter asks what makes sex discrimination differ from race discrimination in this way, making it destructive to both "sides" of the divide at once.

•34•

The Many Meanings of "Reverse Discrimination"

What is the difference—and what are the similarities—between race and sex? Feminist legal scholars have explored the many ways in which the respective histories of race and sex discrimination might offer useful lessons for crafting legal approaches to the achievement of both race and sex equality. There has always been a tension between the law's approach to each, as reflected by the Supreme Court's decision to apply "strict scrutiny" to governmental classifications of race but, at times, only "intermediate scrutiny" to those of sex.

Ironically, the more exacting scrutiny applied to race has made it easier for *white* plaintiffs to bring successful claims of race discrimination and more difficult for governmental affirmative action programs to survive those claims. The African-American community and liberals in general have found these developments disturbing and potentially devastating to the cause of racial equality. In contrast, male plaintiffs have sometimes brought sex-discrimination suits that had as both a purpose and an ultimate effect the *advancement* of women's status in our society.

Differences between the respective roles of race and gender in our lives account for the symbolic and real distinctions between the white plaintiff and the male plaintiff litigating reverse discrimination. Notably, however, these distinctions begin to dissolve in areas, such as interracial marriage, custody, and adoption, that call for permission to love one another across racial lines. (For simplicity, I will address race only in terms of black and white.)

WHY REVERSE DISCRIMINATION SUITS OFTEN HELP WOMEN, BUT RARELY MINORITIES

Interestingly, men rather than women brought quite a few of the most path-breaking Supreme Court cases challenging sex discrimination. In one case, a male applicant successfully sued the University of Mississippi for excluding men from nursing school.[1] In another, the husband of an enlisted woman challenged provisions that allowed military wives to collect benefits automatically but required military husbands to demonstrate their dependence first.[2]

In each of these cases, the men's victories were victories for the women's movement as well. The notions that men should not aspire to become nurses and that men would not rely on their wives for financial support are regressive. The Court's willingness to force the law to move beyond such stereotypes helped not only the men who wanted to become nurses or to collect benefits but also the many women who have aspired to become doctors, lawyers and heads of households.

Thus, reverse discrimination suits by men have often helped to achieve women's rights. Yet reverse discrimination suits by whites almost never have similar positive implications for African-Americans. Why is that?

When white plaintiffs bring race-discrimination suits, it is usually to challenge programs that give minorities benefits that whites feel entitled to have themselves. Examples abound in suits against universities and business enterprises that set aside spaces for minority applicants whose individual credentials might have otherwise precluded (or reduced the odds of) their selection.

Conservatives typically support white plaintiffs in such racial reverse discrimination suits. Liberals tend to oppose them. In contrast, some of the most prominent women's rights advocates have *brought* reverse sex-discrimination suits on behalf of male plaintiffs.

Why has reverse discrimination litigation taken two such distinct paths? Why, to put the question differently, do liberals oppose reverse discrimination in the case of sex but not of race?

REVERSE RACE DISCRIMINATION VERSUS REVERSE SEX DISCRIMINATION

There is no hypocrisy here. The distinction arises because of the peculiar meaning of sex discrimination for men.

The history of sex discrimination is a history of role constraints for both men and women. Though most of these constraints have relegated women to an inferior status sometimes resembling that of slaves, some of the constraints have simply allocated the proper attributes and preferences of life on a sex-typed basis.

The sexist expects, for example, that women will be passive and soft-spoken, submissive, self-effacing, humble, nurturing, and oriented to the needs of others. These expectations are familiar and have not disappeared. They continue to harm women, though to a lesser degree than was once the case. But the sexist has expectations of men as well.

The sexist expects men to be ambitious, aggressive, dominant, economically self-sufficient, excited by sports and money, lustful, and emotionally strong. Men are not supposed to cry very often, display weakness, call for help, or make themselves emotionally available to others (not to mention asking for directions).

Though these expectations are less suffocating and oppressive than the ones aimed at women, they can nonetheless make men who do not or cannot fit the paradigm model of maleness feel inadequate and resentful that the way they might really wish to live would encounter resistance, judgment, and disappointment. The man who wants to become a nurse or stay at home to nurture his children is shunned in a sexist society. And as we saw in chapter 25, the man who falls in love with men is as well.

In contrast, race discrimination does not, to any measurable degree, constrain the roles of white people. Race as a social construct has historically been an instrument of allocating benefits to whites while simultaneously denying them to blacks.

For this reason, when a white plaintiff claims reverse discrimination, the claim virtually always represents an attempt to obtain a job or benefit that has previously been disproportionately or exclusively allocated to whites (but which, in an effort to rectify that historical imbalance, or to serve diversity, is now given preferentially to members of formerly disfavored groups). White reverse discrimination claims, in other words, typically represent a challenge or opposition to affirmative action. It is therefore not surprising that in such cases, one is unlikely to find community between plaintiffs and liberals of all stripes.

WHEN RACE AND SEX ARE SIMILAR: THE LAW OF INTIMATE RELATIONSHIPS

This difference between race and sex, when it comes to reverse discrimination claims, does not hold across the board. Instead, there is at least one area in which reverse race-discrimination claims more closely resemble reverse sex-discrimination claims. This is the area of reciprocal love relationships.

When the law prohibited interracial marriage, it rejected not only the desire of a black person for a white person, but also the reciprocal desire of a white person for a black person. Those white individuals who chose an interracial relationship embraced for themselves the role of spouse or lover to a black person, a role that the law banned for a long time and upon which social custom, at least in some parts of the country, still frowns.

In *Loving v. Virginia*, both members of the couple that sued (successfully) for the fundamental right to marry across racial lines plainly felt committed to breaking out of the roles that a racist society had imposed on them through antimiscegenation laws.[3] As the law may someday recognize as well, and as argued in chapter 25, prohibitions against gay and lesbian relationships (including marriage) are a species of sex discrimination for similar reasons. A man should not be told that by virtue of being a man, his role in life must include finding sexual fulfillment with women.

MORE RACE AND SEX SIMILARITIES: ADOPTION AND CHILD CUSTODY

A second example of how the law has sometimes intervened to prevent the mixing of races is in the area of adoption and child custody. In one case, *Palmore v. Sidoti*, the U.S. Supreme Court struck down a state judge's decision to move a white child from a white mother to a white father after the white mother had taken up with a black man. The Court held that for a judge to consider the surrounding society's private prejudice against interracial families in allocating custody would be to give such prejudice the imprimatur of the state.[4]

In adoption as well, white people and black people might aspire to adopt a child across racial lines. Cross-racial adoption claims and child custody litigation therefore do not represent attempts to enshrine white supremacy. On the contrary, the white people who sue for the right to have an interracial family, by adoption or otherwise, seek the right to care for and love a baby of a different race.

These latter examples may, of course, be more controversial than that of interracial marriage. Many proponents of race-matching in adoption, a practice of questionable legality, are members of minority groups who claim that white parents do not share the African-American commitment to teaching a black child the importance of black identity.[5]

Proponents of race-matching mean well and want the best for the black community. Their view, however, seems short-sighted and wrong to me, because it overlooks the black child as an individual person who—like all children—needs a loving home first, regardless of race.

In reality, a white racist would almost certainly not want to adopt a black child, and would not view the black child as a resource in that sense. And a black child, like the black adult who wishes to marry a white adult, should have the right to join a permanent family without unnecessary delay.

In summary, it is the power of role constraints that usually distinguishes the meaning of reverse discrimination in the race and gender contexts. And it is in loving relationships between people of different races that role constraints can become as stultifying and oppressive for whites as sex roles may be for men. A recognition that such role scripts are wrong, whether their targets are male, female, black or white, would accordingly have beneficial consequences for us all.

POSTSCRIPT

The question of reverse discrimination is an important one, because how we respond to it turns largely on what we think makes "discrimination" wrong. The law generally uses language that is neutral regarding the direction of illegal discrimination. We prohibit discrimination on the basis of a category, such as sex or race, rather than prohibiting discrimination "against" women or "against" minorities. In federal law, for example, it is only the Americans with Disabilities Act[6] and the Age Discrimination in Employment Act[7] that prohibit discrimination in one direction but not the other.

The original purpose of all such laws, however, emerged from a history of discrimination *against* one group and *in favor of* another. It is therefore not obvious that one necessarily ought to treat discrimination against men as violating the principles that animate antidiscrimination law in the same way as discrimination against women does. Nonetheless, as we saw in this chapter, some discrimination against men turns out to entrench the subordination of women. Permitting women an automatic exemption from jury duty upon request, which the U.S. Supreme Court held invalid in *Taylor v. Louisiana*,[8] is just one example. And this reality makes sex-neutrality in antidiscrimination law a wise policy choice. When a policy seems, in other words, to harm men relative to women, the policy—and the apparent direction of the bias—almost always merits a second look.

The final two chapters of this book concern genital mutilation and abortion, two areas in which women's suffering and oppression have rightfully occupied center stage. In these chapters, however, it is men who suffer.

Chapter 35 discusses a proposed bill that would ban male circumcision. Though the practice forms a central part of Jewish and Muslim religious ritual and is otherwise extremely common among even secular families in the United States, it does not appear justified, on strictly medical terms, and it involves a painful and risky procedure. Yet, by contrast to female genital mutilation, there is little outrage. The chapter asks whether this is a species of sex discrimination.

Chapter 36, the last chapter of the book, concerns an abortion practice that should recall the use of wire coat hangers in the days before abortion became legal throughout this country. A teenage boy, at the request of his pregnant girlfriend, terminated her pregnancy by repeatedly beating her abdomen with a baseball bat. Prosecutors in Michigan charged the boy with a felony but did not charge the girl. This chapter raises the question of whether such unequal treatment is fair, when the boy is simply doing the girl's bidding. As minors (and their older counterparts) have a more difficult time obtaining abortions, such practices may become increasingly common. It is therefore important for us to think about who the "culprits" are in the case of these sorts of crimes.

• 35 •

Is Male Circumcision Gender-Based Violence?

Several years ago, a San Diego based group calling itself a health and human rights organization submitted a proposed bill to Congress called the Male Genital Mutilation Bill (MGM bill).[1] The bill, if adopted, would have banned the practice of circumcising baby boys.

The MGM bill did not find a Congressional sponsor and was therefore unlikely to go anywhere at the time of the proposal (or realistically, in the near future). Nonetheless, it raised important questions about the relationship between the protection of children, gender equality, and religious freedom, questions that have ramifications beyond the proposed bill itself.

Reportedly, more than half of the baby boys born in the United States undergo circumcision.[2] For most of these infants, a doctor performs the procedure. For a minority, however, circumcision is a religious ceremony. It ordinarily occurs on the eighth day of a Jewish baby's life. For Muslim children, it may occur on the seventh or eighth day of the boy's life, sometime in his first five years, or during adolescence.

The ceremony serves, for many Jewish and Muslim families, as both a celebration of their children and an assertion of religious identity.

WHAT IS MALE CIRCUMCISION?

Circumcision, in males, involves the cutting and removal of the foreskin, a fold of skin that covers the head of the penis. Because the procedure typically occurs during the baby's first month, anesthesia (other than topical) is generally considered unsafe. This means that a vulnerable newborn infant undergoes the surgical removal of a part of his body that is dense with nerve tissue, without anesthesia.

Notwithstanding the pain suffered during, and in the immediate aftermath of, the procedure, circumcision does not—when performed correctly—prevent the young boy from growing up to be a sexually functioning and fertile man. (Some argue, though, that sex is more enjoyable for the uncircumcised male.)

IS MALE CIRCUMCISION LIKE "FEMALE GENITAL MUTILATION"?

The apparent lack of permanent disabling consequences significantly distinguishes male circumcision from the practice sometimes called female circumcision but also known as female genital mutilation (FGM) or female genital cutting. FGM is prohibited by a federal statute passed in 1996.[3]

FGM typically involves the removal of a girl's entire clitoris (an excision that virtually eliminates the possibility of orgasm). In addition, clitoridectomy is often accompanied by the removal of the girl's labia and the sewing together of remaining raw surfaces, leaving only a small opening for the outflow of urine and menstrual blood, a process known as infibulation. Infibulation itself can have lifelong deleterious consequences, including urinary distress, pain during intercourse, and dangerous complications during labor and delivery of children.

Though the federal statute that prohibits FGM is limited to the protection of female anatomy, the extreme nature of FGM does not have a true analogue in male circumcision. In the light of this reality, it is somewhat misleading for advocates of the MGM bill to claim—as they have—that federal law currently discriminates against boys subjected to genital mutilation by outlawing FGM alone. No modern culture subjects male children as a group to procedures as extreme as clitoridectomy and infibulation. At the same time, however, federal law does prohibit in females even the limited cutting that occurs in males who are subjected to circumcision.

And the practice of male circumcision is not a trivial matter. As described above, highly sensitive and healthy tissue is removed with a knife, generally without anything but a topical anesthetic, and the patient is ordinarily a newborn infant. Though some people suggest that newborn babies do not actually suffer pain, this claim has always been suspect and is now at odds with what is known to the scientific community.

BUT IS THE PAIN "UNNECESSARY"?

The suggestion that circumcision causes *unnecessary* pain is, of course, a controversial one. The reason for the controversy is twofold. First, Muslims and

Jews have performed circumcision on their sons for thousands of years as a religiously required practice. It serves as an affirmation, at a very basic level, of their religion and their culture. To suggest that such a practice is "unnecessary" is accordingly to ignore this feature of circumcision, the fact that it is experienced by many as an essential and imperative component of their religious and cultural identity.

Second, for a long time, there were medical professionals who believed that routine circumcision of infants could be affirmatively beneficial to their later health. Circumcision can prevent infections where hygiene is less than adequate. There were also some studies that suggested that women partners of circumcised men were less likely to develop cervical cancer.

More recently, some have even claimed that circumcision helps to prevent HIV transmission to the circumcised male.[4] The American Academy of Pediatrics, however, issued a statement in 1999 indicating that the data do not support routine circumcision (a retraction of its 1989 statement suggesting a range of possible benefits).

If the evidence continues to provide little or no medical basis for circumcision, that will leave only the religious and cultural reasons for the continuing choice of parents to circumcise their male children.

But those bases are powerful. Many Muslims and Jews continue to circumcise their sons, even when they—the parents—are otherwise not religiously observant. Circumcision is thus, for Jews and Muslims alike, an important identifying mark.

Others continue to circumcise their sons because the practice has been routine in America for some time. Studies suggest, as well, that there may be a cosmetic preference for the look of the circumcised penis. Over time, however, the number of those who continue to circumcise their sons without a religious justification is likely to dwindle, a development that may lead to more support for the outright banning of the practice.

WHEN MAY THE LAW INTERVENE IN RELIGIOUS PRACTICE?

When it comes to matters of religion, legislators are, for good reason, hesitant to ban a practice that represents a religious mandate. The U.S. Constitution itself, however, as construed by the Supreme Court in *Employment Division v. Smith*, does not actually require the accommodation of religious conduct, provided that any prohibition applied to that conduct is part of a neutral, generally applicable law.[5] In the absence of evident discriminatory intent, a prohibition against the cutting of male children's genitals would therefore satisfy the demands of the Free Exercise Clause of the First Amendment.

Moreover, even when the Court interpreted the Free Exercise Clause more broadly, as a requirement that religious practice be affirmatively accommodated, that accommodation did not extend to practices that subjected minor children to health risks on account of their parents' religious observance. In *Prince v. Massachusetts*, for example, the Supreme Court held that a mother could be prosecuted under child labor laws for having her children distribute literature for the Jehovah's Witnesses in the streets, notwithstanding the religious motivation for her actions.[6]

SHOULD THE LAW INTERVENE?

If circumcision turns out to be what many medical professionals are saying that it is—unanesthetized amputation from a newborn child of living, healthy tissue flush with nerve endings, for no medically beneficial result—then it might seem quite proper to prevent parents from subjecting their infants to this cruelty.

Yet there is a worry, and it is significant. The worry is that perhaps, out of the many painful things that people do to their children, the law could ultimately be singling this one out for prohibition at least in part because the practitioners are religiously motivated, and the religions in question are minority religions in the United States.

There is a troubling precedent for this sort of targeting. In Nazi Germany, for example, the law prohibited Kosher slaughter of animals. Though the treatment of so-called food animals and their slaughter—Kosher and otherwise—is indeed extremely cruel, the law in Nazi Germany did not address itself to the whole range of cruelty to the sentient, warm-blooded animals who were and continue to be routinely and unnecessarily killed for food. Rather, it singled out the Jews' religious practice, and it did so out of anti-Semitism rather than any true humane concerns for animals.

We do not live in Nazi Germany, of course, and the proposed law against circumcision does not nominally single out Jewish or Muslim practice. Yet the worry about discrimination has two separate components, one of which applies even to ostensibly neutral laws. The first component is that the law might deliberately aim at harming a minority group. That is what the Nazis were doing in prohibiting Kosher slaughter. The second is about the willingness to pass legislation that might impose serious costs when a majority will not have to worry about bearing those costs.

The second concern animates the idea that a good way to ensure that a majority does not pass excessively burdensome legislation (in which the costs outweigh the benefits) is to require that the burdens of the law fall equally upon everyone. The equality principle, in other words, protects everyone from overreaching by ensuring that the majority truly experiences the negative consequences of its decisions and will therefore—on its own—seek to weigh costs and benefits in an honest fashion.

Because a prohibition against circumcision would not burden every group equally, there is a substantial risk that any cost/benefit analysis performed would largely ignore the true costs to Jews and Muslims, while perhaps exaggerating the benefits of the legislation.

THE BEST SOLUTION: WAIT

Does this mean that religiously motivated practices should be immune from legal intervention, no matter how harmful and abusive? Of course not. The ban on FGM is, in fact, is a good example of appropriate legislation banning a practice embraced by a minority in this country for a combination of religious and cultural reasons. The cost to girls and women who have suffered the procedure is just too great to permit it to continue.

But male circumcision is different. Though professionals have (with some hedging and ambivalence) decided to oppose the practice, it does not pose the obvious risks and harms of FGM, as the latter is generally practiced.[7] Until we can say with certainty that circumcision is truly harmful to male children in a lasting way, we should probably leave it alone.

In the meantime, the groups with the most to lose by a ban on the practice—Muslims and Jews—can absorb the medical evidence and have a chance to respond on their own. If the evidence of harm mounts, it is likely that religious groups will eventually find a way to modify their practices accordingly.

POSTSCRIPT

On July 27, 2005, MGM Bill (the group proposing the ban on circumcision) urged the United Nations to label circumcision as a human rights crime. The U.N. is unlikely to act on this proposal, but it does bring the issue into the public eye, along with the fact that MGM but not FGM seems to fall beneath the general radar of legal condemnation. MGM Bill is likely to continue its advocacy, and even if the law remains the same, practices may change gradually, in response to their efforts.

·36·

Abortion by Baseball Bat

Two years ago, a sixteen-year-old Michigan boy was charged with beating his (also teenage) girlfriend in the abdomen with a baseball bat, with the purpose and effect of terminating her pregnancy.

The unnamed boy, whom I will call "Johnnie Doe," was charged under a Michigan statute passed in 1999. That statute defines as a felony the intentional commission of an act against a pregnant individual, "[i]f the conduct results in a miscarriage or stillbirth by that individual, or death to the embryo or fetus."[1]

This felony would ordinarily have been punishable by up to fifteen years imprisonment. Because of Johnnie Doe's age and his lack of prior crimes, however, his alleged acts fell within the jurisdiction of the juvenile courts.

The pregnant individual in this case—whom I will call "Janie Roe"—allegedly asked her boyfriend Johnnie to help terminate her pregnancy by hitting her in the abdomen. Reportedly, Johnnie went along with the plan, the six-month-old fetus died, and the couple buried the body together.

The statute in question appeared to permit the prosecution of only the boyfriend, despite his girlfriend's arguable status as an accomplice. The case and the underlying law therefore raise significant questions about the relationship between the right to abortion, the freedom of pregnant women from being battered, and the status of third parties who assist women in consensually terminating their pregnancies.

UNUSUAL FACTS

One thing to note about the Doe case is that the fact pattern in question deviates enough from the norm to resemble a law school examination hypothetical. Under ordinary circumstances, pregnant women do not ask to be battered. Furthermore, the statute under which the prosecution was pursuing

Johnnie Doe does not itself appear to anticipate such a scenario. It aims instead at conduct that is independently illegal: assault and battery against a girl or woman who also happens to be pregnant.

A second feature of the Doe and Roe case, to the extent that it implicates abortion controversies, is that the right announced in *Roe v. Wade*[2] as well as the cases that followed does not appear to contemplate this sort of scenario either. The decision in *Roe* notably discusses the privacy of a woman in consultation with her *doctor*—not the privacy of a woman in consultation with her *consensual assailant*—to decide whether or not she will bear a child.

WHICH DIFFERENCES MATTER?

So what? Cases often arise under unusual circumstances. A law need not anticipate the precise contours of a fact pattern for the law to apply to those facts. The problem here, though, is that one must decide how to conceptualize the facts involving Doe and Roe before drawing any conclusions about what truly *ought* to happen.

Let us first examine this as an ordinary case of assault and battery that results in the death of an unborn child. It would make perfect sense for a prosecutor to pursue the boyfriend who attacked a pregnant woman with a baseball bat. He should not be attacking her and her developing baby—regardless of how she feels about her pregnancy—and he should be punished for doing so.

But if the woman's wishes regarding the pregnancy are irrelevant, and the man's actions are criminal, then she too should qualify as a criminal, for having solicited his unlawful conduct. After all, if her request for assistance in terminating her pregnancy does nothing to diminish her boyfriend's culpability in carrying out the assault, then it ought—by the same token—to solidify her own culpability as well.

If the victim in question is the unborn child, in other words, then the boyfriend's responsibility toward that victim necessarily entails his girlfriend's as well. Yet the Michigan statute does not appear to permit prosecution of the woman, and the prosecutor has indicated no intention of otherwise pursuing her. This suggests that a different approach to the case may be appropriate.

Let us assume now that this is more like a case of (voluntarily) induced abortion. If it is, then the woman may be exercising a constitutional right and the prosecutor (as well as the law) would appropriately avoid charging her with a crime. On this approach, however, the third party who facilitated the exercise of her constitutional right—the boyfriend who attacked her on request—should be similarly exempted from criminal liability. Just like the entity that sells contraceptives to those who have the right to use them, the abortion provider is no more subject to liability than his client.

The judge in the case considered whether to classify this as a case of abortion. He asked for briefing on the question of whether the parental consent law in Michigan might bear on Janie Roe's ability under the law to consent to Johnnie's performing an abortion.

Ironically, it could have turned out that if a sixteen-year-old *girl* was, under the law, too young to consent to the acts in question, then—but only then—could a sixteen-year-old *boy* be held criminally responsible for faithfully carrying out that girl's instructions.

A DIFFERENT WAY OF LOOKING AT THESE FACTS

There may be a third way of looking at this case, one that does not force the principled decision maker to choose between condemning both members of the couple and condemning neither of them.

In laws on the books in days past, doctors and others who performed abortions would incur criminal liability, but the women who sought the abortions would not. Stated differently, the person who requests and compensates the others for performing a criminal act would receive a free pass.

If one believes that abortion is murder, this approach is strange indeed. It resembles an exemption from the law of homicide for people who hire a hit man to kill their targets. The only reason that the hit man is in business is that people are hiring him to commit murder. Indeed, the particular individual (rather than someone else) is killed only because the person hiring the hit man has selected that specific target. It would therefore seem odd for the law to place the client beyond the reach of criminal penalties.

Yet an exemption for the pregnant woman in a law prohibiting abortion appears to do exactly that. It treats the person in charge of the killing as bearing no responsibility for it, while her subordinates sustain all of the blame. Why might the law do this?

One way to understand the exemption is by viewing the pregnant woman as not entirely in control of her own actions. If we think of her as less than a fully functioning adult, then it stands to reason that we would not want to punish her as severely (or at all) for acts that were really brought about by the more responsible adults around her.

Like the minor who falls in with a bad crowd, the woman who obtains an abortion—on this view—has fallen under the influence of the doctor and others who assist in terminating her pregnancy. In this scheme, a woman who gets an abortion is a second victim of the provider's wrongdoing, along with her unborn baby.

If we transpose this view of the world to the Doe case, we can now make sense of it. Janie asked her boyfriend to hit her abdomen with a bat and thereby terminate her pregnancy. As a pregnant woman, however (regardless of her age), Janie did not have full emotional autonomy over her decisions and thus should not be held responsible for her actions. By contrast, her boyfriend Johnnie, a male in possession of all of his faculties, could be held responsible under the Michigan statute taking aim at such attacks.

Though perhaps a more coherent approach than the others, this way of conceptualizing the pregnant woman for purposes of Michigan law is both offensive and at serious odds with the entire premise of the right to abortion. The assumption behind *Roe v. Wade*,[3] *Planned Parenthood v. Casey*[4] (the more recent case in which the U.S. Supreme Court declined to overrule *Roe*), and similar decisions is that pregnant women are the equals of men and must have legal control over their own bodily integrity.[5] Particularly in *Casey*, the Court placed gender equality at the center of arguments for reproductive rights—women have to be the ones to decide whether or not they will remain pregnant because they bear the costs of such a decision and are in the best position to weigh all of the considerations.

To assume, then, that women lack the basic capacity to make this decision greatly undermines their entitlement to the right, particularly given a legal regime in which parents may decide whether or not to allow their minor daughters to terminate a pregnancy, however unwise such a regime, as we saw in chapter 10.

SHOULD THEY BOTH BE PROSECUTED?

So what's the solution? Should the statute have been written to authorize a prosecutor to go after Johnnie and Janie? Should it have been written or applied to avoid prosecuting either of them? Or is Johnnie indeed more culpable than his girlfriend?

The answer depends in part on the scope of the right to abortion and on the nature of acceptable legal limitations on that right.

RESTRICTIONS ON THE RIGHT TO ABORTION

In *Roe v. Wade*, the Supreme Court said that even though a woman has the right to an abortion, her right is not absolute. After the first trimester, even prior to viability, the Court held, the government interest in protecting a woman's health allowed for regulation of the right to terminate a pregnancy. Though the state could not prohibit a woman from obtaining an abortion, it could place out of bounds any method that would be particularly dangerous to the woman. An attack on her with a bat would seem to qualify.

For similar reasons, even those jurisdictions that protect the right to a physician's assistance in dying closely regulate the practice. Nowhere can a person who wishes to die simply ask a friend or neighbor to gun her down with an automatic rifle or beat her to death with a tire iron.

As in the First Amendment context, time, place, and manner restrictions may accompany the right to die or to terminate a pregnancy. And the person whose choice is the subject of constitutional protection is no less bound by such restrictions than the various people whom she might recruit to assist in her endeavor.

Nonetheless, the Michigan statute prohibiting attacks on pregnant women who kill their embryos or fetuses most likely contemplates the termination of *wanted* pregnancies, rather than the provision of dangerous (but desired) abortions. Were the latter its objective, the statute would probably have discussed abortion more directly.

As I argued in chapter 3, such termination of a desired pregnancy should qualify as the destruction of a viable pregnancy, regardless of the gestational age of the fetus, because a wanted, developing baby—if left alone by outside assailants—has what he or she needs to survive.[6]

On this theory, however, the events of the Michigan Doe and Roe case, though grotesque and sad, do not seem to implicate the proper concerns of a statute criminalizing attacks on pregnant women resulting in the death of their unborn babies. And for this reason as well, the Michigan prosecutor should probably have stayed his hand.

POSTSCRIPT

The beatings discussed here occurred over the course of three weeks in the Fall of 2004. The defendant ultimately entered a no contest plea and was sentenced to two years probation and 200 hours community service at a pregnancy crisis center.

Conclusion

In October 2002, I adopted a beautiful baby girl from China. While I was waiting to learn when I would travel and who would become my new child, a colleague told me that I was "not showing yet." This joke comes back to me now. Because I was becoming a mother for the first time, the colleague thought of me as in a state of virtual pregnancy, one in which I would eventually begin "showing" but had not yet begun to do so.

Needless to say, the colleague did not make the same joke to my husband, nor would the joke have made any sense—why would he be "showing"? In 2003, however, nine months after adopting my first daughter, I became pregnant with my second.

In addition to the indescribable joy that my two girls have brought to my life, the experience of maternity—in two of its different forms—has been transformative for me. It has made me see more clearly the various gender-related expectations that I and those around me had for me as a mother and, by extension, for other women who have children. In addition, the critical eye that I brought to the adoption process (and the rebuttable presumption of unfitness that necessarily accompanies such a process) was very useful to me in approaching my own pregnancy experience.

Pregnancy, like adoption, has a script in our culture, but the script is one that I might have failed to notice were I not already sensitized to the stereotypes surrounding the physical metamorphosis of a woman into a biological mother. The knowledge of expectations often helped me to dash those expectations, because they no longer struck me as inevitable. One example is the standard overmedicalization of pregnancy and labor in the United States that I narrowly escaped at the last minute when I was able to give birth with a midwife and without painkillers.

Though every woman is either pregnant or not pregnant, she is also a great deal more than that. For many women, pregnancy is not a part of their lives. When this is a result of infertility, we need to think about whether and how the law should respond to that reality—whether reproductive technology should be available to them, for example, and whether that availability should turn on such factors as marital status and sexual orientation. I have suggested that consideration of these factors ultimately amounts to discrimination that ought not to be part of our legal system.

When a woman's nonpregnancy is a choice rather than a consequence of infertility, our laws should support the woman's status and ability to live as she chooses. I have argued that her choices should include birth control, emergency contraception, and abortion, although I do not equate these various options, and I take very seriously the important issues that people opposing abortion have brought to the debate.

As readers will notice from this biographical confession, many of the chapters of this book, not to mention the subject matter of the entire enterprise, reflect experiences that I or others close to me have had in the recent past. That is no accident. Another thing I have learned from being a mother and a writer at the same time is that each experience can—at its best—enrich and inform the other. I hope that people who read this book will become sensitive to the often-hidden realities of life as a woman and the ways in which the law can mitigate or aggravate the darker side of those realities, often unthinkingly. Such sensitivity can become the first step to positive change.

Notes

PREFACE

1. *Geduldig v. Aiello*, 417 U.S. 484 (1970).

2. *Geduldig*, 417 U.S. at 496-97.

3. See, e.g., Tracy E. Higgins, "By Reason of their Sex: Feminist Theory, Postmodernism, and Justice," 80 *Cornell Law Review* 1536 (1995); Scott A. Caplan-Cotenoff, "Parental Leave: The Need for a National Policy to Foster Sexual Equality," 13 *American Journal of Law and Medicine* 71, 75–78 (1987); Edith L. Pacillo, "Expanding the Feminist Imagination: An Analysis of Reproductive Rights," 6 *American University Journal of Gender and Law* 113, 138 (1997); Paula Abrams, "The Tradition of Reproduction," 37 *Arizona Law Review* 453, 495–96 (1995).

4. "Similarly situated," in legal parlance, refers to people who are in a comparable position and accordingly entitled to receive the same or similar treatment under a law demanding equal treatment.

5. See, e.g., Mary Sigler, "By the Light of Virtue: Prison Rape and the Corruption of Character," 91 *Iowa Law Review* 561, 578 (2006). *Cf.* Elizabeth J. Kramer, "When Men are Victims: Applying Rape Shield Laws to Male Same-Sex Rape," 73 *New York University Law Review* 293, 317–18 (1998) (describing the similarity in the dynamic of defense use of prior sexual history against rape victims in cases, respectively, of opposite-sex and same-sex rape, and arguing for similar application of rape shield laws).

6. Invidious discrimination refers to harmful and impermissible discrimination, as opposed to properly distinguishing between different circumstances (e.g., a qualified versus an unqualified applicant for a job, even if sex turns out to be relevant to qualification).

7. Malcolm Gladwell, *Blink: The Power of Thinking without Thinking* (New York: Little, Brown and Company, 2005).

8. See, e.g., Catharine A. Mackinnon, *Feminism Unmodified: Discourses on Life and Law* 8 (Cambridge, MA.: Harvard University Press, 1987). ("Gender is an inequality of power, a social status based on who is permitted to do what to whom. Only derivatively is it a difference.")

CHAPTER ONE

This chapter originally appeared March 16, 2004.

1. Chapter 3, The Inadvertent Murder of an Ex-Girlfriend's Fetus.
2. Chapter 7, Sending out Partial Birth Announcements.
3. Baby Center, "Giving Birth by Cesarean Section," www.babycenter.com/refcap/pregnancy/childbirth/160.html (last updated Oct. 2005).
4. World Health Organization, "Appropriate Technology for Birth," *Lancet* 2 (1985), 436–37. According to the WHO, the C-section rate should be about fifteen percent. See "C-section rate hits record high at 29%," *U.S.A. Today*, June 6, 2002, www.usnews.com/usnews/health/articles/060612/12healy.htm.

CHAPTER TWO

This chapter originally appeared Wednesday, August 11, 2004.

1. See *O'Neill v. Vermont*, 144 U.S. 323, 339 (1892).

CHAPTER THREE

This chapter originally appeared January 28, 2004.

1. *Keeler v. Superior Court*, 2 Cal. 3d 619 (1970), superceded by statute as stated in *People v. Carlson*, 37 Cal. App. 3d, 349 (1974).
2. *People v. Taylor*, 32 Cal. 4th 863 (2004).

CHAPTER FOUR

This chapter originally appeared December 29, 2004.

1. "Case of a Stolen Fetus, Mother's Slaying: *U.S. v. Lisa Montgomery*," *Findlaw*, 17 Dec. 2004, http://news.findlaw.com/hdocs/docs/kidnap/usmntgmry121704aff.html.
2. *Keeler v. Superior Court*, 2 Cal. 3d 619 (1970), superceded by statute as stated in *People v. Carlson*, 37 Cal. App. 3d 349 (1974).
3. See www.usdoj.gov/usao/mow/Montgomery.html.

CHAPTER FIVE

This chapter originally appeared August 28, 2002.

CHAPTER SIX

This chapter originally appeared July 27, 2005.

1. *Roe v. Wade*, 410 U.S. 113 (1973).
2. Blanche Glassman Hersh, *The Slavery of Sex* 210 (Urbana: University of Illinois Press, 1978) ("The feminists preached late marriage and 'moral restraint' within marriage as a means to reduce the frequency of pregnancies. . . . Contraceptive devices, when they became available in the 1840s and 1850s, were considered unnatural and probably associated with nonmarital sex and prostitution"); Steven M. Buechler, *Women's Movements in the United States: Woman Suffrage, Equal Rights, and Beyond* 98 (New Brunswick, N.J.: Rutgers University Press, 1990) ("Although most women reformers in the second half of the nineteenth did not openly support abortion or contraception, they did endorse women's efforts to control their fertility . . . which would make pregnancy, childbirth, and motherhood matters of conscious choice").
3. "Feminists for Life: Women Deserve Better," www.feministsforlife.org/.
4. *Geduldig v. Aiello*, 471 U.S. 484 (1970).
5. 42 USCS § 2000e(k).
6. Frederica Matthewes-Green, "Abortion: Women's Rights . . . and Wrongs," www.feministsforlife.org/FFL_topics/after/rtnwrfmg.htm.
7. Lynette Clemetson and Robin Toner, "Anti-Abortion Advocacy of Wife of Court Nominee Draws Interest," *New York Times*, July 22, 2005, at A1.
8. *Planned Parenthood v. Casey*, 505 U.S. 833, 852 (1992).
9. *Ayotte v. Planned Parenthood*, 126 S. Ct. 961 (2006).
10. 410 U.S. 113 (1973).

CHAPTER SEVEN

This chapter originally appeared June 18, 2003.

1. See www.whitehouse.gov/news/releases/2003/06/20030604-4.html.
2. *Stenberg v. Carhart*, 530 U.S. 914 (2000).
3. *Roe v. Wade*, 410 U.S. 113 (1973).
4. Congressional Record, 149 Congressional Record H4946 (daily ed., June 4, 2003); see also "US Passes 'Partial Birth' Abortion Ban," *The New Zealand Herald*, www.nzherald.co.nz/section/story.cfm?c_id=2&objectid=3505859.
5. See Lilo T. Strauss et al., "Abortion Surveillance—United States, 2002" (2005), www.cdc.gov/mmwr/preview/mmwrhtml/ss5407a1.htm ("Of all abortions for which gestational age was reported, 60% were performed at <8 weeks' gestation and 88% at <13 weeks").
6. President Discusses Stem Cell Research (Aug. 9, 2001), www.whitehouse.gov/news/releases/2001/08/20010809-2.html.

7. Rick Weiss, "400,000 Human Embryos Frozen in U.S.," *Washington Post*, May 8, 2003, at A10.

8. See Gary L. Francione, *Introduction to Animal Rights: Your Child or the Dog?* 14, 17 (Philadelphia, PA: Temple University Press, 2000). Professor Francione writes: "It is in no way necessary for human beings to eat meat or other animal products." *Id.* at 14. He adds: "Yet we choose to eat meat and animal products—we choose animal pain, suffering, and death—and our only justification is human pleasure. But if we take animal interests seriously at all, how can we possibly justify inflicting pain, suffering, and death on animals simply because we like the taste of their flesh?" *Id.* at 17. Most animals killed for food in the U.S. "have spent their entire lives crowded together in factory-farm buildings, automatically fed with unnatural foods on imposed schedules, surgically mutilated to facilitate their crowding, and dosed with drugs and pesticides." Les Inglis, *Diet for a Gentle World, Eating with Conscience* 29 (New York: Avery Publishing Group, 1993). For example, "hundreds of breeding sows and thousands of fattening piglets live in small, cramped pens in long, unheated, often poorly ventilated sheds." Dr. Michael W. Fox, *Eating with Conscience, The Bioethics of Food* 27 (Troutdale, OR: New Sage Press, 1997). Due to the cramped conditions, pigs are "driven to gnaw neurotically on one another's tails and hind ends." *Id.* To resolve this problem, pig producers "routinely amputate the pigs' tails." *Id.* Furthermore, "veal calves . . . are removed from their mothers on their first day of life, put in a crate so narrow that they cannot turn or walk around, deprived of straw and bedding, and kept deliberately anemic, all so that their pale soft flesh . . . can be sold at the highest price." Peter Singer and Jim Mason, *The Way We Eat, Why Our Food Choices Matter* 272 (Emmaus, PA: Rodale Press, 2006). Singer and Mason write that "[w]hat factory farms do to animals . . . they do because people are accustomed to eating these animal products and can't imagine a meal without them, or because they like the way they taste. These are not ethical justifications. . . ." *Id.* at 274. See also Catharine MacKinnon, *Women's Lives, Men's Laws* 98 (Cambridge, MA: Belknap Press of Harvard University Press, 2005). MacKinnon writes: "What is the bottom line for the animal/human hierarchy? I think it is at the animate/inanimate line, and Carol Adams and others are close to it: we eat them. This is what humans want from animals and largely why and how they are most harmed. We make them dead so we can live. We make our bodies out of their bodies. Their inanimate becomes our animate. We justify it as necessary, but it is not. . . . The place to look for this bottom line is the farm, the stockyard, the slaughterhouse. I have yet to see one run by a nonhuman animal."

9. *Carhart v. Gonzales*, 413 F.3d 791 (8th Cir. 2005).

10. *Gonzales v. Carhart*, 126 S. Ct. 1314 (2006).

CHAPTER EIGHT

This chapter originally appeared August 27, 2003.

1. *Wixtrom v. Department of Children and Families*, No. 5 D03-1921 (Fla. App. 5 Dist., June 12, 2003).

2. *In Re Guardianship of J.D.S.*, 864 So. 2d 534 (Fla. 5 Dist. Ct. App. 2004).

CHAPTER NINE

This chapter originally appeared September 7, 2005.

1. Susan J. Lee et al., "Fetal Pain: A Systematic Multidisciplinary Review of the Evidence," *Journal of the American Medical Association* 294 (2005) 947–54.

2. Unborn Child Pain Awareness Act, Senate Bill 51 (2005), http://thomas.loc.gov/cgibin/query/z?c109:S.51.

3. Susan B. Anthony List, "The Unborn Child Pain Awareness Act," www.sba-list.org/urbanchildpain.htm (last accessed July 29, 2006).

4. The last major action on this bill was 1/24/2005 referred to Senate committee. Status: Read twice and referred to the Committee on Health, Education, Labor, and Pensions. See http://thomas.loc.gov/cgi-bin/bdquery/z?d109:s.00051. On Jan. 26, 2005, introductory remarks by Senator Brownback were read on the record. *Id.*

CHAPTER TEN

This chapter originally appeared July 31, 2002.

1. For an engrossing fictional treatment of this issue, see Jodi Picoult, *My Sister's Keeper* (New York: Atria, 2004), a book about a family that conceives a second daughter to save the life of their first, a victim of leukemia, and after years of subjecting the younger daughter to painful bone marrow extractions for transplant, demands that she donate a kidney to save her older sister.

2. *Ohio v. Akron Center*, 497 U.S. 502 (1990). To examine the current Texas and Pennsylvania parental involvement statute, see Tex. Fam. Code § 33.002 (2006); 18 Pa. C.S. § 3206 (2006). There are currently forty-four states that mandate involvement—either consent or notification. See NARAL Pro-Choice America, "Restrictions on Young Women's Access to Abortion," www.prochoiceamerica.org/choice-action-center/in_your_state/who_decides/nationwide_trends/young-women.html.

3. See Carol Sanger, "Regulating Teenage Abortion in the United States: Politics and Policy," 18 *International Journal of Law, Policy, and Family*, 305, 311–2 (2004) (describing the process by which minors must seek to avoid involving their parents in the abortion decision and contending that "judicial bypass hearings serve as a unique and rather clever form of punishment. They are intrusive, humiliating, and meant to punish").

4. *Planned Parenthood v. Casey*, 505 U.S. 833, 894 (1992).

CHAPTER ELEVEN

This chapter originally appeared September 22, 2004.

1. See Mary Anne Ostrom, "Doctor Recounts Embryo-Mistake Drama—Fertility Expert Says 'Wrong Judgment' Led Him to Deceive Two Pregnant Women," *San Jose Mercury News*, Jan. 13, 2005, at 15A.

2. Mary Anne Ostrom, "Doctor's Deceit Unpunished—Called a 'Threat to Public Health,' He Still Practices," *San Jose Mercury News*, Dec. 11, 2004, at 1A.

CHAPTER TWELVE

This chapter originally appeared May 19, 2004.

1. *K.M. v. E.G.*, 13 Cal. Rptr. 3d 136, 146 (Cal. App. 1 Dist. 2004), modified, *K.M. v. E.G.*, 2004 Cal. App. Lexis 873 (2004).
2. *Id.*

CHAPTER THIRTEEN

This chapter originally appeared July 14, 2004.

1. During their halftime performance at the 2004 Super Bowl, Justin Timberlake ripped off part of Janet Jackson's costume, exposing her breast. "CBS spent the rest of the evening apologizing as its main New York switchboard lit up with complaints." Lisa de Moraes, "The CBS-Jackson Nexus—Time to Throw a Flag," *Washington Post*, Feb. 2, 2004, at C7. The Federal Communications Commission, which launched an investigation to determine whether the network had violated its indecency regulations, received "more than a half-million complaints about the incident, double the number of grievances registered for all of 2003." Frank James, "House Bill Increases Fines for Indecent Broadcasts," *Chicago Tribune*, March 12, 2004, at 1. "Outrage at the incident grew nationwide, with the NFL, White House, pro-family groups and talk radio denouncing the display as 'offensive,' 'tasteless' and 'profane.'" Eric Fisher and Jennifer Harper, "FCC to Probe Super Bowl Show—Public Protests Swell Against Jackson 'Stunt'," *Washington Times*, Feb. 3, 2004, at A1. See also CNN, "Apologetic Jackson says 'costume reveal' went awry," www.cnn.com/2004/US/02/02/superbowl.jackson/ (Feb 3, 2004). In this article, Michael Powell, Chairman of the FCC, is quoted as saying:

"I knew immediately it would cause great outrage among the American people, which it did," citing "thousands" of complaints received by Monday morning. "We have a very angry public on our hands"; *USA Today,* "Jackson's halftime stunt fuels indecency debate," www.usatoday.com/sports/football/super/2004-02-02-jackson-halftime-inci dent_x.htm (Feb. 2, 2004) (reporting that NFL commissioner Paul Tagliabue vowed to "change our policy, our people and our processes before the next Super Bowl to ensure that this entertainment is far more effectively dealt with and is of far more appropriate quality for the Super Bowl game").

2. But see *Time,* "Mary Magdalene Saint or Sinner?," www.danbrown.com/media/morenews/time.html (Aug. 11, 2003) (discussing changing interpretations of Mary Magdalene); BBC, "The Real Mary Magdalene," www.bbc.co.uk/religion/religions/features/biblemysteries/mary.shtml (accessed June 16, 2006) (discussing questions of intimacy

between Mary and Jesus); *National Geographic*, "'Da Vinci Code' Spurs Debate—Who Was Mary Magdalene?," http://news.nationalgeographic.com/news/2004/02/0225_040225_davincicode.html (May 17, 2006) (explores these issues in the wake of Dan Brown's novel, *The Da Vinci Code*); MSNBC, "Secrets behind the 'Da Vinci Code,'" www.msnbc.msn.com/id/7491383/ (May 26, 2006) (same).

3. See National Conference of State Legislatures, www.ncsl.org/programs/health/breast50.htm (last updated April 20, 2006).

4. *Id.*

5. Amy Harmon, "'Lactivists' Taking Their Cause, and Their Babies, to the Street," *New York Times*, June 7, 2005, at B3.

CHAPTER FOURTEEN

This chapter originally appeared March 27, 2002.

1. Margaret G. Spinelli, M.D., "Maternal Infanticide Associated with Mental Illness: Prevention and the Promise of Saved Lives," 161 *American Journal of Psychiatry* 1548 (Sept. 2004). For a comparison between the U.S. and British approaches to infanticide, respectively, see http://news.bbc.co.uk/1/hi/world/americas/1401667.stm. For a discussion of international approaches to infanticide, see http://edition.cnn.com/2001/LAW/06/28/postpartum.defense/.

2. "Woman Not Guilty in Retrial in the Deaths of Her 5 Children," *New York Times*, July 27, 2006, at A20.

PART II

1. The Centers for Disease Control and Prevention (CDC) reported that among adults nationwide, more than 300,000 women and over 90,000 men reported being raped in the previous twelve months. National Center for Injury Prevention and Control, *Sexual Violence: Fact Sheet*, www.cdc.gov/ncipc/factsheets/svfacts.htm (last accessed June 25, 2006). The U.S. Department of Justice, by contrast, estimates that approximately 8% of rape victims in 2003 were male. See U.S. Department of Justice, Office of Justice Programs, Bureau of Justice Statistics, Criminal Victimization in the United States, 2003 Statistical Tables, Table 2. Personal Crimes 2003: Number of victimizations and victimization rates for persons age 12 and over, by type of crime and gender of victims (July 2005), www.ojp.usdoj.gov/bjs/pub/pdf/cvus03.pdf.

CHAPTER FIFTEEN

This chapter originally appeared October 23, 2002.

1. See Michelle J. Anderson, "From Chastity Requirement to Sexual License: Sexual Consent and a New Rape Shield Law," 70 *George Washington Law Review* 51, 104–07

(2002) (citing studies conducted over the last two decades indicating that "promiscuity or perceived promiscuity on the part of a rape complainant biases jurors' decision-making processes").

CHAPTER SIXTEEN

This chapter originally appeared September 10, 2003.

1. As of June 2006, Kennedy was "the only person on death row for child rape" and his appeal was still pending. Colin Garrett, "Death Watch: South Carolina Death Penalty for Child Rapists 'Likely to be Unconstitutional,'" *Champion*, June 2006, at 48, www.nacdl.org/public.nsf/freeform/deathpenalty?opendocument. As of September 2006, Louisiana was "the only state with an offender on death row whose crime did not involve murder." Patrick O. Kennedy's case, as of that time, "was still working through appeals courts in Louisiana." See "StandDown Texas Project," Sept. 11, 2006, http://standdown.typepad.com/weblog/2006/09/index.html.
2. *Coker v. Georgia*, 433 U.S. 584, 598 (1977).
3. *Bowers v. Hardwick*, 478 U.S. 186 (1986), overruled by *Lawrence v. Texas*, 539 U.S. 558 (2003).
4. According to Kennedy, "race-of-the-victim disparities in sentencing probably reflect racially selective empathy more than racially selective hostility." Randall L. Kennedy, "*McCleskey v. Kemp:* Race, Capital Punishment, and the Supreme Court," 101 *Harvard Law Review* 1388, 1420 (1988). He contends that white jurors "may show more leniency in black-victim crimes not because of anti-black prejudice but rather because they relate more fully to the suffering of white victims; black victims remain strangers while white victims can be imagined as family or friends." *Id.* Kennedy explains that the tendency to empathize with victims of one's own race stems partially from "a universal dilemma in human relations." Randall Kennedy, *Race, Crime, and the Law* 350 (New York: Pantheon Books, 1997). The dilemma is that people "engage in different valuations of human life according to clannish criteria" including not only race but factors such as family and nationality. *Id.* See also Randall Kennedy, "*McCleskey v. Kemp:* Race, Capital Punishment, and the Supreme Court," 101 *Harvard Law Review* 1388, 1395 (1988) ("[R]ace-of-the-victim sentencing disparities are but one manifestation of a peculiar type of racial oppression—oppression without animus—and . . . race-based devaluations of human life constitute simply one instance of a universal phenomenon: the propensity for persons to empathize more fully with those with whom they can identify").
5. *Coker*, 433 U.S. at 619 n.16.
6. See *In Re Kemmler* 136 U.S. 436, 447 (1890) (noting that "punishments are cruel when they involve torture or lingering death; but the punishment of death is not cruel within the meaning of that word as used in the Constitution"); see also *O'Neill v. Vermont*, 144 U.S. 323, 339 (1892) (stating that cruel and unusual punishments usually refer to "punishments which inflict torture, such as the rack, the thumbscrew, the stretching of limbs and the like . . .").
7. *Lockyer v. Andrade*, 538 U.S. 63 (2003).

CHAPTER SEVENTEEN

This chapter originally appeared October 22, 2003.

1. See, e.g., Alan Dershowitz, "When Child Abuse is a Lie," *Times Union* (Albany, N.Y.), Oct. 17, 1994, at A6 (claiming that "we should take the presumption of innocence very seriously when it comes to accusations of . . . rape . . . since a significant percentage of such charges turn out to be . . . false"). Dershowitz contends that rape complaints are most likely to be exaggerated or false when "the complainant and defendant know each other." Alan Dershowitz, Editorial, "Women's Rights Won't be Served if Accused is Wronged," *Rocky Mountain News*, May 20, 1991, at 42.

2. Bryant's accuser endured degrading and threatening personal attacks while the case was pending. Although the judge issued a decorum order to protect her name from being released, her name, address, phone number, yearbook photo, and e-mail address were available on the Internet shortly after Bryant was charged with rape. Richard I. Haddad, "Shield or Sieve? *People v. Bryant* and The Rape Shield Law in High-Profile Cases," 39 *Columbia Journal of Law and Social Problems* 185, 185 (2005). Websites offered products displaying the name and picture of the accuser including coffee mugs, thongs, and tank tops. Moira E. McDonough, "Internet Disclosures of a Rape Accuser's Identity (Focus on the Kobe Bryant Case)," 3 *Virginia Sports and Entertainment Law Journal* 284, 285 (2004). Digitally enhanced photographs depicting the accuser in "sexual positions with Bryant" were posted on the Internet and websites referred to her as "a lying bitch" and "whore." *Id.* at 285, 308. The accuser received thousands of e-mails, some from men threatening to kill or harm her and others from men looking for a date. Jeff Benedict and Steve Henson, "The Case Against Kobe Bryant Unraveled in a Mock Trial," *LA Times*, Nov. 6, 2004, at A1. Tabloids relentlessly followed the accuser. *Id.* The intense public scrutiny forced the accuser to quit school and leave her home, moving to five different states in the eleven months following Bryant's arrest. "Bryant Accuser Seeks Speedy Trial Date," May 6, 2004, www.cnn.com/2004/LAW/03/25/bryant.hearing/index.html; Jeff Benedict and Steve Henson, "The Case Against Kobe Bryant Unraveled in a Mock Trial," *LA Times*, Nov. 6, 2004, at A1.

3. The judge in the criminal case ruled that evidence of the accuser's sexual conduct during the 72-hour period "end[ing] with her physical examination on . . . the day after her encounter with Mr. Bryant" was admissible. Adam Liptak, "Papers Reveal New Details in Kobe Bryant Rape Case," *New York Times*, Aug. 4, 2004, at A13.

4. Ernst Zundel, "a proponent of white supremacy" who authored a book titled *The Hitler We Love and Why*, was deported to Germany in 2005 to "face charges of denying the Holocaust." Beth Duff-Brown, "Canada Deports Immigrant Who Denies Holocaust; White-Supremacist Sent Back to Germany," *Chicago Sun Times*, March 2, 2005, at 46. Gary Rex Lauck, "an American neo-Nazi publisher who idolized Hitler" and "frequently denied the Holocaust occurred," was sentenced to prison for smuggling neo-Nazi propaganda into Germany. Elizabeth Neuffer, "German Court Convicts U.S. Nazi Publisher; 'Farmbelt Fuhrer' Gets 4 Year Term," *Boston Globe*, Aug. 23, 1996, at A2. Prosecutors claimed Lauck's goal was to "create a Nazi state." *Id.* Ewald Althans, chosen by a group

of former Nazis to head the neo-Nazi movement in Germany at the age of 13, claimed "Hitler is a hero. . . . He opened the door to building a super-civilization, really a paradise on Earth." Marc Fisher, "Youthful Face of Germany's Neo-Nazis; Well-Groomed Leader Works to Create Unified Extremist Bloc," *Washington Post*, March 2, 1992, at A1. Althans also claimed "[t]he Holocaust . . . never happened" and that "[f]ilms and other evidence of the [Holocaust] were 'created by Hollywood' to justify postwar limitations on German sovereignty." *Id.*

CHAPTER EIGHTEEN

This chapter originally appeared November 7, 2001.

1. Susan Estrich. *Real Rape* (Cambridge, MA: Harvard University Press, 1987).
2. Susan Estrich, "Rape," 95 *Yale Law Journal* 1087, 1090 (1986).
3. Stephen Holden, "Cacophony in Three Parts," *New York Times*, Nov. 2, 2001, at E1.
4. U.S. Department of Justice. *Sex Offenses and Offenders: An Analysis of Data on Rape and Sexual Assault* (Washington, D.C.: Bureau of Justice Statistics, 1997), www.ojp.usdoj.gov/bjs/pub/pdf/soo.pdf.
5. Paglia has commented that "it's ridiculous to think that saying no always means no." Camille Paglia, *Sex, Art, and American Culture* 58 (New York: Random House, 1992). She has also stated that "[w]e all know how it goes in the heat of the moment: it's 'no' now, it's 'maybe' later, and it changes again." *Id.* Paglia argues that a woman should not cry rape if she puts herself in a situation with a man where they are "making out and the [woman] decides she does not want to go all the way but the guy forces her to." *Id*
6. Bonnie L. Katz, "The Psychological Impact of Stranger Versus Nonstranger Rape on Victims' Recovery," in *Acquaintance Rape: The Hidden Crime* 251–69 (Andrea Parrot and Laurie Bechhofer, eds., New York: Wiley, 1991) ("Women raped by strangers . . . appear to feel recovered sooner than women raped by nonstrangers"). Victims of acquaintance rape are less likely to seek support from others than victims of stranger rape, which often worsens the psychological trauma. Julie A. Allison and Lawrence S Wrightsman, *Rape: The Misunderstood Crime* 70–71 (Newbury Park, CA: Sage, 1993).
7. *Coker v. Georgia*, 433 U.S. 584 (1977).

CHAPTER NINETEEN

This chapter originally appeared January 15, 2003.

1. *People v. John Z.*, 29 Cal. 4th 756 (2003).
2. See *People v. Vela*, 172 Cal. App. 3d 237 (1985) (overruled by *In Re John Z.*, 29 Cal. 4th 756 (2003)); see also *Battle v. State*, 414 A.2d 1266 (Md. 1980); *State v. Way*, 254 S.E.2d 760 (N.C. 1979).

3. *People v. Vela*, 172 Cal. App. 3d 237 (Cal. App. 5th. Dist., 1985).
4. *Vela*, 172 Cal. App. 3d. at 243.
5. "If a man meets a virgin who is not betrothed, and seizes her and lies with her, and they are found, then the man who lay with her shall give to the father of the young woman fifty shekels of silver, and she shall be his wife. . . ." *Deuteronomy* 22:28–29 (Revised Standard).
6. In Virginia, a man found guilty of raping his spouse can be placed on probation and, upon completion of counseling or therapy, the court may dismiss the charges against him if it "finds such action will promote maintenance of the family unit and be in the best interest of the complaining witness." Va. Code Ann. § 18.2-61(C)(2006). In California, marital rape cannot be prosecuted if it is not reported to authorities within one year of the incident unless "the victim's allegation of the offense is corroborated by independent evidence." Cal. Penal Code § 262(b)(2006.) In South Carolina, marital rape must be reported within 30 days in order for a spouse to be prosecuted. S.C. Code Ann. § 16-3-658 (2005). Several other states exempt marital rape from prosecution as rape if committed against a spouse who is mentally or physically incapacitated. See, e.g., R.I. Gen. Laws § 11-37-2 (2006); Ohio Rev. Code Ann. § 2907.02 (2006); Idaho Code Ann. § 18-6107(2006).
7. Sir Matthew Hale, *The History of the Pleas of the Crown* 629 (1736).
8. *People v. John Z.*, 60 P.3d 183, 187 (Cal. 2003).
9. Antioch College instituted a sexual offense policy in 1990 requiring "'willing and verbal consent' for each individual sex act." Jane Gross, "Combating Rape on Campus in a Class on Sexual Assault," *New York Times*, Sept. 25, 1993, at 1. At a required freshman orientation class, the policy was explained to students as follows: "If you want to take her blouse off, you have to ask. If you want to touch her breast, you have to ask. If you want to move your hand down to her genitals, you have to ask. If you want to put your finger inside her, you have to ask." *Id.* The sexual offense policy was instituted in response to protests by women over the "lack of school policies regarding date rape" following several sexual assaults on campus. *Id.*
10. 75 P.3d 750 (2003).

CHAPTER TWENTY

This chapter originally appeared May 4, 2005.

1. See June 20, 2006, signing statement, ny.gov/governor/press/06/0620062.html.

CHAPTER TWENTY-ONE

This chapter originally appeared February 11, 2004.

1. *Dixon v. State*, 596 S.E.2d 147 (2004).
2. The Prosecution and Defense of Sex Crimes §6.03 (2005). See, e.g., S.C. Code

§16-15-50 ("no conviction shall be had if on trial it is proved that such woman was at the time of the alleged offense lewd and unchaste"). See also Tenn. Code Ann. § 39-13-506 (West 2005) (Comments of Tennessee Sentencing Commission) (noting that the defense of promiscuity of the victim in statutory rape prosecutions was repealed in 1994); *Hernandez v. State*, 861 S.W.2d 908, 910 (Tex. Crim. App. 1993) (Miller, concurring) (noting that the 1993 revisions to the Texas Penal Code eliminated the promiscuity defense to statutory rape); Heidi Kitrosser, "Meaningful Consent: Toward a New Generation of Statutory Rape Laws," 4 *Virginia Journal of Social Policy and the Law* 287, 316 (1997) (citing Fla. Stat. Ann. § 794.05 (West Supp. 1997) (Historical and Statutory Notes)) (explaining that prior to a 1996 amendment, Florida's statutory rape law required a victim to be "'an unmarried person [under eighteen], of previous chaste character'"); Jennifer Ann Drobac, "Sex and the Workplace: 'Consenting' Adolescents and a Conflict of Laws," 79 *Washington Law Review* 471, 546 n.86 (2004) (noting that "in 1998 Mississippi repealed laws requiring that the target [of statutory rape] be 'chaste'").

3. 397 U.S. 358 (1970).

4. *In Re Winship*, 397 U.S. 358 (1970).

CHAPTER TWENTY-TWO

This chapter originally appeared December 1, 2004.

1. Joe Sharkey, "Many Women Say Airport Pat-Downs Are a Humiliation," *New York Times*, Nov. 23, 2004, at A1.

2. 520 U.S. 305, 323 (1997).

3. The TSA announced changes to its security protocols effective Dec. 22, 2005 that extended pat-down procedures to the arms and legs and continued to allow for random selection of passengers for additional screening. Kip Hawley, Assistant Secretary, Transportation Security Administration, Aviation Security Enhancements, Address Before the National Press Club (Dec. 2, 2005), www.tsa.gov/assets/doc/National_Press_Club_speech.doc. The TSA considers random selection to be a "significant component of TSA security measures." Transportation Safety Authority, Office of Privacy Policy and Compliance, Frequently Asked Questions, www.tsa.gov/research/privacy/faqs.shtm. Current TSA procedures for pat-downs provide that "transportation security officers use the front of the hand to screen a passenger's entire back and abdomen, the arms from shoulder to wrist and legs from mid-thigh to ankle. . . . Patting down the chest area may be conducted if there is an alarm from a hand-held metal detector or an irregularity in the person's clothing outline." *Id.*

CHAPTER TWENTY-THREE

This chapter originally appeared January 11, 2005.

1. 392 F.3d 1076 (9th Cir. 2004), *aff'd en banc*, 444 F.3d 1104 (9th Cir. 2006).

2. *Jespersen*, 444 F.3d 1104 (9th Cir. 2006).
3. 490 U.S. 228 (1989).
4. 2006 U.S. App. Lexis 9307 (April 14, 2006).

CHAPTER TWENTY-FOUR

This chapter originally appeared Nov. 16, 2005. *Cf.* Sojourner Truth, "Ain't I a Woman" (1851), in *Women's Rights in the United States* 88-89 (Winston E. Langly and Vivian C. Fox, eds., Westport, CT: Praeger Publishers 1998) (challenging white suffragettes to include black women in their movement and to draw on black women's experience in slavery to support the contention that women are strong and capable of hard work).

1. *Barnes v. City of Cincinnati*, 401 F.3d 729 (6th Cir. 2005).
2. Civil Rights Act of 1964, Pub. L. No. 88-352, 78 Stat. 241 (Title VII codified as amended in sections of 42 U.S.C. beginning with 42 U.S.C. 2000e).
3. 490 U.S. 228 (1989).
4. U.S. Dist. Lexis 6521 (W.D. Pa. Feb. 17, 2006).

CHAPTER TWENTY-FIVE

This chapter originally appeared December 18, 2002.

1. Texas Penal Code §21.06 (2005).
2. *Id.*
3. 478 U.S. 186 (1986).
4. *Id.* at 188 (emphasis added).
5. *Mississippi University for Women v. Hogan,* 458 U.S. 718 (1982); *United States v. Virginia,* 518 U.S. 515 (1996).
6. 388 U.S. 1 (1967).
7. 539 U.S. 558 (2003).

CHAPTER TWENTY-SIX

This chapter originally appeared October 19, 2005.

1. Proposed statute available at www.in.gov/legislative/interim/committee/prelim/HFCO04.pdf.
2. See *Skinner v. Oklahoma*, 316 U.S. 535 (1942) (specifically holding that a class of recidivist criminals could not be singled out for the sterilization penalty, because the fundamental nature of the right to procreate rendered such targeting a violation of the constitutional guarantee of equality).

3. *Skinner v. Oklahoma*, 316 U.S. 535 (1942).

4. See, e.g., Suzanne Goldberg, "Equality Without Tiers," 77 *Southern California Law Review* 481 (2004); William N. Eskridge, Jr., "Some Effects of Identity-Based Social Movements on Constitutional Law in the Twentieth Century," 100 *Michigan Law Review* 2062 (2002); Julie A. Nice, "The Emerging Third Strand in Equal Protection Jurisprudence: Recognizing the Co-Constitutive Nature of Rights and Classes," 99 *University of Illinois Law Review* 1209 (1999).

5. See, e.g., *Planned Parenthood v. Casey*, 505 U.S. 833, 834 (1992); *Griswold v. Connecticut*, 381 U.S. 479, 502 (1965).

6. 405 U.S. 438 (1972).

7. 381 U.S. 479 (1965).

8. See Elizabeth Bartholet, *Family Bonds: Adoption and the Politics of Parenting*, 33–34, 79, 84 (Boston, Houghton Mifflin, 1993). Bartholet writes: "[T]hose seeking to reproduce retain the sense that they are normal rights-bearing citizens. No one asks them to prove that they are fit to parent. They are perceived as having a God-given right to reproduce if they are capable of doing so. . . . Those entering the world of adoption agencies and home studies quickly realize that they have no right to become adoptive parents. Parental screening is the essence of what traditional adoption is all about." *Id.* at 33. She adds that "[b]y subjecting adoptive but not biologic parents to regulation, society suggests that it trusts what goes on when people give birth and raise a birth child but profoundly distrusts what goes on when a child is transferred from a birth to an adoptive parent. The specific nature of adoption regulation constantly reinforces the notion that biologic parenting is the ideal and adoption a poor second best." *Id.* at 34. She explains: "We would not dream of telling fertile people that they have no right whatsoever to produce a child—that childbirth is a privilege to be allowed or not at the entire discretion of the government. . . . Parental screening in the adoption area has always been justified as necessary for the protection of children. But children have much to gain and little to lose from scrapping the system." *Id.* at 79. And in further support of her thesis, she notes that "[t]he studies that exist provide no indication that the objective factors relied on by the current screening system function as useful predictors of good parenting." *Id.* at 84; see also Elizabeth Bartholet, *Family Bonds: Adoption, Infertility, and the New World of Child Production* (Boston, Beacon Press, 1999).

9. See *supra* Chapter 12, Is That Egg Donor My Mommy?

10. 517 U.S. 620 (1996).

11. 539 U.S. 558 (2003).

12. Roberta Braun Curtin, Sara S. McLanahan, and Elizabeth Thomson, "Family Structure, Gender, and Parental Socialization," 54 *Journal of Marriage and Family* 368, 368 (1992) (stating that the "vast majority of single parents are female").

13. See Valerie S. Mannis, "Single Mothers by Choice," 48 *Family Relations* 121 (1999); Terry Brown, Dennis Ferguson, and Dennis K. Orthner, "Single-parent Fatherhood: An Emerging Family Life Style," 25 *Family Coordinator* 429, 431 (1976).

14. See Valerie S. Mannis, "Single Mothers by Choice," 48 *Family Relations* 121 (1999).

CHAPTER TWENTY-SEVEN

This chapter originally appeared January 3, 2001.

1. The U.S. Equal Employment Opportunity Commission: "Decision," www.eeoc.gov/policy/docs/decision-contraception.html (last visited Aug. 8, 2006).
2. 450 U.S. 464 (1981).
3. *Id.* at 473.
4. *Erickson v. Bartell Drug Co.*, 141 F. Supp. 2d 1266 (W.D. Wash. 2001); *EEOC v. UPS*, 141 F. Supp. 2d 1216 (D. Minn. 2001).

CHAPTER TWENTY-EIGHT

This chapter originally appeared February 25, 2004.

1. Gardiner Harris, "Bush Picks F.D.A. Chief, But Vote Is Unlikely Soon," *New York Times*, March 16, 2006, at A18, available at 2006 WLNR 4369947; Gina Kolata, "Debate on Selling Morning-After Pill Over the Counter," *New York Times*, Dec. 12, 2003, at A1, available at 2003 WLNR 5670940. As of that time, the FDA has changed direction, and in August 2006, the FDA's acting commissioner signaled that the agency was prepared to permit the sale of the drug when it scheduled a meeting with the manufacturer to complete plans for approval. Stephanie Saul, "F.D.A. Shifts View on Next-Day Pill," *New York Times*, Aug. 1, 2006, at A1. See also Gardiner Harris, "F.D.A. Gains Accord on Wider Sales of Next-Day Pill," *New York Times*, Aug. 9, 2006, at A13, available at 2006 WLNR 13727054.
2. "Human Sexuality: Resolving Conflicting Beliefs About Condoms," www.religioustolerance.org/condom5.htm (last visited Aug. 8, 2006); "Human Sexuality: Condoms: Life Savers or Killers," www.religioustolerance.org/condom3.htm (last visited Aug. 8, 2006).
3. "'Morning-after' Pill on Hold," *Washington Times*, Feb. 15, 2004, at Nation/Politics. But see Mike Dorning, "Morning-after Pill Fight Pits Science v. Policy," *Chicago Tribune*, Nov. 14, 2005, at News, available at 2005 WLNR 23382324 (stating that "many who follow the issue suspect the Bush administration, as long as it can, possibly leaving the issue unresolved for the rest of the president's term"). Specifically, because "many in the anti-abortion movement oppose Plan B," while the "Republican moderates in Congress generally support Plan B," some believe "from the administration's perspective, the colliding political imperatives argue for 'just trying to run the clock and delay the decision.'" *Id.*
4. U.S. Government Accountability Office, "Decision Process to Deny Initial Application for Over-the-Counter Marketing of the Emergency Contraceptive Drug Plan B was Unusual" (2005), www.gao.gov/new.items/d06109.pdf.
5. U.S. Food and Drug Administration press release, "FDA Approves Over-the-Counter Access for Plan B for Women 18 and Older; Prescription Remains Required for

Those 17 and Under," available at www.fda.gov/bbs/topics/NEWS/2006/NEW01436.html (last visited Nov. 21, 2006).

CHAPTER TWENTY-NINE

This chapter originally appeared November 2, 2005.

1. The states were Arizona, Arkansas, California, Georgia, Indiana, Maryland, Michigan, North Carolina, Rhode Island, South Dakota, Tennessee, Texas, Vermont, West Virginia, and Wisconsin. Of these states, Arkansas, California, Georgia, and South Dakota have now enacted such bills into law. Pharmacist Conscience Clauses: Laws and Legislation, www.ncsl.org/programs/health/conscienceclauses.htm (last visited Nov. 22, 2006).

2. 410 U.S. 113 (1973).

3. 432 U.S. 464 (1977).

4. "Four States (Arkansas, Georgia, Mississippi, and South Dakota) have passed laws allowing a pharmacist to refuse to dispense emergency contraception drugs. Illinois passed an emergency rule that requires a pharmacist to dispense FDA approved contraception. Colorado, Florida, Maine, and Tennessee have broad refusal clauses that do not specifically mention pharmacists. California pharmacists have a duty to dispense prescriptions and can only refuse to dispense a prescription, including contraceptives, when their employer approves the refusal and the woman can still access her prescription in a timely manner." Pharmacist Conscience Clauses: Laws and Legislation, www.ncsl.org/programs/health/conscienceclauses.htm (last visited Nov. 22, 2006).

5. Michael Barbaro, "In Reversal, Wal-Mart Will Sell Contraceptive," *New York Times*, March 4, 2006, at C4, available at 2006 WLNR 3661600 ("Relenting to pressure from state government officials, Wal-Mart stores said yesterday that it would begin carrying Plan B, an emergency contraception pill, in all of its United States pharmacies by the end of the month. . . . Wal-Mart, which has 3,700 pharmacies, had been the only major chain that refused to sell the so-called morning-after pill, which can prevent pregnancy when taken within 72 hours of intercourse").

6. *Id.* The Complaint was filed on Feb. 7, 2006, and alleged a violation of the Massachusetts Board of Pharmacy Regulation 247 C.M.R. § 6.02(4) and the Massachusetts Consumer Protection Act, M.G.L. c93A, § 2(a). The complaint further alleged that the plaintiffs were injured by Wal-Mart's refusal to stock the pills because it delayed and hindered them from obtaining a validly prescribed medication. Plaintiff's complaint, *McCarty et al. v. Wal-Mart stores, Inc.*, available at http://walmartwatch.com/img/documents/complaint_plan_b.pdf.

7. Michael Barbaro, "In Reversal, Wal-Mart Will Sell Contraceptive," *New York Times*, March 4, 2006, at C4, available at 2006 WLNR 3661600 ("Wal-Mart said that it would allow pharmacists who object to filling a Plan B prescription to refer customers to another pharmacist and, in some cases, to another pharmacy").

CHAPTER THIRTY

This chapter originally appeared January 26, 2005.

1. On June 25, 2006, a committee of the National People's Congress (NPC), the legislature of China, decided to eliminate that portion of a draft criminal law amendment that dealt with banning nonmedical sex-selective abortions before taking a final vote on the amendment. *NPC Unlikely to Criminalize Selective Abortions*, NPC, June 25, 2006, www.npc.gov.cn/zgrdw/english/news/newsDetail.jsp?id=220101&articleId=349882.
2. David Glenn, "A Dangerous Surplus of Sons? Two Political Scientists Warn that Asia's Lopsided Sex Ratios Threaten World Peace," *The Chronicle of Higher Education,* April 30, 2004, at A14; Paul Wiseman, "China Thrown Off Balance as Boys Outnumber Girls," *USA Today*, June 19, 2002, available at 2002 WLNR 4503018; see Peter Harmsen, "UN Warns of 'Alarming Gender Issues' Affecting 600 Million Chinese Women," *Agence France Presse English Wire*, March 25, 2004.
3. Murray Scot Tanner, *Chinese Government Responses to Rising Social Unrest* 5 (2005), http://www.rand.org/pubs/testimonies/2005/RAND_CT240.pdf.
4. James B. Jacobs and Kimberly Potter, *Hate Crimes: Criminal Law & Identity Politics* (New York: Oxford University Press, 1998).
5. 505 U.S. 833, 852 (1992).
6. 410 U.S. 113 (1973).

CHAPTER THIRTY-ONE

This chapter originally appeared March 9, 2005.

1. Carla K. Johnson, "Unexpectant Father Can Sue For Distress," *Associated Press*, Feb. 25, 2005, available at 2005 WLNR 24314484.
2. 505 U.S. 833, 896 (1992).
3. 505 U.S. at 852.
4. Abdon M. Pallasch, "Doctor Says Ex-Fiancee Saved Sperm To Impregnate Herself; Court Allows Lawsuit Claiming Outrageous Conduct To Proceed," *Chicago Sun-Times*, Feb. 25, 2005, at 3; see Carla K. Johnson, "Unexpectant Father Can Sue For Distress," *Associated Press*, Feb. 25, 2005, available at 2005 WLNR 24314484; Michelle Oberman, "Sex, Lies, and the Duty to Disclose," 47 *Arizona Law Review* 871, 918 n.268 (2005).
5. *Id.*

CHAPTER THIRTY-TWO

This chapter originally appeared March 21, 2006.

1. Most recently, an Intervening Defendant, the Attorney General for the State of Michigan, filed a motion to dismiss and Plaintiff replied with a Brief in Opposition to the

Motion. Intervening-Defendant's Motion to Dismiss, *Dubay v. Wells et al.*, No 1:06-cv-11016 (E.D. Mich. 2006); Response to Motion to Dismiss and Brief in Opposition to Intervening-Defendant's Motion, *Dubay v. Wells et al.*, No 1:06-cv-11016 (E.D. Mich. 2006). On July 17, 2006, District Judge David M. Lawson granted the Michigan Attorney General's motion to dismiss the case. See www.traversecityfamilylaw.com/Documents/Dubey_v_Wells_Opinion_Order.pdf.

2. Susan Dominus, "The Fathers' Crusade," *New York Times*, May 8, 2005, available at 2005 WLNR 7206953.

3. John Tierney, "Men's Abortion Rights," *New York Times*, Jan. 10, 2006, at A25, available at 2006 WLNR 502474 (stating that "the term was coined by Frances Goldscheider, a professor of sociology at Brown University who studies family issues").

4. Ann Fessler, *The Girls Who Went Away: The Hidden History of Women Who Surrendered Children for Adoption in the Decades Before Roe v. Wade* (New York: Penguin Press, 2006) (bringing to light the tragic pressure that families and social workers brought to bear on young girls to surrender their babies in the decades prior to *Roe v. Wade*).

5. In her 2002 *Columbia Law Review* article, Professor Joan Williams stated that "while 'the gap in pay between women and men has been narrowing, the gap between women with children and those without children has been widening' in the past few decades. 'Having children had positive or no effects for men, but very strongly negative effects for women, and these effects increased from 1980 to 1991.' By 1991, the pay gap between mothers and others was larger than the pay gap between men and women. Single mothers (whether never married or divorced) fare worse than married mothers." Joan Williams, "'It's Snowing Down South': How to Help Mothers and Avoid Recycling The Sameness/Difference Debate," 102 *Columbia Law Review* 812, 827 (2002). In addition, in performing her analysis, Professor Williams relied on recent data collected by economist Jane Waldfogel, stating that between 1980 and 1991, the wage gap between males and females decreased (in log points) from .46 to .21. In contrast, between 1980 and 1991, the wage gap between non-mothers and mothers increased (in log points) from .17 to .25. Jane Waldfogel, "Understanding the 'Family Gap' in Pay for Women with Children," 12 *Journal of Economic Perspectives* 137, 147 (1998).

CHAPTER THIRTY-THREE

This chapter originally appeared July 18, 2001.

1. *State v. Oakley*, 629 N.W.2d 200 (WI 2001).

2. 316 U.S. 535 (1942).

3. 532 U.S. 318 (2001).

4. *In Re Bobbijean P.*, 800 N.Y.S. 2d 342 (2005) (Table). According to the New York Civil Liberties Union (NYCLU) website, "attorneys for Stephanie P. filed a motion to appeal on January 20, 2005" and "the [Reproductive Rights Project] continues to work closely with [the couple's] attorneys at the Monroe County Public Defenders Office in

preparing the appeal." NYCLU: "In the Courts—Active Cases," www.nyclu.org/rrp_courts.html#bobbijean (last visited Jan. 1, 2007).

5. *State v. Talty*, 814 N.E.2d 1201 (Ohio 2004).

6. "Man Gets Probation in Child Support Case," *The Courier-Journal* (Louisville, Kentucky), Sept. 6, 2002, at 3B.

7. See *Smith v. Superior Court of State In and For Coconino County*, 725 P.2d 1101 (Ariz. 1986); *People v. Pointer*, 199 Cal. Rptr. 357 (1984); Kristyn M. Walker, "Judicial Control of Reproductive Freedom: The Use of Norplant as a Condition of Probation," 78 *Iowa Law Review* 779 (1993).

8. *Cf. Mississippi University for Women v. Hogan*, 458 U.S. 718 (1982) (finding that a policy prohibiting men from enrolling in a nursing program for credit violated the Equal Protection Clause of the Fourteenth Amendment).

CHAPTER THIRTY-FOUR

This chapter originally appeared April 11, 2001.

1. *Mississippi University for Women v. Hogan*, 458 U.S. 718 (1982).

2. *Frontiero v. Richardson*, 411 U.S. 677 (1973).

3. 388 U.S. 1 (1967).

4. *Palmore v. Sidoti*, 466 U.S. 429 (1984).

5. Twila L. Perry, "Transnational Adoption and Gentrification: An Essay On Race, Power, Family and Community," 26 *Boston College Third World Law Journal* 25 (2006); Twila L. Perry, "The Transracial Adoption Controversy: An Analysis of Discourse and Subordination," 21 *New York University School of Law Review of Law & Social Change* 33 (1994).

6. Pub. L. No. 101-336, 104 Stat. 327 (1990).

7. Pub. L. No. 90-202, 81 Stat. 602 (1967); *Gen. Dynamics Land Sys. v. Cline*, 540 U.S. 581 (2004) (stating that the Age Discrimination in Employment Act does not prohibit favoring the old over the young).

8. 419 U.S. 522 (1975).

CHAPTER THIRTY-FIVE

This chapter originally appeared April 6, 2005.

1. The organization's website is located at www.mgmbill.org. The bill was resubmitted Feb. 6, 2006.

2. National Center for Health Statistics, www.cdc.gov/nchs/products/pubs/pubd/hestats/circumcisions/circumcisions.htm (stating that "in 1999, the latest year these data are available, 65.5 percent of white newborns and 64.4 percent of black newborns were circumcised").

3. 18 U.S.C. §116 (2005).

4. Sharon LaFraniere, "Circumcision Studied in Africa as AIDS Preventative," *New York Times*, April 28, 2006, at A1, available at 2006 WLNR 7141527; R.S. Van Howe, "Circumcision and HIV Infection: Review of the Literature and Meta-Analysis," 10 *International Journal of STD & AIDS* 8 (1999).

5. 494 U.S. 872, 879 (1990), superseded by statute, Religious Freedom Restoration Act of 1993 (RFRA), Pub. L. No. 103-141, 107 Stat. 1488, statute limited by *City of Boerne v. Flores,* 521 U.S. 507 (1997) (holding that Congress exceeded its power under the Fourteenth Amendment's enforcement clause to enact the RFRA, invalidating RFRA as applied to state and local governments, but not as applied to the federal government through Congress' Article I enforcement powers).

6. 321 U.S. 158 (1944).

7. World Health Organization (WHO): Female Genital Mutilation Fact Sheet (2000), www.who.int/mediacentre/factsheets/fs241/en/ (last visited June 27, 2006) (stating that "the most common type of female genital mutilation is excision of the clitoris and the labia minora, accounting for up to 80% of all cases; the most extreme form is infibulation, which constitutes about 15% of all procedures").

CHAPTER THIRTY-SIX

This chapter originally appeared April 20, 2005.

1. Michigan Compiled Laws §750.90b (2005).
2. 410 U.S. 113 (1973).
3. See *supra* Chapter 32, note 2.
4. 505 U.S. 833 (1992).
5. *Planned Parenthood v. Casey*, 505 U.S. 833 (1992).
6. See *supra* Chapter 3: The Inadvertent Murder of an Ex-Girlfriend's Fetus.

Index

About the Author

Sherry F. Colb is Professor of Law and Judge Frederick B. Lacey Scholar at Rutgers University School of Law. A former law clerk to Associate Justice Harry A. Blackmun, she is a regular columnist for FindLaw's Writ, a layperson's online source for legal commentary. She lives in New York City.

DEC 0 5 2007
JUL 2 8 2008

KF 3760 .C65 2007

Colb, Sherry F., 1966-

When sex counts
10/2007